The problem of
revolution in Germany,
1789-1989

The Problem of Revolution in Germany, 1789–1989

German Historical Perspective Series
General Editors:
Gerhard A. Ritter and Anthony J. Nicholls

German Historical Perspectives/XII

The Problem of Revolution in Germany, 1789–1989

Edited by
REINHARD RÜRUP

Oxford • New York

First published in 2000 by
Berg
Editorial offices:
150 Cowley Road, Oxford, OX4 1JJ, UK
838 Broadway, Third Floor, New York, NY 10003-4812, USA

Berg is the imprint of Oxford International Publishers Ltd.

Library of Congress Cataloging-in-Publication Data

A catalogue record for this book is available from the Library of Congress.

British Library Cataloguing-in-Publication Data

A catalogue record for this book is available from the British Library

ISBN 1 85973 276 3

Typeset by JS Typesetting, Wellingborough, Northants.

Contents

Editorial Preface

The purpose of this series of books is to present the results of research by German historians and social scientists to readers in English-speaking countries. Each of the volumes has a particular theme that will be handled from different points of view by specialists. The series is not limited to the problems of Germany but will also involve publications dealing with the history of other countries, with the general problems of political, economic, social and intellectual history as well as international relations and studies in comparative history.

We hope the series will help to overcome the language barrier that experience has shown obstructs the rapid appreciation of German research in English-speaking countries.

The publication of the series is closely associated with the German Visiting Fellowship at St Antony's College, Oxford, which has existed since 1965, having been originally funded by the Volkswagen Stiftung, later by the British Leverhulme Trust, by the Ministry of Education and Science in the Federal Republic of Germany, and starting in 1990, by the Stifterverband für die Deutsche Wissenschaft with special funding from C. & A. Mode Düsseldorf. Each volume is based on a series of seminars held in Oxford, which has been conceived and directed by the Visiting Fellow and organized in collaboration with St Antony's College.

The editors wish to thank the Stifterverband für die Deutsche Wissenschaft for meeting the expenses of the original lecture series and for generous assistance with the publication. They hope that this enterprise will help to overcome national introspection and to further international academic discourse and co-operation.

Gerhard A. Ritter   Anthony J. Nicholls

Foreword

This book is devoted to the question of what significance we should accord the phenomenon of revolution in modern German history. To this day, the notion of Germany as the 'land without a revolution' persists in both scholarly and political literature, and historians continue to explain the catastrophes of recent German history, particularly the Nazi regime, not least in terms of the absence of successful revolutionary sparks to political and social development. The authors of this volume, in dialogue with recent scholarship and against the background of the political experience of 1989, ask instead whether German history is indeed characterized by a strikingly low tendency towards revolution and a failure of revolutionary efforts, which distinguishes it from the rest of European history. It would seem to make sense here to abandon the widespread notion that successful revolutions represent a sort of 'normal case' in European history. Quite the opposite is true: Europe has seen far more failed or arrested revolutions than successful ones, and, apart from the special case of the Russian revolutions of 1917, there has been nothing comparable to the epochal significance of 1789. Thus it would seem more fruitful to seek explanations for the few decisive successes of revolutions than to enquire into the particular causes of their more frequent failures.

Moreover, scepticism has increased about whether the antagonistic juxtaposition of revolution and reform, like that which arose in reaction to the revolution of 1789, and later particularly in the socialist tradition influenced by Marx, is actually justified. Such doubts have also been formulated in recent historical scholarship, but they draw their legitimacy not least from an analysis of the disintegration process of the communist system. It was precisely the efforts at reform that revealed the unreformability of 'state socialism' or 'socialism as it actually exists' and led to a change of system that was not planned as a revolution, but whose consequences possessed a revolutionary quality. People wanted to reform the existing system and instead brought about a revolution. This had already been the case in 1789, but 200 years later the traditional pathos of revolution was missing, even at the moment of success. The people who pushed through the changes no longer believed in revolutions as 'locomotives' of the historical process. They were sceptical of utopian models of the future and placed their hopes instead in immediately tangible improvements in political, economic and social conditions. They no longer thought in the categories developed by Marx, but rather agreed with Walter Benjamin, who grappled critically with the socialist understanding of revolution in his *Notizen über den Begriff der Geschichte* and remarked quite sceptically: 'Marx says that revolutions are the locomotives of world history. But perhaps matters are quite different. Perhaps revolutions represent the travellers on this train reaching for the emergency brake.'

The authors of this volume address the fundamental questions of the German history of revolution, and in addition discuss the effects of reforms as well as war, counter-revolution and defeat on the societal modernization process in Germany. The contributions make clear that the relationship between revolution and reform is ambiguous and highly contradictory. Both successful interventions in existing conditions and blocked reforms can lead to revolutions. Failed or arrested revolutions can hinder reforms but also, at least in the medium term, promote them. For reformers, the widespread fear of revolution was a means to speed the political and social changes they believed necessary, whereas conservatives feared that reforms were only the first stages of revolution, which they understood as a total overturning of political and social circumstances. But the majority of middle-class liberals and social democratic labour leaders were equally mistrustful of the dynamics of the revolutionary process. Plagued by fears that the masses, once moved, could go out of control, they argued for a quick stabilization of the new circumstances after the political upheaval, a stabilization that generally worked against any deeper transformation. Those who desired reform but were forced to take the path of revolution usually sought to keep the phase of revolutionary conflict as brief – and as bloodless – as possible in order to return to a politics of reform.

The Centre for European Studies at St Antony's College Oxford and the financial support of the Stifterverband für die deutsche Wissenschaft made it possible for leading German and British historians to elucidate these and other questions. All of the authors were invited to give lectures within the framework of a seminar at Oxford between January and March 1996. I am particularly grateful to Anthony J. Nicholls, director of the Centre for European Studies, for his hospitality and unfailing helpfulness and not least for his constant intellectual presence, which contributed greatly to the seminar's success. I also thank all of the authors, whose contributions summarize many years of research and reflection, for making them available for publication in slightly revised form, supplemented by notes. I would also like to express my gratitude to those other colleagues in Oxford, particularly Peter Pulzer, Hartmut Pogge-von Strandmann and Jonathan Wright, who attended the seminar regularly and enriched the discussions with their own contributions. The editor and the authors thank Mark Hewitson, David Higgins, Mary Elise Sarotte, and Pamela Selwyn for taking on the difficult job of translating most of the contributions.

In order to avoid misunderstandings, I would like to emphasize that the final essay is not intended as a summary of the seminar's conclusions. It presents instead an individual view of the history of revolution, which deviates in several respects from what other authors have to say in their contributions to this volume.

Reinhard Rürup

REINHARD RÜRUP

Revolution and Reform: Germany and the French Revolution of 1789

Germany and the French Revolution – this is indisputably one of the great themes of German history, and it is all the more astonishing that German historiography, up until the Second World War and beyond, paid very little attention to this topic. Historians of the period 1789 to 1815 were interested primarily in the process of external and internal state building, which, from their predominantly national point of view, meant that they were mainly interested in the territorial reorganization of Germany during the era of Napoleon and the Prussian reforms. Thus, significantly, it was three non-German historians who first made Germans' intellectual responses to the French revolution the object of detailed study: George Peabody Gooch in Cambridge (1920), Alfred Stern in Zürich (1928), and Jacques Droz in Clermont-Ferrand (1949). As far as German historiography was concerned, the first comprehensive account that rested on modern research appeared in 1959 with Kurt von Raumer's major contribution to the *Handbuch der deutschen Geschichte*.[1] The 1960s witnessed the start of research into so-called 'German Jacobins', in which the Marxist-Leninist historians of the German Democratic Republic played an important part. This was followed in the early 1970s by seminal studies of the Napoleonic 'model states' and the introduction of the *Code Napoléon* in Germany, and by intensive research into the reforms of the states belonging to the Confederation of the Rhine. Such studies were, in turn, accompanied by a rapidly increasing number of economic and social history monographs, which examined the dissolution of the old feudal society and the beginnings of a capitalist mode of production, as well as concomitant social tensions and conflicts.

1

The revolutionary and Napoleonic decades were increasingly recognized as constituting a period of radical transformation in Germany, a time of accelerated transition towards the modern world. Consequently, historians inquired with a new intensity into the internal and external forces motivating political and social change, into the Enlightenment and those strata which disseminated it, into the potential and limits of enlightened absolutism in Germany and into the continuities and discontinuities of the reform movement. Naturally, they also asked why no revolution occurred in Germany, in contrast to France. As early as 1959, Golo Mann began his *German History in the Nineteenth and Twentieth Century* with the French Revolution. Similarly, Ernst Rudolf Huber appended the words 'since 1789' to the title of his seminal, if not uncontroversial, *German Constitutional History*. Although the bicentenary celebrations of the French Revolution also gave rise to an abundance of publications in Germany, including several impressive anthologies, both the debate and our current state of knowledge is still represented by the concise account of Elisabeth Fehrenbach, which came out in 1981, and by the first volume of Hans-Ulrich Wehler's *History of German Society*, which was published in 1987. For the period between 1789 and 1815, Wehler gives the heading *Defensive Modernization: the German Reaction to the French Revolution and Napoleon*. In this particular understanding he differs little from James Sheehan's major book on German history from 1770 to 1866 (Oxford History of Europe), where the same era falls under the heading *Germans and the French Revolution*.[2]

Thirty years ago, as I first became interested in the subject of 'Germany and the French Revolution', it was relatively simple to gain an overview of the topic and its state of research. That is no longer the case today, when even specialists feel increasingly helpless given the steadily growing number of works, above all of regional and local history, many of which are extremely valuable. Any historian who is familiar with the Rhineland cannot, as a rule, claim the same level of familiarity with Bavaria or East Prussia. Moreover, there are the highly varied themes and methods of different historians in the field. Research is characterized by an ever more threatening degree of fragmentation, and the so-called 'big questions' of interpretation are often handled at too great a distance from current research projects. This is a phenomenon, of course, which can be seen in other branches of research too, but which stands out all the more markedly if scientific enquiry has, over a long period, stagnated and then suddenly revived. Under these conditions, it is not possible for me to discuss the results of new research in detail here.[3] I will therefore concentrate on three sets of issues: (1) reactions to the French revolution up until the territorial reorganization of Germany under Napoleon; (2) the politics of reform, above all in Prussia and the states belonging to the Confederation of the Rhine; (3) the relationship between reform and revolution, as it was understood at the time and as it is seen today.

I.

I begin with the more or less 'classic' question about immediate reactions to the revolution and about the intellectual debate that this revolution occasioned. It is a theme that lends itself to quotation – a temptation that I too will not completely resist. In the meantime, the older view of the completely unpolitical German has been discredited. There was not only a strong movement of Enlightenment in Germany, but there was also, from 1770 onwards at the latest, a political public sphere, which manifested itself in newspapers and journals, reading societies, orders of freemasons, enlightened societies and clubs of various kinds. This public sphere was shaped by the thoughts of the Enlightenment, and this Enlightenment was far from being merely speculative, but rather was practice-oriented and in favour of reform. The fact that contemporaries counted on the princes as allies in the struggle against the old order and the inherited privileges of the Churches, the aristocracy and the guilds was neither an expression of unusual naivety nor proof of a specific deference to authority. Rather it was a recognition of given circumstances and can be defined as a thoroughly realistic strategy. Enlightened absolutism was by no means purely fictional, even if its limitations soon became clear. In Germany, not only Frederick II in Prussia and Joseph II in Austria, but also a considerable number of other rulers, including prince bishops, had oriented their policies at least in part towards the demands of the Enlightenment. Practical successes remained limited in nature, but should not be discounted completely. Changes in polity and society, which were regarded as necessary by German enlightened thinkers, could at least be passed in principle, if unevenly, by an alliance with the princes. Not only in private, but also in public, there were discussions about human rights and civic freedoms, about the abolition of estates' rights, about economic and social reforms, about political reforms and even about constitutions – the American events were followed attentively after 1776. There was no deep-seated political crisis in Germany: rather, contemporaries believed that they were living in an era of progress, increasing justice, and freedom.[4]

In these circumstances, it is hardly surprising that the revolution in France was greeted joyfully by the great majority of German intellectuals, but it was not understood as a signal that Germany should act in the same way. The epoch-making character of the revolution was recognized very quickly, with the Swiss historian Johannes von Müller, who lived in Germany, describing the day on which the Bastille was stormed as 'the best day since the fall of the Roman Empire'. The well-known scholar and publicist August Ludwig Schlözer wrote in Göttingen under the immediate impression of the news from Paris: 'One of the greatest nations in the world, the first in general culture, is finally throwing off the yoke of tyranny, which she had borne both tragically and comically for a century and a half. Doubtless God's angels in heaven have started to sing a Te deum laudamus.' And against the objection that 14 July was associated with bloody excesses, he added immediately: 'Where is it possible to think of revolution without excesses! One does not cure cancer with rose-water. And even if innocent blood has been spilled (and still far less than that spilled by the pillaging despot Louis XIV in one unjust war alone): this blood is on the hands of you despots and your notorious instruments, who have made this revolution necessary.' Müller and Schlözer were no exceptions, but thoroughly representative of the German public sphere of academics and artists. Naturally, there was a silent majority, as well as figures such as Goethe, who was sceptical of the revolution. Nevertheless, when one looks at the journals, books and diaries of the time, it is possible to speak of widespread enthusiasm in Germany for the revolution during its first months, and of clear and preponderant support continuing into 1791 and 1792.[5]

It is conspicuous that the revolution was understood as the result of theory, as a consequence of the Enlightenment, which, in view of the inability of the French political system to reform itself, became inevitable. Georg Forster, one of the radical partisans of the revolution, wrote as early as the end of July 1789 in Mainz: 'It is nice to see what philosophy has allowed to grow in the minds of men and then has been put in place in the state, without one having an example that so complete a change ever cost so little blood and devastation.' Friedrich Gentz, who later became a close collaborator of Metternich, declared himself to be decidedly in favour of the revolution as late as December 1790: 'I would hold the failure of the revolution to be one of the most severe accidents that have ever struck mankind. It is the first practical triumph of philosophy, the first example of a form of government, which is based on principles and on a coherent, logical system.' Only a short time later, Gentz belonged to those who polemicized against the French revolution because of the predominance of 'abstract principles'. The dialectic relationship between the needs of the masses and theory was, by contrast, well formulated by Friedrich Maximilian Klinger, the 'storm and stress' poet:

> Voltaire, Montesquieu, Rousseau, Mably, Diderot, the economists and the encyclopaedists are supposed to have created the revolution through their writing; so say the emigrants, and, in imitation, those who cannot think. They forget (the emigrants know why) the intrigues, pride, greed and licentiousness of those who have been in power since the adolescence of Louis XV. Still, who would like to linger over that? And what would have come out of the revolution without the genii? Precisely that which would occur in Turkey, if a political revolution should take place there. Yet more gruesome scenes and complete disintegration . . .

The revolutionary crisis was not the result of theory, but without theory it was impossible to create a future. The idealist foundation of the revolution was later formulated most impressively by Georg Friedrich Wilhelm Hegel in his *Lectures on the Philosophy of History*. Hegel claimed:

> The idea of law and justice made itself felt all of a sudden, and the old structure of injustice could manage no resistance to it. A constitution founded on legal thought has now been established, and everything should be based on this foundation from now on. For as long as the sun has stood in the firmament and the planets have orbited around it, it is unheard of that man stands on his head, that is, stands on thought and builds reality according to it.

The formulation is well known and we know, too, that Karl Marx then endeavoured to put man back on his feet again, instead of on his head – rarely, however, has the victorious power of thought been depicted with such force. The fact that the revolution and the society that resulted from it, needed theory, has seldom been formulated so impressively.[6]

The debate over the French revolution did not, as Jacques Droz has shown, remain limited to a small circle of intellectuals. Recent research has proved that the 200 or so German newspapers, in which revolutionary events were reported in detail – and, initially, almost entirely with approbation – reached some three million people. It is to be assumed, therefore, that a large number of those who took part in social unrest in Germany also had reasonably precise knowledge of the developments in France. It was believed until relatively recently that, to a great extent, Germany had escaped social conflicts during the period of the French revolution. Yet, as has been shown, conflicts were anything but rare exceptions. There were disturbances and revolutionary upheavals on both the left and the right side of the Rhine, in the Electorates of Mainz and Cologne, in the Palatinate, in the Duchy of Berg, in the Bishopric of Speyer and in the Austrian Breisgau, as well as in south German cities, in Hessen-Kassel, Saxony and the Prussian province of Silesia (this list of the regions that were affected is by no means exhaustive). As a rule, acute signs of hardship and crisis led to antifeudal revolts, during which it was evident that the French paradigm was alive and well, even if concrete demands aimed at the reestablishment of old rights. In the cities, there were journeymen's riots and, in the countryside, agricultural disturbances in which, in 1790, more than 10,000 people participated in Saxony alone. These disturbances should not be overestimated, however: they remained thoroughly isolated, and neither in the cities nor in rural areas did they run out of control. No revolution came out of the disturbances, and the contrast with France remains, despite all our new knowledge, not merely a matter of degree. This had, amongst other things, to do with the fact that the disturbances were not only quashed violently, but in many cases were also defused by means of limited concessions. Moreover, it was significant that the legal and social predicament of the peasantry in Germany was, as a rule, clearly better than in France, as has been shown by comparative studies.[7]

The lower orders, who had been stirred into action, lacked political leadership. There was no democratic movement in Germany that enjoyed even the semblance of broad support amongst the people. The gap between radical intellectuals and the suffering masses was even wider than was previously thought. Intensive research into 'Jacobins' in the 1960s and 1970s proved that there were, in Germany, not only isolated radical writers, but also organized groups of people, which pushed for quick and decisive changes akin to those of the French revolution. The aim of uncovering previously concealed democratic traditions has, to a large extent, been achieved. This same research has overreached itself, however, in attempting to prove, at the same time, the existence of genuinely revolutionary currents in Germany. The so-called 'German Jacobins' were not only different from their alleged exemplars in France, but they belonged in many instances to the group of decided critics of French Jacobinism. The assumed 'revolutionary-democratic' philosophy of the leading protagonists amongst them cannot be proved from the sources. One cannot really talk of a sharp distinction between them and liberal positions. Their revolutionary objectives were oriented towards the first phase of the revolution and towards the constitution of 1791, whereas the period of the Terror was rejected and there was even talk of a 'Jacobin counter-revolution'. They were for the most part Girondins rather than Jacobins, in the words of one recent study. They viewed violence with hesitation and the popular masses with scepticism. Even in the Mainz Republic of 1792–3 the division between radical intellectuals and the populace was obvious. This was also true of the Viennese conspiracy, which was uncovered in 1794. Its members, many of whom were hanged or imprisoned for many years, had cited the French example in order to protest against the abandonment of reforms in Austria.[8]

That which is usually brought together under the collective name of 'German Jacobinism' is in fact closer to the liberal 'spirit of 1789' than to the radical experiments of the years 1793–4. Nevertheless, the representatives of this tendency stood on the extreme left of the burgeoning political camps in Germany. These political currents had their origins not in the reaction to the French revolution, however, but in the 1770s, as Fritz Valjavec was able to show in a pioneering study of 1951. The initiative lay with those who pushed for political and social changes in the spirit of the Enlightenment, yet, even before 1789, conservative counter-currents had formed, sometimes publicly. Klaus Epstein demonstrated this convincingly in 1966 in his broad-ranging work *The Genesis of German Conservatism*. The French revolution effected a clear acceleration in the building-process of political strands, but it did not stand at the start of that process. And it was the rule of Napoleon that first provoked a clear politicization of German nationalism, which until then had oriented itself towards the concept of a 'cultural nation' or *Kulturnation*.[9]

II.

It has been said that the French revolution reached Germany in the years after 1800 under the hegemonic power of Napoleon, which is true, if one excludes the areas on the left bank of the Rhine, which stood under French rule from 1792 onwards. Within a few years, the dissolution of the old Holy Roman Empire and a reorganization of German territory took place, the radical nature of which would have been unimaginable only short time beforehand. French conquests on the left bank of the Rhine and the revolutionary demand that the Rhine was the 'natural border' of France constituted the trigger. The recognition of these claims by Prussia, Austria and the Empire, as well as the simultaneous agreement of compensation for territorial losses left of the Rhine, led, from 1797 onwards, to intensive negotiations, which were dominated by Napoleon and which, after an interruption because of war, came to a preliminary arrangement in 1803 and to a final conclusion in 1805–6. Historians of the nineteenth century already correctly talked of a 'revolution of the princes', who had disregarded existing law and historically established structures. Within three years the number of independent political units had been reduced to little more than a tenth of the previous number, and this figure takes no account of the 1,500 or so fiefs that had belonged to the imperial knights. The means that were used were secularization and 'mediatization'. Secularization meant that the Church principalities were abolished and their territories were added to lay principalities. The Catholic Church, which had previously been so powerful, thereby lost its entire temporal areas of authority. Moreover, secularization was also understood to involve the taking over of Church property, in particular the monasteries, by the new rulers. Catholic states such as Austria and Bavaria were especially rigorous in the execution of these directives. In Bavaria, for example, 70 per cent of all peasants after 1806 resided on state land, over half of which came from former monastic property. 'Mediatization' meant that the great majority of small principalities, almost all imperial cities, and all the imperial knights, lost their political independence and were added on to the remaining states and principalities. This reallocation of land – the so-called *Flurbereinigung* – meant at the same time an expansion and consolidation of forty or so states that survived. The notion of 'compensation' for losses suffered disappeared quickly into the background, because territorial gains in Baden were six times, in Württemberg four times, and in Prussia five times as large as the cession of land on the left bank of the Rhine. South Germany, in particular, witnessed the advent of so-called *Mittelstaaten* (middle-size states) such as Bavaria, Württemberg, and Baden, which became influential in shaping nineteenth-century German history. That all these changes contributed to the destruction of the German Empire was obvious. In this respect it only required one more step, which was taken in July 1806 with the founding of the Confederation of the Rhine, which was dominated by Napoleon and to which, initially, sixteen and, later, thirty-nine German states belonged. Francis II, a Habsburg, thereupon abdicated the German imperial crown and declared the Empire dissolved. Although he was by no means authorized to make such a declaration, it was challenged by no one – the political meaninglessness of the Empire was too conspicuous. It was – and there can be no doubt about it – Napoleon who fundamentally altered the German polity, but the German princes were willing accomplices, and to this extent the concept of a 'princely revolution' is thoroughly justified. In recent literature, this has been described as 'the real Napoleonic revolution' on German soil. Remarkably, after the submission of Napoleon, the Vienna Congress did not reverse the fundamental decisions that were made between 1803 and 1806. The new political structures proved themselves to be viable, notwithstanding the considerable transformation that occurred with the creation of the German nation state in the Bismarck period.

In 1983, Thomas Nipperdey opened his great *German history of the nineteenth century* with the well-known sentence: 'In the beginning, there was Napoleon.' He was, on the one hand, speaking of territorial reorganization, but, on the other, he was also alluding to the fact that the real 'process of modernization' in Germany first began under Napoleon. Timothy Blanning objected to this formulation several years ago, claiming that it expressed an impermissible underestimation of enlightened absolutism, and he pointedly summarized his reflections by suggesting an alternative formulation: 'In the beginning, there was Frederick the Great.' It might, however, be more appropriate to stress the significance of the French revolution. For Napoleon appeared in Germany not only as a conqueror, but also as the heir and executor of the revolution.[10] There is no doubt – and this is stressed much more determinedly in recent research than was previously the case – that there were profound changes in the political and social conditions during the years of Napoleonic rule in Germany. 'The first fifteen years of the nineteenth century can be seen in many respects', according to the judgement of Lothar Gall, one of the best authorities on the history of the nineteenth century, 'as the real revolutionary years in German history. It is then, and this is even more the case in the South than in the North, that the foundations were laid for subsequent development in its entirety, and no caesura until 1945 has proved itself more decisive than this one.' Reinhart Koselleck's judgement of the significance of the Prussian reforms runs along similar lines: 'The reforms of Stein and Hardenberg – as an answer to the French revolution – had in many ways a more revolutionary effect than the revolution of 1848.' Whereas the Prussian reforms – certainly in conservative interpretations – have always been accorded a place of honour in German history writing, the positive assessment of reforms in the south German states has only gained acceptance since the 1970s.[11]

When we talk of changes in Germany under the influence of the revolution and Napoleon, it is sensible to distinguish between several extended regions. A radical break with the political and social conditions of the pre-revolutionary period occurred in the areas on the left bank of the Rhine, which had been occupied from 1792 onwards and which were annexed in 1802. Here, French laws were in force, and more than two decades of French rule were long enough to leave behind lasting traces. Although the majority of the population was sceptical of, or opposed to, French rule, many basic innovations found widespread acceptance, from economic freedoms and the removal of feudal dependencies to the introduction of French civil laws (the Napoleonic code), the new constitution for the courts, and the reorganization of local government. As a result, they were defended stubbornly after 1815 as so-called 'Rhenish institutions', as these areas became part of Prussia, Hessen-Darmstadt, and Bavaria: It is by no means a coincidence that these areas became the centre of the liberal and democratic movement in Germany. By contrast, the 'French era' or *Franzosenzeit* remained a mere episode without far-reaching consequences in the extensive area of north Germany that was annexed by France in 1810.[12]

In a certain sense, this was also true of the two states that Napoleon created from scratch in 1808: the Kingdom of Westphalia and the Grand Duchy of Berg. They were intended not only to be bulwarks of Napoleonic power, but also to be 'model states', which constituted a form of advertisement for the new order. Thus wrote Napoleon towards the end of 1808, as he despatched the constitution of Westphalia to his brother Jérôme, the new king of Westphalia: 'Which people would want to return to the arbitrary rule of Prussia, when it has tasted the merits of a wise and liberal constitution? The peoples of Germany, France, Italy and Spain demand civic equality and liberal ideas.' Under these circumstances, it was not surprising that French legislation was transferred to the two states practically in its entirety. Characteristically, the Westphalian constitution was drafted in Paris and personally authorized by Napoleon. That, at best, only the beginnings of a prototypical regime came into being was attributable not merely to the fact that here, too, there was insufficient time to anchor the new legal system firmly in society, but also to the fact that the imperial interests of Napoleon were always given precedence over the specific interests of the two states. The generous gifts of land that were made to the newly created military and service aristocracy of the Empire stood in crass contradiction to the intended end of feudalism, on the one hand, and to the financial needs of the new states, on the other. Elisabeth Fehrenbach appositely summarized this problem: 'In the conflict of aims between moral victories and financial exploitation, between the consolidation of power through social reform and the stabilization of his rule by building up a new, economically-secure elite, the uncouth actions of Napoleon demonstrated that a satellite state was more important to the emperor than a model state.' Westphalia and Berg remain two particularly interesting examples, however, of an attempt to restructure society in a radical and progressive way under the aegis of military power.[13]

Reforms, which were partly prompted and partly demanded directly by Napoleon, constituted a component of Napoleonic power politics, especially in the south German states that belonged to the Confederation of the Rhine. If Napoleonic rule was not, over the longer term, going to rest exclusively on military power, then it was necessary, as Napoleon was convinced, to make the dependent states converge as far as possible with the social and political constitution of France. The interests of foreign policy demanded domestic reforms, particularly in immediately neighbouring states. It would, however, certainly be wrong to understand reforms in Bavaria, Württemberg, Baden, and the new Grand Duchy of Frankfurt or Nassau exclusively as a product of Napoleonic interests and interventions. These states had a strong self interest, which resulted in the first instance from the necessity of integrating very heterogeneous new territories. For example, in Baden, the area of which had more than quadrupled, extremely diverse legal and social conditions had to be unified in the interests of internal state building. In view of this situation, 'the adoption of the French system, with its abstract, rational and universally binding principles' was one obvious solution. Moreover, the tradition of enlightened absolutism, whose efforts had pointed in the same direction, was still alive and well, so that French ideas and models fell on relatively well-prepared ground. The new generation of leading civil servants consisted of reformers, who had been shaped by the Enlightenment and who now saw a chance of realizing their schemes of reform – which were, without doubt, considerably more radical and gave far less attention to existing conditions, than had previously been thought possible. The reforms in the states belonging to the Confederation of the Rhine were, under these circumstances, anything but a mere import or an expression of foreign rule, as German historiography claimed for almost one-and-a-half centuries. But Napoleon 'played', as Eberhard Weis phrased it, 'the role of a catalyst, which allowed the reform of state and society to become possible, necessary and pressing'.[14]

It is not possible to discuss reforms in the states belonging to the Confederation of the Rhine individually, nor, even, to present the leading characters such as Montgelas in Bavaria, Reitzenstein in Baden, or King Frederick in Württemberg. It is now agreed that Montgelas, Reitzenstein, and their immediate colleagues were just as advanced as the leading minds of the Prussian reform period, both in their political conceptions and in their concrete achievement of reform. Montgelas was always an attentive observer of the French revolution: 'What a great performance', he wrote as early as 1791, 'provided that we have the good fortune to profit from it (. . .), that is to say, that the French lessons are not lost.' For Germany too he sought in 1792 a 'more equal form of (political) representation, the extension of important human rights to all classes of society, equal tax liabilities without exceptions'. Montgelas's Ansbach memorandum of 1796 has, in the meantime, been recognized to be just as significant (but much earlier!) as the famous Prussian reform memoranda. The so-called 'administrative revolution' – the centralizing, rational restructuring of the entire administrative machine from the communes to the highest echelons of the state, which ignored inherited structures – constituted the very kernel of the reforms. This was necessary for the integration of the newly acquired territories, but, at the same time, it meant a consistent and ruthless exclusion of the competing claims to power of the nobility, of the Churches, and also of city corporations. Administrative reform created opportunities for the political participation of citizens and for necessary economic and social reforms. In Baden, a modified version of the Napoleonic code was introduced, and everywhere the constitution of the courts was altered at least in the direction of the French model. Measures against agrarian feudalism and for a liberalizing reform of crafts, trades and professions proved more difficult. On the other hand, political reforms pushed further in the direction of a representative constitution than, for example, in Prussia. The Bavarian constitution of 25 May 1808 was the first constitution to be both drafted and introduced in Germany, whilst Württemberg, Baden and the Grand Duchy of Hessen followed this example about a decade later. On the whole, the energetic endeavours of the reformers in south and south-west Germany succeeded in achieving for their states the breakthrough to modernity, even if there was still much to be done. Without the French revolution and Napoleon, this breakthrough would not have been possible. It was important for the history of Germany in the nineteenth century – above all in comparison to Prussia – that political reforms were carried forward more decisively, so that the more precocious states of the Confederation of the Rhine evinced a clear lead in the development of the constitution and, thereby, also in the development of the liberal and democratic movement until 1848. It was above all its proximity with France, its greater receptivity to the political reforms of the 1789 revolution, which allowed south-west Germany to become the heartland of German liberalism in the nineteenth century.[15]

If we examine briefly the much better known reforms in Prussia, the first thing to stress is that it was not a question here, as it was in the states belonging to the Confederation of the Rhine, of the internal consolidation of a new or considerably expanded state. Rather it was a question of the consequences resulting from an unusually heavy military and political defeat, with the Prussian state losing 49 per cent of its territory and 46 per cent of its population (so that it found itself to be of a similar order of magnitude as the newly founded Kingdom of Westphalia). That, under these conditions, a comprehensive reform programme was embarked upon, with all the risks which are necessarily associated with decisive structural changes, was intimated both by the political far-sightedness and the courage of the reform party, which was led by Stein and then, above all, by Hardenberg. That they were well aware of the risks is shown by Ludwig von Vincke's remark, that one would have 'to renounce most reforms', 'if one first had to investigate what they cost'.[16]

The programme of this 'revolution from above', as it was called in the relevant memoranda, was summarized in 1811 by Hardenberg:

The new system – the only one on which prosperity can be founded – rests on the idea that each inhabitant of the state, being personally free, can also freely develop and use his potential, without being hindered by another's arbitrary use of power; that no one one-sidedly bears a burden, which is not borne in common and with the same effort; that equality before the law is guaranteed to each state subject, and that justice is implemented stringently and on time; that merit, in whichever estate it finds itself, can rise unhindered; that unity, order and strength are laid down in the administration; that, finally, through education, through true religiousness and through an appropriate arrangement (of the whole), one national consciousness, one interest and one feeling can be created, on which our well-being and our security can be firmly grounded.

It was the reformers' belief that only a society that was based on the freedom and security of the individual and of property, which overcame the privileges and limitations of an estates-based, feudal society, could do justice to the needs of both individuals and the state. A strong state, a liberal economy and civic freedoms were the aim, although the accent differed between reformers. It was obvious that this programme went well beyond the reforming efforts of enlightened absolutism, and that it was beholden to Adam Smith as well as to the 'ideas of 1789'.[17]

Koselleck summed up those reforms which aimed to set free a liberal, capitalist society by claiming that the reformers 'consciously [opted] for Adam Smith against Napoleon', 'in order to drive out one with the other'. It is true that the reforms had the task of strengthening the Prussian state against Napoleon. But it is equally true that those reforms were not only used tactically, but that they had long-term goals. The 'October Edict' of 1807 did not simply announce the personal freedom of the dependent rural population, it also abolished estates-based limitations with regard to the acquisition and use of landed property and to the pursuit of trades. The complete freedom of trades was introduced in Prussia with the laws on trade of 1811–12 (and with the edict of 1812, Jews too were freed from almost all previous restrictions). Although the laws took a long time to come into effect in the economic sector, with compromises being made in the interest of the nobility, the steps towards the creation of a modern, economically oriented society were, on the whole, so successful that they laid the foundations for Prussian economic supremacy in Germany. Education and the army enjoyed a very high priority in the reform programme. In both cases, the reforms succeeded in a civic and liberal sense, and were perceived for a long time to be exemplary, even outside Prussian and German borders.[18]

An essential precondition of the whole programme was believed, from the start, to be the reform of the administration. With the creation of modern ministries, the institution of collegiate state government and the tight organization of administrative authorities down to the level of the local districts, an efficient system of government and administration was established, which came to characterize the Prussian state. Certainly, the participatory interests of the populace were, for the most part, ignored, so that it has rightly been said that on the political level the reforms actually only meant a transition from monarchical absolutism to the new form of 'bureaucratic absolutism'. The cities' right to self-government remained limited, and a constitution including representative state bodies – which was anyway conceived as a coping stone rather than as a foundation stone of reform – remained an unfulfilled promise until 1848. How important the constitutional plans were to the leading reformers is still a matter of debate amongst researchers. As late as 1815, the historian and reformer Niebuhr judged 'that freedom rests far more on administration than on the constitution'. This corresponded with the predominant self-confidence of reformist civil servants and it could find partial confirmation in the fact that any Prussian parliament at that time, however it was elected, would – it seems certain – have refused to back most reform laws. Those social strata that were meant to form the backbone of the new order were still much too weak in comparison with those whose privileges would be revoked or, at least, brought into question. The abandonment of reform after 1815 has often been interpreted as the failure of the reform movement. In fact, with the strengthening of the forces of opposition – after the successful restoration of the Prussian state's position of power – the result was that coexistence of economic 'progress' and political 'backwardness' that was typical of Prussia in the nineteenth century. Nevertheless, the Prussian reforms were, without doubt, a successful attempt in many respects to use the challenge of the French revolution to found, in a systematic way, a new civil and capitalist society.[19]

In order to counter the impression that the reaction to the French revolution consisted, almost with the necessity of nature, in reform, it is worth noting, in parenthesis, that the Austrian example shows that this reaction could consist in abandoning reform. Here there was no 'era of reform', but only a crude defence against all liberal tendencies in economy and politics. The reforms of Joseph II had preempted much that was addressed for the first time in south Germany and Prussia during the reform period, but they had also aroused strong forces of opposition, which saw themselves vindicated by the outbreak and course of the French revolution. From 1792 onwards, Austria tried for more than half a century to deliver proof that a strong state could exist without reforms.

III.

The question of why there was no revolution in Germany at the end of the eighteenth century has been discussed endlessly by historians. In such discussions, it has been pointed out that the policy of enlightened absolutism had not, by that juncture, been discredited, and that the capability of the German states to enact reforms had not yet fundamentally been brought into question. The confrontation between a princely state and a developing civil society was less starkly defined than was the case in France, and the signs of social crisis were regarded as less acute. Furthermore, there was the political fragmentation of Germany. There was no centre in which political decisions could be imposed. Disturbances and revolts remained isolated, the political nation was one of books and journals, not of the spoken word. One could examine other aspects in detail. It seems more important to me, however, to realize that the question is, in fact, wrongly formulated. A revolution such as that which occurred in France is itself evidently a special case, which is in need of explanation, rather than attempting to explain why, in Germany, and everywhere else, no revolution took place. The idea, which is still widespread, that revolutions are necessary in the transition from one type of society to another is just as tenuous as the assumption that revolutionary upheavals are a matter of political hygiene.[20]

The fact that the transition from the pre-civic to the civic world was introduced in France by revolution and in Germany by series of reforms, has been interpreted recurrently by German historiography right up until the present as a fundamental discrepancy of political style and content between the two countries – or even more generally: between Germany and 'the West'. It is without doubt correct that the revolution of 1789 in France, despite all of its faults, created a positive, identity-building national tradition, whereas in Germany the Prussian reforms were stylized in an anti-revolutionary tradition as a 'German way' to modernity. By contrast, those critical historians who pointed to a German *Sonderweg*, described the reform period as a turning point, in which Prussia-Germany uncoupled itself from the development of Western democracy and took its own specifically 'German' course, which diverged from the Western course of freedom and equality.[21] If one examines contemporary discussions and conduct more closely, however, the difference between revolution and reform is much smaller, and above all less fundamental. What revolution and reform obviously had in common was the demand that given circumstances should be altered 'according to fixed principles', as it was termed time and again, i.e. on the basis of enlightened theory. What distinguished the two were the means that were employed towards this end and, as soon became clearer, the agents of this process of change. In France, too, reformers had believed, by the strength of their arguments, that they could convince rulers to implement their plans until, confronted with the impossibility of achieving results in this way, there was a shift towards the use of violence. Still more important was the fact that, in France, the people eventually took over political power and demanded sovereignty, whereas, in Germany, changes were to be effected with and through the princes against the privileged estates.

As early as 1792/3, there were already voices in Germany amongst those who had welcomed the revolution enthusiastically, which now distinguished clearly between revolution and 'evolution'. 'We Germans need reforms; things must not always (...) remain as they are; but protect us from revolutions, dear God!' wrote Schlözer in 1793. The polemic of Johannes von Müller against the 'fury of the mob' and the 'scorn of demagogues' sounded much the same: 'I am for all evolutions, but not for a single revolution.' Experience of violence and terror belonged henceforth to the most important arguments against revolution, even if many continued to acknowledge that the two were not necessarily linked to revolution.[22] In this context, the question of when a people is 'mature' enough for freedom was debated extensively in Germany. The sudden lapse of the French revolution into violence and terror was seen to prove the French populace's lack of 'maturity' and to demonstrate the necessity of education over a longer term. Such was the public judgement of Wieland, for example, as early as 1791: 'A people, which wants to be free and in two full years has not learned that freedom is not possible without unconditional and unlimited obedience before the law (...) is, to put it as mildly as possible, not yet mature enough for freedom.' It was Kant who wrote, in 1793, that he could not get used to opinions that maintained that 'a certain people (which is in the process of working out its legal freedom) is not mature enough for freedom'. And he went on to argue:

> According to such an idea, however, freedom would never arrive: for one can not become mature enough for it, if one is never put in a position of freedom. The first attempts are admittedly raw, and are also bound up with more arduous and dangerous conditions, since one previously stood

not only under the orders, but also under the welfare of others; one only
matures enough for freedom through one's own experiments (for the
making of which, one must be free).

This classic liberal opinion admittedly remained a minority position
in Germany, whilst the majority believed, in the tradition of the
Enlightenment, in the education of people for a better future. For
Friedrich Schiller, this meant that one needed an 'improved' human
race for the 'political and civic freedom' that he, too, desired: 'One
must begin to create citizens fit for the constitution before one can
give citizens a constitution.' Scepticism *vis-à-vis* the unenlightened
popular masses and fear of unchecked actions 'from below' was
widespread in Germany (nor was it lacking in France).[23]

Leading reformers formulated in countless different ways the claim
that there was no discrepancy of aims between revolution and reform,
but merely one of means. Looking back, Clausewitz explicitly formulated, with regard to the Prussian reforms, 'that the aim of the French
revolution had been accepted, even though the means had been
rejected'. As early as 1809, he had formulated the thesis that Europe
could not, indeed, escape 'a great and general revolution': and only
those kings 'who know how to keep a step ahead of it, by entering
into the true spirit of the Reformation, will be able to survive'. It was
in this sense that talk of a 'revolution from above' was to be understood, whether it came from Montgelas, from Hardenberg, or other
reformers in Prussia. Governments should push through all changes
that were recognized to be desirable or necessary, even against the
will of society, but within the bounds of law and order, without
disturbances or participation 'from below'. Action lay within the
competence of rulers and their governments, not within that of the
people. Reformers entrusted their programmes to the unlimited
ruling power of the prince, although they aimed unambiguously to
replace the prince gradually with the 'state'. The new concept of 'state
citizen', which was introduced systematically by Hardenberg, aimed
at this transformation (and was for this reason rejected just as
dogmatically by the Prussian king after the reform period had
ended).[24]

Employed first by Klaus Epstein, and then by Elisabeth Fehrenbach,
the concept of 'defensive modernization' has in the meantime come
to constitute the core of Hans-Ulrich Wehler's interpretation in his
Deutsche Gesellschaftsgeschichte. What is meant is that reforms were more
or less forced upon German states through the French revolution and

Napoleon and that they were adopted in the first instance to avert the danger of revolution or, in other words, for defensive reasons. This is, however, to underestimate the considerable degree of conviction amongst reformers that structural changes were desirable and necessary. They operated within a theoretical framework that was determined to a significant extent by the Enlightenment, liberal economic theory and the 'ideas of 1789', and, in this sense, they acted 'offensively' and not 'defensively'. Certainly, the constraints imposed by Napoleon played an important role – but the decisive fact is that the reforms were meant to plan and structure the future. Their historical significance, which is no longer questioned, rests on the results achieved in this way. There was no realistic alternative to the decision in favour of reform. In Germany, the way to modernity at this juncture could only be the way of reform.[25]

If reformers in the period under discussion here did not differ significantly in their aims from revolutionaries – in economic questions they could even be more radical – these circumstances soon changed after 1815. Reforms were now increasingly understood to be limited alterations, which remained mindful of historical institutions and practices. In the German National Assembly of 1848, Friedrich Bassermann, for example, argued: 'We have no *tabula rasa* in Germany, we have given conditions, and it is necessary to reform, and not to revolutionize.'[26] On this understanding, those who wanted reforms operated on the basis of existing conditions, whereas supporters of revolution championed a change of system. This unambiguous antithesis between reform and revolution became, for many decades, a core element of the programme of the socialist workers' movement – and the majority of historians, too, still tend to think in terms of these outdated categories. It is all the more important to recall today, therefore, that, in the era of the French revolution and Napoleon, the similarities between reformers and revolutionaries were still greater than the differences between them.

In conclusion, I would like to stress the following points:

1. It remains incontestable that no revolution took place in Germany and, moreover, that all attempts to create a revolutionary crisis, including attempts to exploit the revolutionary will of parts of the population, failed. It is equally clear, however, that Germany did not lack a political public sphere, that there were social disturbances and conflicts in much greater number than was previously believed, and that the traditions of the Enlightenment

and of enlightened absolutism were stronger than had, for a long time, been claimed.

2. It is, likewise, undisputed that, despite the absence of a revolution such as had occurred in France, fundamental changes were wrought in Germany between 1800 and 1815. These did not only involve political and territorial changes, but also the transformation of the old order into a modern society. If revolutions are measured by the depth and duration of the changes achieved, then the period up until 1815 constitutes one of the most important revolutionary upheavals in German history.

3. These changes were realized in Germany by means of reform. In this respect, the reforms in a series of states belonging to the Confederation of the Rhine were not less far-reaching and forward-looking than the Prussian reforms, which have traditionally been studied more closely and judged more favourably. For all these reforms, the tradition of enlightened absolutism played an important role.

4. Nevertheless, it required the French revolution and the rule of Napoleon to inaugurate an 'era of reform' in Germany. The French revolution served, on the one hand, as a shock and, on the other, it opened up opportunities for genuinely reformist policies. Reform was described as the 'real revolution', and reform and revolution were, in fact, not as far from each other in their aims as used to be – and still is – commonly believed. Both strove for a new political and social order, which was to be based on the freedom and security of the individual and of property. To this extent, the interpretation of the reforms in Germany as 'defensive modernization' misses the central point. The concept of a 'revolution from above' comes closer to reality than critics of both right and left usually allow. Reform and revolution were two paths of the 'process of modernization' that was characteristic of European development – and revolution was the exception, not reform.

Notes

1. George Peabody Gooch, *Germany and the French Revolution*, London 1920; Alfred Stern, *Der Einfluß der Französischen Revolution auf das deutsche Geistesleben*, Stuttgart 1928; Jacques Droz, *L'Allemagne et la Révolution Française*, Paris 1959 (cf. Jacques Droz, *Deutschland und die Französische Revolution*, Wiesbaden 1959); Kurt von Raumer and Manfred Botzenhart, *Deutschland um 1800. Krise und Neugestaltung 1789–1815*, in Leo Just (ed.)

Handbuch der deutschen Geschichte, vol. 3, part 1, Konstanz 1959 (revised and enlarged version, Wiesbaden 1980).

2. Golo Mann, *The History of Germany since 1789*, London 1968 (first German edition: Frankfurt am Main 1958); Ernst Rudolf Huber, *Deutsche Verfassungsgeschichte seit 1789*, vol. 1: *Reform und Restauration 1789 bis 1830*, Stuttgart 1957; Elisabeth Fehrenbach, *Vom Ancien Régime zum Wiener Kongreß*, Munich 1981; Hans-Ulrich Wehler, *Deutsche Gesellschaftsgeschichte*, vol. 1: *Vom Feudalismus des Alten Reiches bis zur Defensiven Modernisierung der Reformära, 1700–1815*, Munich 1987; James J. Sheehan, *German History, 1770–1866 (Oxford History of Modern Europe)*, Oxford 1989.

3. See inter alia Jürgen Voss (ed.), *Deutschland und die Französische Revolution*, Munich 1983; Helmut Berding, Etienne François and Hans-Peter Ullmann (eds), *Deutschland und Frankreich im Zeitalter der Französischen Revolution*, Frankfurt am Main 1989; Arno Herzig (ed.), *'Sie und nicht Wir.' Die Französische Revolution und ihre Wirkung auf Norddeutschland und das Reich*, 2 vols, Hamburg 1989; Elisabeth Fehrenbach, 'Deutschland und die Französische Revolution', in Hans-Ulrich Wehler (ed.), *200 Jahre amerikanische Revolution und moderne Revolutionsforschung*, Göttingen 1976, pp. 232–53; Gonthier-Louis Fink, 'Die Französische Revolution im Spiegel der deutschen Literatur und Publizistik', in Hans-Otto Mühleisen, *Die Französische Revolution und der deutsche Südwesten*, Munich 1989, pp. 60–147; Helmut Reinalter, *Österreich und die Französische Revolution*, Wien 1988; Holger Böning (ed.), *Französische Revolution und deutsche Öffentlichkeit. Wandlungen in Presse und Alltagskultur am Ende des 18. Jahrhunderts*, Munich 1992.

4. See Rudolf Vierhaus, *Deutschland im 18. Jahrhundert. Politische Verfassung, soziales Gefüge, geistige Bewegungen*, Göttingen 1987; Hamish M. Scott (ed.), *Enlightened Absolutism. Reform and Reformers in Late Eighteenth Century Europe*, Ann Arbor 1990; Wolfgang Ruppert, *Bürgerlicher Wandel. Studien zur Herausbildung einer nationalen deutschen Kultur im 18. Jahrhundert*, Frankfurt am Main 1981. On the German Reactions to the American Revolution see in particular Horst Dippel, *Germany and the American Revolution 1770–1800. A Socio-historical Investigation of Eighteenth-Century Political Thinking*, Chapel Hill 1977; Horst Dippel, 'Die Auswirkungen der amerikanischen Revolution auf Deutschland und Frankreich', in H.-U. Wehler (ed.), *200 Jahre amerikanische Revolution*, pp. 100–21.

5. Johannes von Müller, quoted in G. P. Gooch, *Germany and the French Revolution*, p. 47; August Ludwig von Schlözer, *Staats-Anzeigen* 13, 1789, pp. 467f. Cf. Eberhard Bahr and Thomas P. Saine (eds), *The Internalized Revolution. German Reactions to the French Revolution, 1789–1989*, New York 1992. For useful collections of source material see Claus Träger (ed.) *Die Französische Revolution im Spiegel deutscher Literatur*, Leipzig 1979; Horst Günther (ed.), *Die Französische Revolution. Berichte und Deutungen deutscher Schriftsteller und Historiker*, Frankfurt am Main 1985; Theo Stammen and Friedrich Eberle (eds), *Deutschland und die Französische Revolution, 1789–1806*, Darmstadt 1988.

6. Georg Forster in a letter to his father in law Christian Gottlob Heyne, Mainz, 30 July 1789, in Georg Forster, *Sämmtliche Schriften*, vol. 8, Leipzig 1843, pp. 84 f; Friedrich Gentz in a letter to Christian Garve, Berlin, 5 December 1790, in Friedrich Carl Wittichen (ed.), *Briefe von und an Friedrich von Gentz*, vol. 1, Munich 1909, pp. 177 f; Friedrich Maximilian Klinger, *Werke*, vol. XI, Leipzig 1832, quoted in Werner Krauss, *Perspektiven und Probleme. Zur französischen und deutschen Aufklärung und andere Aufsätze*, Neuwied 1965, p. 245f; Georg Wilhelm Friedrich Hegel, 'Vorlesungen über die Philosophie der Geschichte', quoted in Pierre Aubenque, 'Kant, Hegel und die Französische Revolution', in Hans-Albert Steger (ed.), *Die Auswirkungen der Französischen Revolution außerhalb Frankreichs*, Neustadt an der Aisch 1991, p. 2.

7. Cf. Helmut Berding (ed.), *Soziale Unruhen in Deutschland während der Französischen Revolution*, Göttingen 1988; Arno Herzig, *Unterschichtenprotest in Deutschland 1790–1870*, Göttingen 1988.

8. 'Girondins rather than Jacobins': Volker Reinhardt, 'Reformer oder Revolutionäre? Deutscher und italienischer Jakobinismus im Vergleich', in *Zeitschrift für Historische Forschung* 21, 1994, pp. 203–20, especially p. 208. On the 'German Jacobins' see in particular Heinrich Scheel, *Süddeutsche Jakobiner. Klassenkämpfe und republikanische Bestrebungen im deutschen Süden Ende des 18. Jahrhunderts*, 2nd edn, Berlin 1971; Walter Grab, *Norddeutsche Jakobiner. Demokratische Bestrebungen zur Zeit der Französischen Revolution*, Frankfurt am Main 1967; Axel Kuhn, *Jakobiner im Rheinland. Der Kölner Konstitutionelle Zirkel von 1798*, Stuttgart 1976; Hellmut G. Haasis, *Morgenröte der Republik. Die linksrheinischen deutschen Demokraten 1789–1849*, Frankfurt am Main 1984; Helmut Reinalter, *Der Jakobinismus in Mitteleuropa. Eine Einführung*, Stuttgart 1981; Helmut Reinalter, *Die Französische Revolution und Mitteleuropa. Erscheinungsformen und Wirkungen des Jakobinismus. Seine Gesellschaftstheorien und politischen Vorstellungen*, Frankfurt am Main 1988; Helmut Reinalter, 'Volksbewegung und Jakobinismus in Mitteleuropa. Zur Dialektik von materieller Basis und Ideologie', in *Jahrbuch für Geschichte* 39, 1990, pp. 255–70; Walter Grab, *Ein Volk muß seine Freiheit selbst erobern. Zur Geschichte der deutschen Jakobiner*, Frankfurt am Main 1984. On the situation of the peasantry in France and Germany see Eberhard Weis, *Deutschland und Frankreich um 1800. Aufklärung und Revolution*, Munich 1990, pp. 67–81.

9. Fritz Valjavec, *Die Entstehung der politischen Strömungen in Deutschland 1770–1815*, Munich 1951; Klaus Epstein, *The Genesis of German Conservatism*, Princeton 1966; Frederick C. Beiser, *Enlightenment, Revolution, and Romanticism. The Genesis of Modern German Political Thought, 1790–1800*, Cambridge 1992.

10. Thomas Nipperdey, *Deutsche Geschichte 1800–1866. Bürgerwelt und starker Staat*, Munich 1983, p. 11; Timothy C. W. Blanning, 'The French Revolution and the Modernization of Germany', in *Central European History* 22, 1989, p. 114.

11. Lothar Gall, *Der Liberalismus als regierende Partei. Das Großherzogtum Baden zwischen Restauration und Reichsgründung*, Wiesbaden 1968, p. 3; Reinhart Koselleck, *Preußen zwischen Reform und Revolution. Allgemeines Landrecht, Verwaltung und soziale Bewegung von 1791 bis 1848*, Stuttgart 1967, p. 13.

12. Cf. Timothy C. W. Blanning, *Reform and Revolution in Mainz 1743–1803*, Cambridge 1974; Timothy C. W. Blanning, *The French Revolution in Germany: Occupation and Resistance in the Rhineland, 1792–1802*, Oxford 1983; Hansgeorg Molitor, *Vom Untertan zum Administré. Studien zur französischen Herrschaft und zum Verhalten der Bevölkerung im Rhein-Mosel-Raum von den Revolutionskriegen bis zum Ende der napoleonischen Zeit*, Wiesbaden 1980; Josef Smets, *Les pays Rhénans (1794 à 1814). Le comportement des Rhénans face à l'occupation française*, Berlin 1997.

13. Napoleon's letter to his brother Jérome, quoted in Elisabeth Fehrenbach, 'Verfassungs- und sozialpolitische Reformen und Reformprojekte in Deutschland unter dem Einfluß des napoleonischen Frankreich', in *Historische Zeitschrift* 228, 1979, p. 290; 'conflict of aims': Fehrenbach, 'Verfassungs- und sozialpolitische Reformen', p. 291. On the 'model states' see Helmut Berding, *Napoleonische Herrschafts- und Gesellschaftspolitik im Königreich Westfalen 1807–1813*, Göttingen 1973; Elisabeth Fehrenbach, *Traditionale Gesellschaft und revolutionäres Recht. Die Einführung des Code Napoléon in den Rheinbundstaaten*, 2nd edn, Göttingen 1978; Bettina Severin, 'Modellstaatspolitik im rheinbündischen Deutschland. Berg, Westfalen und Frankreich im Vergleich', in *Francia* 24, 1987, pp. 181–204.

14. The 'adoption of the French system': E. Fehrenbach, 'Verfassungs- und sozialpolitische Reformen', p. 292; 'the role of a catalyst': Eberhard Weis, 'Der Einfluß der Französischen Revolution und des Empire auf die Reformen in den süddeutschen Staaten', in *Francia* 1, 1973, pp. 569–83. On reforms in the Rheinbundstaaten see inter alia Eberhard Weis, *Montgelas, 1759–1799. Zwischen Revolution und Reform*, Munich 1971; Eberhard Weis (ed.), *Reformen im rheinbündischen Deutschland*, Munich 1984; E. Fehrenbach, 'Vom Ancien Regime', pp. 76–88, 170–8; E. Fehrenbach, *Traditionale Gesellschaft und revolutionäres Recht*; E. Fehrenbach, *Der Kampf um die Einführung des Code Napoléon in den Rheinbundstaaten*, Wiesbaden 1973; Walter Demel, *Vom aufgeklärten Reformstaat zum bürokratischen Staatsabsolutismus*, Munich 1993; Paul Nolte, *Staatsbildung als Gesellschaftsreform. Politische Reformen in Preußen und den süddeutschen Staaten 1800–1820*, Frankfurt am Main 1990; Manfred Hettling, *Reform ohne Revolution. Bürgertum, Bürokratie und kommunale Selbstverwaltung in Württemberg von 1800–1850*, Göttingen 1990; Andreas Schulz, *Herrschaft durch Verwaltung. Die Rheinbundreformen in Hessen-Darmstadt unter Napoleon (1803–1815)*, Stuttgart 1991; Jörg Engelbrecht, *Das Herzogtum Berg im Zeitalter der Französischen Revolution. Modernisierungsprozesse zwischen bayerischem und französischem Modell*, Paderborn 1996.

15. Montgelas as quoted in Eberhard Weis, *Montgelas*, pp. 224, 188; cf. H.-U. Wehler, *Deutsche Gesellschaftsgeschichte*, vol. 1, p. 371. On the history of German liberalism see James J. Sheehan, *German Liberalism in the Nineteenth Century*, Chicago 1978; Wolfgang Schieder (ed.), *Liberalismus in der Gesellschaft des deutschen Vormärz*, Göttingen 1983; Dieter Langewiesche, *Liberalismus in Deutschland*, Frankfurt am Main 1988; Dieter Langewiesche (ed.), *Liberalismus im 19. Jahrhundert. Deutschland im europäischen Vergleich*, Göttingen 1988.

16. Vincke as quoted in H.-U. Wehler, *Deutsche Gesellschaftsgeschichte*, vol. 1, p. 539; on the Prussian reforms see especially R. Koselleck, *Preußen zwischen Reform und Revolution;* Barbara Vogel, *Allgemeine Gewerbefreiheit. Die Reformpolitik des preußischen Staatskanzlers Hardenberg (1810–1820)*, Göttingen 1983; Barbara Vogel (ed.), *Preußische Reformen 1807–1820*, Königstein 1980; Bernd von Münchow-Pohl, *Zwischen Reform und Krieg. Untersuchungen zur Bewußtseinslage in Preußen 1809–1812*, Göttingen 1987; P. Nolte, *Staatsbildung als Gesellschaftsreform*; Otto Büsch and Monika Neugebauer-Wölk (eds), *Preußen und die revolutionäre Herausforderung seit 1789*, Berlin 1991.

17. Hardenberg's speech before the assembly of Prussian notables in 1811, quoted in Hans Hausherr, *Hardenberg. Eine politische Biographie*, part 3, 2nd edn, Cologne 1965, p. 232.

18. 'Adam Smith against Napoleon': R. Koselleck, *Preußen zwischen Reform und Revolution*, p. 14.

19. Ludwig Freiherr von Vincke, *Darstellung der inneren Verwaltung Großbritanniens*, edited by Barthold Georg Niebuhr, Preface, quoted in R. Koselleck, *Preußen zwischen Reform und Revolution*, p. 72. On the missing constitution see Herbert Obenaus, *Anfänge des Parlamentarismus in Preußen bis 1848*, Düsseldorf 1984.

20. See my essay on 'Problems of Revolution in Germany' in this volume.

21. For a critical discussion of the German *Sonderweg* thesis see David Blackbourn and Geoff Eley, *The Peculiarities of German History. Bourgeois Society and Politics in Nineteenth-Century German History*, Oxford 1984; for a positive assessment of a modified *Sonderweg* thesis see H.-U. Wehler, *Deutsche Gesellschaftsgeschichte*, vol. 3, Munich 1995, pp. 449–86.

22. August Ludwig Schlözer, quoted in A. Stern, *Der Einfluß der Französischen Revolution*, p. 67; Johannes von Müller, quoted in A. Stern, *Der Einfluß der Französischen Revolution*, p. 88.

23. Christoph Martin Wieland, quoted in A. Stern, *Der Einfluß der Französischen Revolution*, p. 111; Immanuel Kant, 'Die Religion innerhalb der Grenzen der bloßen Vernunft', quoted in A. Stern, *Der Einfluß der Französischen Revolution*, p. 178; Friedrich Schiller in a letter to Herzog Friedrich Christian von Augustenburg, 13 July 1793, in Claus Träger (ed.), *Die Französische Revolution im Spiegel der deutschen Literatur*, p. 269.

24. Carl von Clausewitz, 21 May 1809, quoted in H.-U. Wehler, *Deutsche Gesellschaftsgeschichte*, vol. 1, p. 532.

25. K. Epstein, *Die Ursprünge des Konservatismus,* p. 692; E. Fehrenbach, 'Verfassungs- und sozialpolitische Reformen', p. 308; H.-U. Wehler, *Deutsche Gesellschaftsgeschichte,* vol. 1, pp. 343–546.

26. Friedrich Daniel Bassermann in a speech in the German National Assembly on 19 June 1848, quoted in Reinhart Koselleck, 'Revolution', in *Geschichtliche Grundbegriffe,* vol. 5, Stuttgart 1984, p. 752.

RÜDIGER HACHTMANN

Success and Failure:
The Revolution of 1848

It is difficult to state conclusively whether the German revolution of 1848 was a success or a failure. I take a more sceptical view of the positive consequences of this revolution view than many recent historians of the period, at least in Germany. In order to explain and substantiate this position, I will begin by outlining a few theses taking a closer look at the character of the German revolution of 1848 and its social and political base. Then I shall discuss the question of the 'success or failure of the revolution' and the long-term effects of the events and developments of the year 1848. In the following I shall concentrate primarily on Prussia as the centre of the later German Empire, and I shall focus particularly on the situation in the cities.[1]

I.

From a socioeconomic standpoint, in the 1830s and 1840s (an era referred to in the historical literature as the *Vormärz* or pre-March period) German society was in the midst of radical changes. The traditional corporate order had been disintegrating for some time. In Prussia the guilds had been abolished as compulsory organizations (*Zwangsorganisationen*) in 1810–11. They persisted nevertheless as private associations. Apart from those of the aristocracy, estates in the classic sense had ceased to exist, but social classes (in the Marxist or Weberian sense) had not yet formed. The boundaries between the social strata were fluid. For this reason it is difficult to separate the various social strata from each other statistically with any precision. If we take existing local history studies for Germany as a basis, then at mid-century in cities with more than 10,000 inhabitants, the proportion of the 'upper class', that is, the bourgeoisie (*Bürgertum*) in the narrower sense, was about 5 per cent, and that of the lower middle classes (*Mittelschichten*) 10 to 20 per cent. More than three-quarters of urban dwellers, between 75 per cent and 85 per cent, belonged to the lower classes (*Unterschichten*).

Although these figures can only describe general trends, they make clear that a small bourgeois upper class existed alongside a numerically gigantic 'proletariat' (as contemporaries already disparagingly referred to the lower classes). The proletariat of 1848 had little in common with the industrial proletariat of the last third of the century, however. The lower classes were so deeply divided internally, not only socioeconomically, but also culturally and politically, that the labour movement that arose during the year of the revolution could take root only in certain segments of the early proletariat, primarily among journeymen and skilled factory workers. In the light of the quite different development in England, one must also emphasize that in all cities life trades remained strongly craft dominated throughout the 1840s and in many cases long beyond. This was also true of the European revolutionary metropolises of Berlin, Vienna, Paris and those cities on the Continent that had already experienced the vigorous beginnings of industrialization in the 1830s.

For both reformist and revolutionary movements, a society in the midst of radical change was both a burden and an opportunity. Social conditions on the eve of the revolution represented an opportunity because everybody had come to recognize that 'society' was not something played out according to unchanging rules, not a closed system, but rather an open structure. The revolutionary developments in the fields of the natural sciences and technology during the first half of the nineteenth century, and the radical political changes that had occurred particularly in France, Germany's western neighbour, since the end of the eighteenth century had opened up new perspectives. They turned many contemporaries into political optimists and believers in progress. History no longer appeared as immutable destiny. To be sure, the openness of history and the attendant insecurity about what the future might bring aroused fears as well as hopes. Many members of the bourgeoisie and the lower middle classes were afraid of downward mobility and of the social and political demands being made by the numerically gigantic and seemingly unpredictable proletariat.

From the beginning, the revolution of 1848 was shaped by yet another burden: society was splintered into many social strata that had little to do with each other. The bourgeoisie included the economic or propertied bourgeoisie (*Wirtschaftsbürgertum*) – the great merchants, bankers and manufacturers –, the higher civil servants on the state and municipal levels (who included, however, numerous members of the nobility) and, last but not least, the educated classes and free professions. The lower classes included journeymen, skilled factory workers and commercial clerks alongside day labourers, domestic servants and other mainly unskilled groups of workers, as well as impoverished master artisans who were frequently reduced to the status of homeworkers and, finally, the subproletariat. The lower middle classes were similarly heterogeneous.[2] The varying socio-economic positions frequently occasioned quite divergent, and from time to time conflicting, social and political interests. Even those social forces seeking reforms frequently had very different goals in mind. Germany's fragmentation into numerous smaller and larger states made coordinated efforts particularly difficult. A lack of simultaneous action and coordination, together with the divergent interests of the reformist and revolutionary movements, made the revolution's failure probable from the outset. The rather adroit operations of the old elites and traditional authorities after they had digested the initial shock in March 1848 were additional factors. I should like to address these points in more detail in what follows.

II.

I shall begin with a thesis: the revolution of 1848 was not a bourgeois revolution – at least not if one has the bourgeoisie as a social class in mind. The bourgeoisie, to the extent that it took an oppositional stance at all, did seek political changes in the form of freedom of the press, assembly and opinion, as well as the right to a say in the political decision-making process. These, however, were reforms to be wrested from the crown, and they were not supposed to go too far. At any rate the great majority of the bourgeoisie and the petty bourgeoisie did not want a revolution. The rigid and clumsy behaviour of the old authorities did provoke revolutionary uprisings in the capitals of the Habsburg and Hohenzollern monarchies. Under pressure from 'the street' in March 1848 all German states were transformed into constitutional monarchies. This did not, however, render obsolete the politics of avoiding revolution through cautious reform, which characterized the majority of the oppositional bourgeoisie. It did change its character and political thrust, though. From now on the primary goal was to prevent a radicalization of the revolution through reform policies in agreement with the old powers, by 'arrangement' with the sovereign. To 'calm the general unrest' was the first order of the day, as Heinrich von Gagern was later to describe the viewpoint of the liberal majority among the deputies to the 'preliminary parliament', which met in Frankfurt's St Paul's Church from 31 March to 3 April 1848, and to the German National Assembly.[3]

The political rift, present from the beginning, between bourgeois-influenced liberalism and radical democracy, with its roots primarily in the lower classes, was only temporarily papered over during the euphoria of the first days after the March revolution. To be sure, in 1848 both camps were united initially in their desire for the abolition of the pre-March restrictions on the freedoms of association, assembly and the press. There was already great controversy, however, over how these attainments were to be organized in practice. The lower classes' demands for freedom had a strongly sociopolitical flavour, but the overwhelming majority of the bourgeoisie feared the consequences of their own wishes for reform. Fearing democratic 'anarchy' and social revolts, instead of insisting on the unrestricted right to assembly and association they became, after the March revolution, increasingly emphatic in their calls for barriers to what they regarded as 'excessive liberties'. The majority of the bourgeoisie rejected the vociferous demands for participation that the lower classes made during the revolutionary year. The lower classes, large segments of whom were highly suspicious of the authorities, and the oppositional bourgeoisie taken as a whole, shared few, if any, positive objectives, and then only on individual points, and only temporarily.

In order to give some indication of the extent of the political differences between pro-reform liberals and the democratic-revolutionary movement, which also included the nascent labour movement, I shall offer two examples here: the debates surrounding the suffrage and the arming of the people. Unlike the democrats, most liberal bourgeois did not favour universal and equal manhood suffrage, preferring instead a census suffrage, which excluded 'dependent' individuals and weighted votes according to the voter's income and property. In addition most of them wanted a bicameral parliamentary system. The monarch was also to retain a strong position. (England and Belgium were important models for the moderate liberals here.) To be sure, no census stipulations were introduced for the elections to the German National Assembly. The pressure from the democratic-revolutionary movement was still too great in April 1848. In most states, however, the criterion of 'independence' could be established as a condition for participation in the elections. By these means up to one-quarter of the adult male population could be excluded from the suffrage – mainly wage-dependent members of the lower classes, most of whom embraced democratic attitudes. The liberals also succeeded, against the resistance of the democrats, in introducing an indirect electoral system. This meant that the primary voters did not elect the deputies themselves, but only so-called electoral delegates (*Wahlmänner*), who then elected the actual members of the German National Assembly. (A similar system was also introduced for elections to most parliaments of the individual states.) The 'independence' clause and the indirect method of election were filters built into the franchise that significantly weakened the democratic movement within the parliaments. Moreover, no true political parties existed in April 1848; the men elected were mainly prominent personalities. All of this explains why the German National Assembly and most provincial parliaments were dominated by moderate bourgeois notables, while the democratic currents in the revolution were underrepresented.[4] The actions of leading representatives of the bourgeois strata were guided in large measure by the desire to end the revolution as quickly as possible. This fact was also reflected in attitudes towards the questions of 'arming the people' and the reorganization of the police and military's functions in maintaining order in the larger cities. Above all, the lower classes were to be given no instruments of power that might allow them to insist effectively on the realization of their political and social demands. For this reason, during the founding and expansion of the civic guards (in German *Bürgerwehr* – the name says it all) only men who possessed municipal citizenship were accepted as members. Members of the lower classes were, as a rule, excluded from the right to bear arms.

The reasons why no reform coalition developed between the upper and lower classes become clearer when one examines the economic, social and political interests of particular segments of the bourgeoisie more closely. The economic bourgeoisie never favoured the 'revolution', even if they were reluctant to say so too loudly at the beginning. They were sceptical of even moderate political reforms. Only weeks after the March revolution, for example, the Berlin merchants' corporation, which represented the interests of the Prussian capital's bankers, merchants and entrepreneurs, demanded in an internal document in no uncertain terms that the ministry and the city government (*Magistrat*) must secure 'peace in public life and [restore] lost faith in the public administration of the laws'. In the face of the 'danger which, under present circumstances, has deeply shaken all social relations, threatens property and prosperity', drastic measures were necessary. If the authorities did not take the 'most energetic measures' to oppose the supposed excesses of the proletarian and democratic movements, the merchants' corporation feared the 'dissolution of all social relations, a general state of emergency' and the 'horrors of anarchy'.[5] This attitude of the Berlin merchants' corporation cannot, to be sure, simply be generalized to include the entire Prussian, let alone German economic bourgeoisie. There were considerable regional differences. While the entrepreneurs of the Prussian capital were emphatically anti-revolutionary, their West German counterparts had more liberal attitudes and were more open to substantial reforms. The assertion of a basically conservative stance is even truer of the higher civil servants on the state and municipal levels. As a rule, they continued to feel an obligation of absolute loyalty towards the old authorities. Beginning in the summer of 1848, when it became clear that the political winds were blowing against the democratic-revolutionary movement, the civil servants, most of whom had remained in their posts, more openly demonstrated their conservative opinions and let democrats and 'simple folk' feel that the old masters were also the new ones.

If the economic bourgeoisie and the higher civil servants kept aloof from the revolution, this also reflected the fact that the 'modernizations' these strata believed desirable had already been realized in their essentials, at least in Prussia, long before 1848. One should mention in particular the introduction of freedom of trade in 1810–11 and the founding of the German customs union (*Zollverein*) in 1834. In the same measure as it had proved politically 'reactionary' during the pre-March (*Vormärz*), the Hohenzollern monarchy had shown itself favourable to economic modernization. Contemporaries in 1848 had no reason to believe that this would change in future. Moreover, developments in trades and industry had been rather adversely affected by the political tremors of 1848. Absolute 'peace and order' – under whatever political conditions – appeared to entrepreneurs to be the best guarantee of a renewed economic upswing, which did indeed set in at the end of 1848. The great self-assurance and faith in the future of the economic bourgeoisie in particular, the feeling that aristocratic privilege could no longer touch their own firm economic and political position, facilitated the decision to oppose any substantial democratization of society. Moreover, many bourgeois did not need the revolution of 1848, and the countless lower-class tumults and revolts of that year, to make them enemies of revolution. Recollections of the great French revolution, above all of the phase between 1792 and 1794, of the Napoleonic occupation, and of the Paris July revolution of 1830, which had also been echoed in the German states, had become deeply engraved in the collective memories of these classes. The political and social fears were merely rekindled in 1848. It is not true that broad sections of the economic bourgeoisie and also the lower middle classes did not understand their 'objective interests' when they maintained a great reserve towards the upheavals of the revolution. The opposite is the case. It was precisely because the complete political equality of every citizen of the state, regardless of his social and economic position, contradicted their interests, at least in 1848, that the majority of the better-off classes of society did not embrace the revolution.[6]

A majority, but not the entirety, of the bourgeoisie rejected the revolution. The political behaviour of the educated classes, including the 'free professions', the third significant subgroup of the bourgeoisie, had very different contours from that of the civil servants and the economic bourgeoisie. Many members of the educated classes occupied leading positions in the democratic clubs. They were spokesmen at revolutionary mass meetings and demonstrations. The grassroots of the democratic-revolutionary movement in most larger towns were 'proletarian', but the leadership was bourgeois and educated. This group was dominated by young men of the starving writer variety, as well as journalists and members of related occupations, and finally, students, a sort of 'free-floating intelligentsia'. The educated classes by no means all belonged to the democratic camp, however. Rather, there was a sharp generational conflict: younger people in particular, who had been influenced by the religious conflicts and oppositional movements of the pre-March,[7] by radical democratic ideas and, in some cases, by the ideas of early socialism, were the ones who became enthusiasts of the 'new era'. It was also mainly younger people who were particularly active in the professional reform movements of physicians, university lecturers and teachers and who articulated demands in 1848 that were to remain relevant for many years to come, some of which were only realized in the twentieth century. Older men, in contrast, who were established in their professions and who had received their political socialization through the Wars of Liberation between 1813 and 1815, or the 'terrors' of the older French revolutions, or at least through the (mild) shock of the 1830 July revolution, maintained a reserved attitude. If one looks at the social group of the bourgeoisie as a whole, then, only a small minority, namely a substantial portion of younger educated men, embraced 'revolutionary' ideas. In the face of political polarization the bourgeois-influenced political centre, liberalism, melted away rapidly – at least in Prussia, if more slowly in the smaller states of central, western and southern Germany.

III.

        The revolution of 1848 was thus not a 'bourgeois revolution' – at least not if one takes the social class of the bourgeoisie as a yardstick. The German term *Bürgertum,* which I have translated here for the sake of simplicity as 'bourgeoisie', is however a multilayered one. It can also refer to *Staatsbürger,* the citizen of the state. If one uses this sense of the term *Bürger,* then the revolution of 1848 was indeed a 'bourgeois revolution': to be more precise, a revolution of citizens or a democratic revolution whose content was the establishment of 'bourgeois civil society', in German, *bürgerliche Gesellschaft.* After all, the agenda of 1848 – in abbreviated form – was the achievement of equal political rights for all men, independent of their social and economic status. In 1848 in Germany (in contrast to France), no side demanded social revolution, that is, the overturning of property relations or at least major interventions in the socioeconomic fabric. Even the early labour movement and the radical democrats did not pursue this as an immediate goal. In some German cities, however, socialist tendencies did gain in weight as it became apparent that the liberal March Cabinets had no intention of meeting the lower classes' social demands. Other subgroups within the revolutionary movement combined anticapitalism with pre-bourgeois utopias, such as the ideal of a closed guild society. The concept of 'bourgeois civil society' did not encompass the goals of all participants in the revolution. Nevertheless, even if those manning the barricades and leaving their mark on the subsequent events of the revolution were mainly members of the lower classes, 1848 was no 'proletarian' revolution. If one insists on a label, one might say that it was a revolution of citizens (*bürgerlich* in the sense of *staatsbürgerlich*).

        The German revolution of 1848 was a profoundly paradoxical phenomenon. If one looks at the centres of revolutionary action, proletarian strata, particularly journeyman artisans, impoverished ('proletaroid') independent artisans, commercial clerks and factory workers were the main actors. More than 85 per cent of the approximately 1000 Berlin barricade fighters known by name who were killed, wounded, or arrested by the military on 18 March 1848 belonged to the lower social strata. Similarly, members of the lower classes also made up the majority of insurgents in the Vienna March revolution, the storming of the Berlin armoury, and the October battles in Vienna.

In contrast, the parliaments and March Cabinets, which one might refer to as the 'institutionalized revolution', were dominated by the higher social classes: civil servants (particularly jurists), older educated men who were generally long established in their careers, and a significantly smaller number of bankers and early entrepreneurs.[8] In light of the basic attitudes prevalent among these social groups, it is not surprising that the liberal majorities in the German National Assembly as well as the provincial parliaments were interested in political reforms. There was, however, no majority in the parliaments of 1848 for fundamental social reforms that might have substantially improved the miserable conditions among the urban lower classes. A radicalization of the revolution was to be avoided at all costs. Most deputies did not realize that social reforms were the most effective preventive measure against social revolution. And even the political reforms proposed by liberals were based on a limited concept of citizenship encompassing only the bourgeoisie and segments of the lower middle classes.

Fear of the lower classes explains why a majority of the upper classes greeted the end of the revolution with undisguised relief. This can be followed particularly well in Berlin, where in mid-November 1848 a state of siege was declared, and where repression was thus especially harsh in the months that followed. The price that the bourgeoisie paid for the crown's victory – above all restrictions on the freedoms of assembly, association and the press – appears high only at first glance. In fact, the prohibitions on assembly primarily affected the lower classes. They were those most likely to assemble spontaneously in the streets. Their politics did not require formal organizations or elaborated programmes, agendas or committees. A brief description of their method of political action during the revolution might read as follows: journeymen, labourers and other members of the lower classes, including many women, gathered around the often very large placards posted by the clubs, the authorities, or individuals. They commented upon them loudly and argued with fellow onlookers who uttered contrary opinions or expressed their agreement with equal vociferousness. This was how the 'political corners' typical of Berlin and many other cities in 1848 arose. They not infrequently became the starting point for spontaneous mass actions and (thus) for revolutionary events.[9] Politically active bourgeois, in contrast, including those who espoused democratic ideas, preferred self-contained, coherent organizations with predictable structures and enclosed meeting spaces. Clubs with a fixed membership and a formalized associational life as well as parliaments were (viewed from the perspective of ideal types) the political forms suitable for the bourgeois activist; he generally remained sceptical of vast and incalculable mass rallies and spontaneous demonstrations.[10]

The sceptical or even hostile attitude of most bourgeois and petty bourgeois, of whatever political persuasion, towards the forms of politics common among the lower classes explains why these strata in Prussia were relatively willing to dispense with the right of assembly that they had fought for in March. This does not, however, explain why the bourgeoisie and lower middle classes also largely accepted the restrictions placed on the freedom of association. Only the bourgeois democrats and left-liberals, a minority within the bourgeoisie and petty bourgeoisie, clung firmly to the principle of democratically structured mass organizations. If a substantial majority of the better-off strata of society accepted the limitations on freedom of association announced in November 1848 without much protest, it was mainly for two reasons. Firstly, political associations were by no means universally prohibited. The authorities proceeded much more selectively than that. The radical democrats were hardest hit by the restrictions on association, followed by the moderate democrats and left liberals. The majority of liberal, conservative, or 'apolitical' citizens were largely unaffected. Secondly, most liberals preferred the model of the party of notables. Conservatives were fundamentally opposed to true political parties. Both right-wing liberals and conservatives remained suspicious of associations founded on the equality of all their members. After all, associations organized along democratic lines also permitted, as a matter of principle, the equal participation of members of the lower classes, a terrifying vision for wealthy citizens who feared social revolution and the overthrow of traditional property relations. Their terror grew when it became clear, in the summer of 1848, that the radical democratic clubs in Vienna, Berlin, Cologne and elsewhere actually possessed a broad and stable base among 'workers'. This was the main reason why the banning of the democratic and (left-)liberal clubs in mid-November 1848 and the return to traditional forms of politics were met largely with relief by conservatives and also many liberals among the bourgeoisie and petty bourgeoisie. Finally, restrictions on the press also affected primarily the radical democratic press, which (as the low print runs show) was scarcely read in bourgeois circles anyway, and thus were also accepted there without complaint.

These assertions apply primarily to Prussia, above all to the core provinces, but less to Silesia and the Rhine Province. In the smaller German states, particularly in the south west and Saxony, and here mainly in smaller towns where social and political polarization were less marked, the bourgeois and petty bourgeois strata were more strongly integrated into the revolutionary movement. If the majority of the Prussian bourgeoisie, in particular, increasingly followed the monarchy, the resentments and fears mentioned above were not the only decisive factors. Unlike the Habsburg monarchy, for example, the Prussian crown proved itself quite capable of learning political lessons from the revolution. It was well aware of the political and social fears of broad segments of the bourgeoisie and, from mid-1848 onward, it increasingly incorporated them into its political delibera-tions. In the face of the successful March revolution and a strong democratic movement, the Prussian monarchy saw itself compelled to seek additional allies in order to maintain power. It found them in the bourgeoisie and petty bourgeoisie.

To be sure, the counter-revolution of November 1848 was the political work of the monarchy and the old non-bourgeois elites. In fact, however, it was no accident that from a legal as well as a political standpoint Berlin, Prussia and Germany had a different, more bourgeois face after 1848 than they had before. Although it continued to draw support largely from the traditional elites, the Prussian crown saw itself forced to make concessions to the guild-oriented artisanal petty bourgeoisie as well as to the economic bourgeoisie in order to gain the loyalty of these strata and to expand and stabilize its social base. These concessions included, among other things, dissolving the union-like organizations of the early labour movement by the summer of 1850 and amending the Prussian trade regulations (*Gewerbeordnung*) on 9 February 1849. The last action was a political gift to the conserva-tive artisanal middle classes. It gave the trade guilds (*Innungen*) more influence by granting them greater authority in the training of apprent-ices, the admission of new craft firms and the like. More important, perhaps, than the actual content of these and other post-revolutionary reforms was the political message they sent to the bourgeoisie and the lower middle classes: post-revolutionary Prussia was open to bourgeois and petty bourgeois wishes, and a thorough overturning of the political system was thus superfluous. Political moderation and loyalty to the monarchy, it was suggested, were the only paths to the realization of their goals that stood any chance of success.

The liberal constitution promulgated by the Prussian crown on 5 December 1848 was addressed to the same social strata and additionally nourished this attitude. The Hohenzollern monarchy proved itself politically more flexible than the Habsburg monarchy, particularly in this regard. While Prussia formally remained a constitutional state even after the amendment of the constitution in January 1850, in Austria the constitution promulgated on 4 March 1849 was repealed altogether in 1851. The introduction in Prussia on 30 May 1849 of a franchise linked to a property qualification, replacing both the old corporate provincial diets and the national assemblies of 1848 elected by universal and equal manhood suffrage, can be regarded as a concession to the dominant tendency within the bourgeoisie. It met the wishes of many bourgeois to separate themselves, socially and politically, from the classes beneath them. The three voter classes, which were organized according to tax revenues, corresponded to the bourgeois ethic of achievement and increased the influence of the propertied bourgeoisie, which was overrepresented in the lower chamber of Parliament. Later liberal critiques complained less of the inequality of the suffrage than of the parliament's relatively limited or vaguely defined rights.

The liberals, who were also internally split, were nevertheless only partial victors: the reform of the military, which they, like the democrats, hoped to achieve, if in a more moderate form, did not materialize. The dominance of the old pre-bourgeois elites remained unbroken. The liberals had also not wanted the draconian political and legal restrictions that became common in the 1850s. In the face of the supposedly looming threat of social revolution, however, the right-wing liberals, at least, were prepared to accept all of this as the lesser evil.[11] Moreover, many liberals, at least in northern and central Germany, regarded Prussia as the state most likely to succeed in uniting Germany. This goal became increasingly important after 1849. To be sure, not all liberals were willing to postpone or relinquish altogether demands for a reform of the political system in order to achieve national unity, but many were.

IV.

Even in 1848 serious differences had existed between the main political tendencies over what a united Germany would look like and under what political circumstances national unity should be achieved. The very terms 'nation' and 'German unity' could be invested with widely diverging contents. In order to get to the bottom of these differences, I shall enlist the help of the terms 'patriotism' and 'nationalism', whereby 'patriotism' aims at the coexistence of equal nations, and 'nationalism' implies the superordination of the German nation to other nations. Who could be regarded as a patriot according to this definition, and who, as a nationalist, became particularly clear in Prussia during late April and early May when the Poles of the Prussian Grand Duchy of Posen staged a revolutionary uprising to secure their own sovereign state.

By this definition, not only the conservatives, who were highly sceptical of German unification anyway, but also a substantial group among liberals in 1848 must be considered 'nationalist': for them, the maintenance of so-called 'German national traditions' (*deutsches Volkstum*) in the Prussian Grand Duchy of Posen had priority. At the same time they denigrated the Poles as an inferior nation and built up the Germans, at least culturally, into a superior nation who possessed the right to rule over supposedly inferior peoples. On 15 April 1848, the widely-read *Spenersche Zeitung,* for example, declared 'that it was an indisputable fact that the German folk character has always been called to a deeper and more perfect formation and a richer life development than the Slavic, that it unites within itself all the elements that entitle it to a complete representation of political and religious freedom'. To give in to the Poles' desire for political sovereignty would be 'nothing less than to reduce the higher life-element, the more mature and perfectly formed folk character, to a subordinate level' and to 'sacrifice' the German minority to 'a more immature nationality'. The left-liberal *National-Zeitung* also asserted (on 11 July 1848) that 'the Slavs were always behind the Teutons at all points in their development'. To grant political sovereignty to the Poles and other Slavs was thus 'impossible at present'. Attitudes such as these apparently met with a positive response among broad segments of the better-off population. They were uttered not least in the parliaments. The speech of the author and deputy Wilhelm Jordan, held during the so-called Polish debate on 24 July in Frankfurt's St Paul's Church, became famous. Jordan referred to the democratic deputies' demand that the Poles also be granted national sovereignty, as 'idiotic sentimentality'. It was 'high time' that the Germans shed their 'dreamy self-forgetfulness and foolish enthusiasm for all manner of nationalities' and developed a 'healthy national egotism'. 'The superiority of the German tribe over most of the Slavic tribes' belonged to the 'facts of natural history'. He considered those who supported the Poles' right to national self-determination, and who were thus willing to 'cast adrift' the 500,000 Germans living in Posen, 'unconscious traitors to their people, at the very least'. He apparently spoke for a large proportion of the German National Assembly's members, for his speech ended in 'loud peals of applause that went on for some time'.[12] Other parliamentarians who sat on the right wing of St Paul's church were seduced by national conceit into quite other visions. In an 1848 work the Austrian deputy Karl Moering had referred to 'the Germanic element as the most numerous, physically beautiful, morally refined, intelligently pure, which best unites beauty and strength, permanency and goodness. For this reason it deserves to rule over the world'.[13] Viewed in retrospect, these phrases did not bode well. Clearly, segments of the movement for national unification were beginning to shed their emancipatory origins and to develop an aggressive brand of nationalism.[14] Although Jordan's chauvinistic speech also received the approval particularly of the liberal factions in St Paul's church, and Moering's opinions were well-received beyond the borders of the multi-ethnic Austrian state, most liberals could not adopt such notions. Admittedly, the trouble with the liberal concept of nation was that its content tended to be vague and was thus open to broad interpretations. For many liberals, the idea of nation also had an integrative function; the struggle for national unity was supposed to unite the various political positions and currents and also include the German princes. This concept was not wholly unrealistic, since monarchs such as Frederick William IV also looked to German unity as a lofty goal. The Prussian king, however, associated quite clear political objectives with 'national unity': only he and the other princes should be able to decide who would wear the imperial German crown. This excluded any substantial liberal participation in the decision on the constitutional form of German unification and on the identity of the head of state.

While the liberal idea of nation was thus also open to conservative, pre-revolutionary concepts of German unity,[15] the democrats' notion of national unification was directly tied to securing and expanding the political and social order that developed in the wake of the March revolution. For the democrats even a partial sacrifice of the achievements of the revolution and of further reforms in the name of German unity was out of the question. In their view, as in that of the labour movement, it went without saying that the Poles had as much right to national and thus political autonomy as the Germans.[16] On this matter, the left was admittedly largely isolated in St Paul's Church and no doubt among the bourgeois public more generally. The German National Assembly rejected by a three-quarters majority their motion to 'declare the partition of Poland a disgraceful injustice' and to recognize it as 'the German people's sacred duty' to 'participate in the restoration of Poland'.[17]

The democratic patriotic movement for a unified German state was additionally weakened by the greatly varying importance attached to the German question by the revolutionary movements in the various states. For the democratic movement in Prussia, the call for national unity was, on the whole, only one demand among many. Here it was above all a welcome instrument in the day-to-day struggle against a strongly Prussian-flavoured conservatism.[18] In southern and western Germany, by contrast, the national question appears to have been a sort of focal point for the revolutionary movement, including the liberals. The reasons for this, in my view, deep-seated difference between Prussia and the south-west German middle states can only be touched on here. In south-western Germany, even before the revolution, relatively 'modern' quasi-constitutional monarchies had been established, despite strong corporate roots. Baden had had a constitution since 1818, and Württemberg since 1819. Both states had liberal electoral laws that granted the vote to relatively broad segments of the male population. For both states and their local liberal and democratic movements, national institutions, namely the German Confederation, which was dominated by the hegemonic powers of Austria and Prussia, represented the most important obstacle to more extensive reforms. For this reason, south-west German democrats and liberals placed demands for national unity in the foreground. Only unification seemed to hold out the promise of expediting the democratization of political structures in their own states. The situation in Prussia was altogether different. In the Hohenzollern monarchy external factors were not the main obstacles to political development. Here, a repressive domestic policy blocked even timid attempts to democratize society. For the Prussian democrats, at least, basic reforms in their own country had first priority. From their standpoint the political unification of the nation could only be a secondary goal.

All of these fundamental contradictions and tactical differences within the national movement in 1848 in turn made it easier for the Prussian king, Frederick William IV, to refuse the imperial crown which the German National Assembly offered him. To be sure, Frederick William IV was not opposed on principle to German unity. He had no intention, however, of wearing an imperial crown that bore the 'vile stench of the revolution of 1848'. He did not want to be crowned with 'such an illusory hoop, baked of filth and rags'.[19] The only imperial unification he could accept would come 'from above' – without or against the revolution.[20]

V.

The heterogeneity of the social base of the revolution and the multiplicity of political currents and lines of conflict were not the only factors that determined the 'fate' of the revolution.[21] The revolutionary and reformist movements of the Habsburg and Hohenzollern monarchies, in particular, carried an additional handicap: they had had no opportunity before 1848 to articulate their critiques of the authorities or to engage in 'party' politics within autonomous clubs or on the parliamentary stage. This was in contrast to south-western Germany, where parliaments and party-like organizations had existed as training grounds for many years. A further burden was the overwhelming and seemingly complete initial success of March 1848. Once the old ministers abdicated and the monarchs uttered a few political promises, the revolutionaries of Vienna and Berlin believed they had attained all their objectives. The March movements intimidated the old powers, to be sure, but they failed to deprive them of real power. No far-reaching political changes were made. The superficiality of the structural alterations in turn determined the failure of the revolution. When in the summer the left discovered the importance of demanding a democratization of the army and substantial reforms in such areas as the bureaucracy and the justice system, it was already too late. The old powers had consolidated. The revolution could be carried no further, and the counter-revolution was all but unstoppable.

The revolution of 1848 ended in defeat – not only in Germany, however, but all over Europe (with the exception of Switzerland). The revolution was not, however, a complete failure. The feudal rights and bonds that still existed in the agrarian sector were largely abolished. Broad segments of the population had been profoundly politicized. The establishment of the various political currents on a national level was also a great step towards modernity.[22] The emancipation of the Jews was extended and, on a formal level, at least, largely completed.[23] Formally, large parts of Germany and here particularly Prussia became 'constitutional states' in 1848. Many historians regard this as the greatest success of the revolution.[24] I take a more sceptical view. Doubtless the mere existence of a constitution is important. There is no question that the catalogue of basic rights compiled in St Paul's church and the Prussian constitutions of 1848 and 1850 were of great historical significance as models for the imperial constitutions of 1867 and 1871, the Weimar Constitution and the Basic Law of the Federal Republic. More important, however, is 'constitutional reality' and the actual functioning of a political system.

A basic problem with the Prussian constitution of December 1848, and to a lesser extent with the amended constitution of January 1850,[25] was that they were granted from above. Ultimately, however, the promulgation of a constitution by unilateral royal decree, and with it the possibility that the king can restrict or repeal it altogether at any time, and a 'constitutional state' are mutually exclusive. From the beginning, the constitutions equipped the monarchy with a structural predominance. The promulgation of the constitution of 5 December 1848 testifies above all to the psychological skill of influential circles. Leopold von Gerlach, one of the closest and most influential ultraconservative advisers to the Prussian King Frederick William IV, aptly summarized the Crown's intentions when he asserted that, with an eye to broadening the monarchy's social base, the crown could not and would not abolish the constitution. It was, rather, a matter of 'weakening it with substructures' and rendering it 'anti-revolutionary'.[26]

In the face of these so bluntly uttered intentions, which influential circles in Prussia pursued with the promulgation of the constitution, it is scarcely surprising that the most extensive liberties contained in the constitution were not matched in political practice. Instead, the basic rights guaranteed by the Prussian constitution were systematically undermined in the 1850s. In some respects, the period between 1850 and 1859 fell behind even the constitutionless pre-March period.[27] It was no accident that the promulgation of the constitution was accompanied by the appointment of the government official Karl Ludwig von Hinckeldey as chief constable of the Berlin police and his subsequent rise to the position of informal minister of police in Prussia. Hinckeldey, who was also one of Frederick William

IV's closest confidants, was responsible for a whole series of decrees and laws introduced in 1849 and 1850, which severely curtailed the freedoms of association, assembly and the press formally guaranteed by the constitution. Hinckeldey is known not least as the creator of the modern Prussian secret police, which covered the entire country with a tight network of informers in order to prevent the democratic movement from regaining strength.[28]

The Prussian monarchy created for itself a constitutional façade that included a parliament possessed of only very limited substantial rights in relation to the crown. The constitutional conflict between a liberal-influenced Prussian chamber of deputies on the one hand and William I and Bismarck on the other a decade-and-a-half later expressed this dilemma quite conspicuously. In addition, the deputies of the Prussian lower house were selected by a non-democratic suffrage. To be sure, this can be regarded to some extent as a 'bourgeois success', since the three-class voting system introduced in Prussia on 30 May 1849 accommodated (right-wing) liberal ideas by giving substantial weight to the propertied bourgeoisie and excluding the lower classes, for all intents and purposes, from political codetermination. When compared to the democratic suffrage that had been introduced for the elections to the German and Prussian National Assemblies in 1848, the three-class voting system doubtless represented a significant regression.

Viewed in retrospect, 1848 cast long shadows over the decades that followed. The defeat of the revolution lastingly strengthened the antidemocratic powers of the old regime. The experience that revolutions were possible not just in France but also in Germany and Prussia forced the traditional elites to break out of their condition of political rigidity. The ultraconservatives became consummate masters of the modern instruments of mass influence. It is no concidence that the notorious *Kreuz-Zeitung*, a widely-distributed ultraconservative daily newspaper, was founded in 1848. In particular, however, the revolution forced the pre-bourgeois elites to form social coalitions that enabled them to maintain power for much longer than they would have if the revolution had never exerted pressure on them. In a sense, the Prussian constitutions of December 1848 and January 1850 represented the official seal of approval on the coalition between the old and new elites.

VI.

In conclusion, I would like to mention one result of the revolution of 1848 that, as I believe, had a particularly lasting influence. The outcome of this revolution confirmed and fortified a specific political character and mentality in Germany. It can be roughly characterized as follows:

1. The defeat of the revolutionary movement corresponded with the beginning of a renaissance of 'blueblooded arrogance'. The bourgeoisie by no means relinquished its own values and cultural guidelines, but it made only a limited effort to impose them on society more generally. In this regard Prussia-Germany was, to be sure, no exception in the European context.[29] It is important nevertheless that the old elites' leading role in the sociocultural and especially in the political field remained unchallenged and even gained in social influence after 1849.

2. In view of the later history of Prussia and Germany it was especially unfortunate that, after the Prussian army's 1849 'successes' in Saxony, the Palatinate and Baden, military 'virtues' received a more positive response among broad segments of the population. To be sure, here too there are obvious lines of continuity reaching farther back into the past, particularly to vaunted glories of the Seven Years' War (1756–63) and the Wars of Liberation (1813–15). 1848, though, represents a missed opportunity to break with this tradition. Even the army's oath of loyalty to the constitution, which had been promised by the king, never came about. After 1849 the army was dazzlingly rehabilitated from the disgrace of 18 March 1848, and its social importance greatly increased. The ultraconservative military leadership's dream in 1848 of extending and elevating military virtues to universal social virtues in order to immunize the population against revolutionary ideas[30] became at least partial reality in the second half of the century. Military values, titles and modes of behaviour gained increasing approval among bourgeois civilians. Even many of those who in 1848 had made no secret of their disdain for the Prussian military, its deeply undemocratic structures and 'glorious past', changed after 1866 into uncritical and at times enthusiastic proponents of Prussian military strength.

3. The defeat of the revolutionary movement confirmed a deep-seated attitude towards the authorities in Prussia, one with roots

in the 'enlightened absolutism' of Frederick II and above all in
the Prussian reforms of 1806–15, which many older people had
experienced personally: the hope for a 'revolution from above'.
It was, in turn, this same attitude that made Bismarck's 'white
revolution' possible in the first place. With the defeat of the
revolutionary movement of 1848 the opportunity to found a
strong, democratic and non-authoritarian tradition in Prussia and
Germany, and with it an antithesis to the subservient mentality
was also lost.[31]

4. The striving for national unity in 1848 was combined by many,
    but not all people, with a nationalism that denied other nations
    the right to political sovereignty. Even a partially successful
    democratic revolution would have allowed a patriotism that
    respected the rights of other peoples to attain much greater
    influence *vis-à-vis* an arrogant and aggressive nationalism.

The failure of the German, and in this case Prussian, revolution of
1848 confirmed and heightened fateful basic attitudes. Without the
experience of the defeat of the revolution, a solution of the constitutional conflict of 1862 to 1866 in Bismarck's favour would have been
scarcely possible. William I – if the so-called 'case-shot prince' had
even been considered a candidate for German sovereign – would not
have been offered the imperial crown by the rulers of the German
states, but by a parliamentary deputation. Above all, had imperial
unification been accomplished from below rather than from above,
the political system of imperial Germany would have borne clear
democratic and constitutional characteristics. The trauma of the
failed revolution 'from below', in contrast, made many democrats
surrender, sooner or later, to a successful practitioner of power politics.
It made them receptive to the blessings of a revolution 'from above'.

Certainly, one should not overinterpret the revolution's negative
consequences. There was no direct path from 1848 to '1914' or even
'1933'. A whole series of developments and events pointed German
history in the direction that it actually took.[32] This does not mean,
however, that 1848 was inconsequential. The result of the revolution
of 1848 was a pseudo-constitutional Prussian monarchy, which in turn
became the main constitutional as well as the political model for the
German empire founded in 1871. The strong position first of the
Prussian king and then of the German *Kaiser* blocked political reforms
that would have cleared the way for a truly parliamentary monarchy.
Reform remained backed up, despite the constitution of 1871, and

despite Bismarck's social legislation. First thwarted and then defeated, the first German revolution made a second radical political change necessary. This second democratic revolution of 1918–19 failed because of '1848' – not least because of the political characteristics that had been decisively reinforced by the first revolution. The particular tragedy of both revolutions was that their failure rendered the 'Caesarist stance'[33] more acceptable, and respectable. A good fourteen years after the March revolution of 1848 the first modern German 'Caesar', Otto von Bismarck, began to determine the fortunes of Prussian-German politics. A good fourteen years after the November revolution of 1918 a much more terrible 'Caesar' assumed power, whose regime would bring war, terror, and misery to all of Europe.

We should not become too fixated on this negative German tradition, though. The revolution of 1848, or, to be more precise, the left liberals, the democrats, and the early labour movement as the political currents that carried the revolution, also founded a positive tradition. They offered democratic self-confidence as an alternative to the spirit of subservience. Instead of arrogant nationalism they postulated a patriotism that respected other peoples' right to self-determination; they also showed signs of beginning to think and act in terms of a democratic Europe. In place of the pseudo-constitution promulgated by the Prussian crown they posited the concept of a parliamentary and social democracy. This tradition of the revolution of 1848 has put down strong roots in Germany since the end of the Second World War. It is to be hoped that it will continue to grow in strength in future.

Notes

1. The concentration on developments in the cities has certain problems because three-quarters of all inhabitants of the German states at mid-century lived in the countryside. At the same time, the mainly uncoordinated and spontaneous agrarian revolts of March and April 1848 as well as later social-revolutionary movements in the countryside did not have a major impact on the revolution, at least in the German states. The revolution of 1848 remained largely urban. The best overviews of the German revolution are Wolfram Siemann, *Die Deutsche Revolution von 1848/49*, Frankfurt am Main 1985; and Dieter Hein, *Die Revolution von 1848/49*, Munich 1998. On the revolution of 1848/49 as a European phenomenon see, particularly, Jonathan Sperber, *The European Revolutions, 1848–1851. New Approaches to European History*, Cambridge 1994; Manfred Botzenhart, *1848/49: Europa im Umbruch*, Paderborn 1998; Dieter Dowe,

Heinz-Gerhard Haupt and Dieter Langewiesche (eds), *Europa 1848. Revolution und Reform*, Bonn 1998.

2. In order to offer at least a rough impression of the internal differentiation and scope of the various substrata, it may be useful to give some more figures for Berlin (for which, in contrast to most other cities, excellent statistics already existed before 1848): the (upper) middle classes or bourgeoisie (*Bürgertum*) of the Prussian capital claimed a scant 5 per cent of the Berlin population. The propertied or economic bourgeoisie (*Wirtschaftsbourgeoisie*) and higher civil servants each made up 0.6 per cent, the educated classes 2.2 per cent. Other people who belonged to the bourgeoisie in the broad sense were rich rentiers and pensioners, with 0.8 per cent, and students and others who were training for a bourgeois profession with 0.7 per cent of the city's population. The (lower) middle classes (*Mittelschichten*), approximately 12 per cent of the population, included well-off master artisans (4 per cent), middling and 'smaller' shopkeepers (1.5 per cent), self-employed people engaged in transport and the like (1.5 per cent), middle and lower civil servants and salaried employees (2.1 per cent) and the remaining rentiers and pensioners (3 per cent). The Berlin lower classes (*Unterschichten*) were also composed of four sub-groups, namely the 'proletaroid self-employed' (some 13–14 per cent of the total population), skilled labourers (37–38 per cent), unskilled labourers including most female domestic servants (approximately 27 per cent) and the subproletariat, whose numbers are very difficult to calculate, but which, according to official statistics, made up some 5 per cent of the population, a figure that is doubtless too low, however. For more on this see Rüdiger Hachtmann, *Berlin 1848. Eine Politik- und Gesellschaftsgeschichte der Revolution*, Bonn 1997, pp. 70–81. All the following details on Berlin are taken from this work.

3. My discussion here follows Manfred Botzenhart, *Deutscher Parlamentarismus in der Revolutionszeit 1848–1850*, Düsseldorf 1977, p. 117. The German National Assembly, in contrast to the Prussian National Assembly, was not formally obliged to reach an 'agreement' with the sovereigns in regard to politics or the constitution. The deputies in St Paul's church practised a *de facto* voluntary politics of agreement, however, a politics of unilateral handicaps in which they appealed at many points to the reigning monarchs, failed to incorporate the central imperial authority into a democratic parliamentary system, and created a legal stopgap, a substitute emperor in the form of the Imperial Governor (*Reichsverweser*), in the hope that the princes would at least offer their blessing after the fact.

4. On the local level, too, the bourgeois and petty bourgeois strata did their best to exclude the lower classes from political participation. This can be demonstrated particularly well for Berlin. Here, new elections to the town council were set for May 1848. The majority of town councillors in the Prussian capital decided to retain the principle introduced for the

1809 council elections, according to which only Berlin citizens were eligible to vote. These represented scarcely one-third of the city's total male population. The democratic or left-liberal minority in the city parliament proposed a motion to introduce universal, equal suffrage, but this was rejected by a large majority.

5. Resolution of the elders of the KKB ad. No. 383, 12 May 1848, Landesarchiv Berlin, Stadtarchiv, Rep. 200-01, No. 348, p. 3.

6. On this see, for example, David Blackbourn and Geoff Eley, *Mythen deutscher Geschichtsschreibung. Die gescheiterte bürgerliche Revolution von 1848,* Frankfurt am Main 1980 (published in a revised version as *The Peculiarities of German History: Bourgeois Society and Politics in Nineteenth-Century Germany,* Oxford 1984). It is senseless to construct a *Sonderweg* (for Germany) and a 'normal path' (for France or England). For the behaviour of the 'bourgeoisie' (*Bürgertum,* in many cases also used in the general sense of 'middle class') – also often an excessively inclusive category – the point in time of revolutionary events, before 1789 or after 1794, is decisive. The nightmare of a radicalization of the revolution, as it had occurred between 1792 and 1794 in France, and of the political rule of the lower classes, or at least their partial participation in power, was omnipresent for most bourgeois in 1848, whether implicitly or explicitly, and influenced their behaviour in large measure. If the German *Bürgertum* (or at least large segments of the German bourgeoisie in the narrower sense) appears to have been more 'conservative' or 'reactionary' than its English or French counterparts, this was not a matter of national character. Instead, it was a result of the fact that in the German states revolutionary situations only matured long after 1789 or 1792–94, and historical memory was thus wholly different.

7. See, particularly, Sylvia Paletschek, *Frauen und Dissens. Frauen im Deutschkatholizismus und in den freien Gemeinden 1841–1852,* Göttingen 1990; Jörn Brederlow, *'Lichtfreunde' und 'Freie Gemeinden': Religiöser Protest und Freiheitsbewegung im Vormärz und in der Revolution von 1848/49,* Munich 1976.

8. See the figures on the social composition of the German and Prussian National Assemblies in M. Botzenhart, *Deutscher Parlamentarismus,* pp. 161 and 517. In France, in contrast, the proportional weight of the propertied or economic bourgeoisie among the deputies to the Assemblée Nationale was much greater. See Heinrich Best, *Die Männer von Bildung und Besitz. Struktur und Handeln parlamentarischer Führungsgruppen in Deutschland und Frankreich 1848/49,* Düsseldorf 1990, p. 59 (Table 1).

9. On the typical popular forms of protest, more generally, namely what is known in German as *Katzenmusik* (literally, cats' music), which often began with such spontaneous gatherings, see the work of E.P. Thompson, especially '"Rough Music": Le charivari anglais', in *Annales E. S. C.* 27, 1972, pp. 285–312; for Germany see, in particular, Manfred Gailus, *Straße und Brot. Sozialer Protest in den deutschen Staaten, unter besonderer Berücksichtigung Preußens 1847–1849,* Göttingen 1990, pp. 142–50. For a detailed

discussion of the political mentality, social actions, and organizational behaviour of the lower classes and (in contrast) of the bourgeoisie, cf. Hachtmann, *Berlin 1848*, pp. 478–502, and R. Hachtmann, 'Zwischen konservativer Beharrung und demokratisch-sozialistischer Utopie. Politische Einstellungen und Organisationsverhalten von Bürgertum, Mittelstand und Proletariat während der Berliner Revolution von 1848', in *Berlin in Geschichte und Gegenwart. Jahrbuch des Landesarchivs Berlin* 14, 1995, pp. 101–29.

10. The early labour movement's understanding of politics remained strongly influenced by bourgeois notions. Typically, they expressly distanced themselves from the spontaneous political forms of the unorganized lower classes and were equally and fundamentally opposed to the non-bourgeois way of life typical of the 'culture of poverty', with its emphasis on living for the moment. See Hachtmann, *Berlin 1848*, pp. 478–85.

11. To be sure, developments since the summer of 1848, in particular, demonstrated that the term 'liberalism' is too all-encompassing. In fact, liberalism as a political tendency was highly fragmented. Since the end of 1848 the various liberal trends could no longer be brought together under one umbrella; from this point forward their points of contact to neighbouring political camps often increased. It was no accident that in Prussia democrats and left-liberals on the one hand and right-wing liberals and conservatives on the other formed coalitions for the January 1849 elections to the provincial parliaments and also organized within joint associations.

12. *Stenographischer Bericht über die Verhandlungen der deutschen constituierenden Nationalversammlung zu Frankfurt a.M.*, ed. F. Wigard, Frankfurt am Main 1848–49, vol. 2, pp. 1143 and 1145 f; see also Günther Wollstein, *Das 'Großdeutschland' der Paulskirche. Nationale Ziele in der bürgerlichen Revolution 1848/49*, Düsseldorf 1977, pp. 146–9. The occasion of the debate was the partition of the mainly Polish Prussian province of Posen according to nationality, which was undertaken by the Prussian government in early June 1848 and sanctioned by a clear majority of the Frankfurt Assembly after the debate on 24 July.

13. Quoted in G. Wollstein, *'Großdeutschland'*, p. 270, n. 18. On the response to Moering's ideas among the deputies to the German National Assembly, see pp. 268–71.

14. On the whole, nation and nationalism possessed quite another status in the Europe of 1848–9 than they had during the revolutions of previous decades. In contrast to 1789, when the self-determination and self-assertion of the 'grande nation' *vis-à-vis* outside forces became a prerequisite for the success of the French revolution at home, in 1848 the various nationalisms within the European framework largely cancelled each other out, to some extent with the vigorous assistance of the old powers. The Habsburgs were particularly successful in their efforts to pit the national movements of the Croats and so forth in the

Hungarian half of the empire against the Magyar independence movement. See Sperber, *European Revolutions*, especially pp. 246 ff.

15. On the ambivalence and political function of the liberal concept of unification see, in particular, Reinhard Rürup, *Deutschland im 19. Jahrhundert 1815–1871*, Göttingen 1984, pp. 184–5.

16. Many democrats, though, were not completely immune to the nationalist frenzy, as clearly evidenced by the debates and resolutions of the German National Assembly on the South Tyrolian and 'Bohemian–Moravian Question'. The democratic deputies could not bring themselves to grant the Italians and Czechs, who represented the majority of the population in both regions (or in individual districts), the complete national sovereignty they desired.

17. Ernst Rudolf Huber (ed.), *Dokumente zur deutschen Verfassungsgeschichte*, vol. 1, 3rd edn, Stuttgart 1978, p. 271.

18. This can be demonstrated at least for the cases of Cologne and Berlin. On Cologne, see Marcel Seyppel, *Die demokratische Gesellschaft in Köln 1848/49. Städtische Gesellschaft und Parteienentstehung während der Bürgerlichen Revolution*, Cologne 1992, pp. 81 and 206. On Berlin, see R. Hachtmann, *Berlin 1848*, pp. 683–4. The labour movement, in contrast – at the latest after the June battles in Paris, which were interpreted as the beginning of European class warfare – began to emphasize 'internationalist' goals over efforts at national unification.

19. Letter from Frederick William IV to the Prussian ambassador to England, Karl Josias von Bunsen, 6 December 1848, quoted in Leopold von Ranke, *Aus dem Briefwechsel Friedrich Wilhelms IV. mit Bunsen*, Leipzig 1873, p. 234.

20. On the Prussian politics of unification, which pursued just this goal, and then failed because of the intervention of the great powers Austria and Russia, see the overview by Wolfram Siemann, *Gesellschaft im Umbruch. Deutschland 1849–1871*, Frankfurt am Main 1990, pp. 26–36.

21. A further decisive factor was Germany's fragmentation into numerous smaller and larger states, which, ultimately, seriously weakened the revolutionary movements. Political decentralization and the multitude of armies (which also remained largely resistant to revolutionary 'temptations') allowed the old powers to catch their breaths and regenerate their forces. To be sure, the political and military decentralization typical of Germany enabled the revolutionaries to win some victories in individual arenas, but at the same time it also prevented them from maintaining them in the longer term. Where one centre of action was weakened, the other remained stable.

22. One should certainly not overestimate this aspect, though. On the whole the various political currents managed only to a limited extent to establish organizations on a national level. The early labour movement was the most successful with its Workers' Alliance (*Arbeiterverbrüderung*) founded at the beginning of September 1848. The democrats were far

less successful; the Central Committee of German Democrats (*Central-Ausschuß der deutschen Demokraten*) elected in June 1848 remained a top-heavy organization that barely managed to paper over the internal heterogeneity and local eccentricities of the democratic clubs. The Central March Club (*Zentralmärzverein*), which had a large membership, was founded at the end of 1848 under the massive pressure of counter-revolution, at a time when the revolution's defeat was a foregone conclusion. The liberal-constitutional clubs were even less successful than the democrats in their efforts to coordinate at a national level.

23. Here, in particular, though, theoretical rights continued to coexist with a frequently very restrictive practice. On the emancipation movement during the revolution and the significance of 1848 for the long-term process of emancipation, see Reinhard Rürup, 'The European Revolutions of 1848 and Jewish Emancipation', in Werner E. Mosse, Arnold Paucker and Reinhard Rürup (eds), *Revolution and Evolution: 1848 in German-Jewish History*, Tübingen 1982, especially pp. 17–22 and 52–3; and Reinhard Rürup, 'Der Fortschritt und seine Grenzen. Die Revolution von 1848 und die europäischen juden', in D. Dowe, H.-G. Haupt and D. Langewiesche (eds), *Europa 1848*, pp. 985–1005.

24. See (to name only those syntheses that also summarize the various currents of historiography on the revolution) Thomas Nipperdey, *Deutsche Geschichte 1800–1866. Bürgerwelt und starker Staat*, Munich 1983, p. 670; and Hans-Ulrich Wehler, *Deutsche Gesellschaftsgeschichte*, vol. 2: *Von der Reformära zur industriellen und politischen 'Deutschen Doppelrevolution' 1815–1848/49*, Munich 1987, p. 778.

25. Formally, the constitution was agreed upon by Crown and Parliament between July 1849 and January 1850, as had been intended in April 1848. In fact, however, the constitutional decree of December 1848 was merely legalized after the fact.

26. Leopold von Gerlach, *Denkwürdigkeiten aus dem Leben von Leopold von Gerlach. Nach seinen Aufzeichnungen hrsg. von seiner Tochter*, vol. 1, Berlin 1891, p. 628.

27. Dirk Blasius has provided impressive evidence of this for the important area of the justice system in his *Geschichte der politischen Kriminalität 1800–1980*, Frankfurt am Main 1983, pp. 41–53. On the 'Age of Reaction' more generally see the overview in Siemann, *Gesellschaft im Umbruch*, pp. 32–83.

28. Admittedly, Hinckeldey also contributed much to the creation of a modern infrastructure in Berlin by reorganizing and expanding poor relief, street-cleaning, the fire brigade, etc. On Hinckeldey's role between 1848 and 1856 see Wolfram Siemann, *'Deutschlands Ruhe, Sicherheit und Ordnung'. Die Anfänge der politischen Polizei 1806–1866*, Tübingen 1985, pp. 343–96.

29. See, in particular, Jürgen Kocka's summary in the introduction to J. Kocka (ed.), *Bürgertum im 19. Jahrhundert. Deutschland im europäischen Vergleich*, vol. 1, Munich 1988, pp. 65–8.

30. This was formulated with particular clarity by Gustav von Griesheim, the *éminence grise* in the Prussian Ministry of War and one of the most influential military men in 1848, in his treatise *Die deutsche Zentralgewalt und die Preußische Armee*, Berlin 1848. See, above all, Manfred Hettling, 'Bürger oder Soldaten? Kriegsdenkmäler 1848–1854 und die Mentalität der Gegenrevolution', in Reinhart Koselleck and Michael Jeismann (eds), *Der politische Totenkult. Kriegerdenkmäler in der Moderne*, Munich 1994, pp. 165 ff; Manfred Messerschmidt, 'Die preussische Armee während der Revolution in Berlin 1848', in M. Messerschmidt, *Militärgeschichtliche Aspekte der Entwicklung des deutschen Nationalstaates*, Düsseldorf 1988, pp. 56 ff; Gordon A. Craig, *The Politics of the Prussian Army*, Oxford 1955, pp. 112 ff; Rüdiger Hachtmann, 'Die Potsdamer Militärrevolte vom 12. September 1848: Warum die preußische Armee dennoch ein zuverlässiges Herrschaftsinstrument der Hohenzollern blieb', in *Militärgeschichtliche Mitteilungen* 57, 1998, pp. 333–69; Sabrina Müller, *Soldaten in der deutschen Revolution von 1848/49*, Paderborn 1999.

31. In this respect the difference between Germany and France in particular is significant. To be sure, the French revolution of 1848 also failed. (The presidency and empire of Napoleon III was certainly a modern form of restoration.) The critiques of the authorities and the democratic, anti-authoritarian traditions that had underlain the French revolutions of 1789 to 1799 and (to a limited extent) 1830 were by no means interrupted, let alone reversed by this defeat.

32. On the *Sonderweg* (special path) debate, see, among others, Jürgen Kocka, 'German History before Hitler: The Debate about the German Sonderweg', in *Journal of Contemporary History* 23, 1988, pp. 3–16; Richard J. Evans, *Rethinking German History. Nineteenth-Century Germany and the Origins of the Third Reich*, London 1987, pp. 96 ff.

33. The term (coined with William II in mind) is used in Martin Broszat, 'Der Zweite Weltkrieg: Ein Krieg der "alten" Eliten, der National-sozialisten oder der Krieg Hitlers?', in M. Broszat and Klaus Schwabe (eds), *Die deutschen Eliten und der Weg in den zweiten Weltkrieg*, Munich 1989, pp. 33 ff.

HANS-ULRICH WEHLER

The German 'Double Revolution' and the Sonderweg, 1848-79

The concept of a 'double revolution' was introduced by Eric J. Hobsbawm in his *Age of Revolution*, where he referred to the political revolution in France and the industrial revolution in England since the 1780s. He focused upon the very distinct qualities and the cumulative effects of both revolutions in the long run, first in Western Europe, then in other European and non-European countries. The effort to combine these two revolutions was, however, originally made by Jacob Burckhardt and Friedrich Engels.[1]

It will be one of my basic arguments that the German-speaking countries of Central Europe experienced their industrial and political revolutions at the same time and that the German version of the 'double revolution' created extremely difficult and highly specific problems during the process of modernization.[2] I am therefore not going to stress the impact of traditions, but rather the turning point between the early 1840s and the late 1870s when the overlapping and interaction of complex economic, social, political, and cultural processes of transformation generated dangerous strains within a rather short time, yet their effects lasted for a long time to come.

I shall use the term 'industrialization' in a specific sense, meaning the 'take off' – the rapid economic changes – of the 'Industrial Revolution'. I shall also include social change as a consequence of industrialization: the formation, as Max Weber put it, of 'market-conditioned classes'. I shall exclude, however, the question of cultural conditions that operated in favour of, or against, socioeconomic changes.

What happened in Germany was the creation of a new state, a 'great power' in economic and political terms. For the first time a centralized

55

state was founded in an area that had seen loose federations of various political systems for centuries. This specific German development can also help us to understand and explain in a comparative perspective the murderous results of the Nazi dictatorship and Germany's relapse into barbarism. The idea of this *Sonderweg* has by now been vigorously debated and challenged for decades.

There are two useful concepts for the analysis of the industrial 'takeoff' period:

First, the concept of regional industrialization, which helps us to avoid the trap of describing entire national states as being industrialized and to avoid the illusion created by highly aggregate data. It focuses instead on regions with a specific capacity for economic growth where it originates, expands, and slowly spreads to other areas.

Second, the concept of leading sectors where technical innovations, financial and human capital, and know-how crystallize and stimulate other sectors of the economy to follow suit. In the German context it is railway construction that was the leading sector *par excellence* for approximately thirty years, from the mid 1840s to the mid 1870s.

Railroad construction was the force behind modern economic growth in Germany. Coal mining, iron and steel production and machine construction became other leading sectors and together they formed, within a very short time, the growth engine that pulled forward the German economy since the early 1840s.[3]

There followed an explosive surge forward. Growth was briefly interrupted by the revolution of 1848–9, then it reached unprecedented levels in the 1850s until the first world economic crisis of 1858–9 hit the German-speaking countries; but afterwards growth accelerated again and was hardly affected by the Austro-Prussian war of 1866. There were fabulous growth rates until 1873. Then the second world economic crisis of 1873 interfered. Growth, however, did continue, and although a very severe depression hit the German economy for six years, between 1873 and 1879, it turned out by then that industrial capitalism was deeply anchored and institutionally capable of surviving the vicious impact of those fluctuations.[4]

Whenever we talk about the rise of a modern market economy the most important market is the labour market. The capacity of the labour market influences and changes the basic organizing principles of societies. The German industrial revolution and the emergence of a full-blown market economy was therefore accompanied by the rise of a market society. We can observe the rise of a German bourgeoisie, a term that includes different social formations. But between the early

1840s and the early 1870s there emerged 'bourgeois classes', an expression also used by Bismarck. These new classes were often perceived by the traditional power elites – for example, the nobility, the officer corps, and the upper-rank bureaucracy – as a threat to the establishment.

Liberalism is not simply the ideology of a rising bourgeoisie, but the liberal ideas and parties in Germany in the 1860s were supported to a large extent by this new bourgeoisie. Among the liberals were members of the new professions as well as university-trained civil servants. In this market economy there now appeared a new class: the nucleus of the industrial proletariat. At the end of the 1860s two socialist parties had emerged, one Marxian, one Lassallean; they eventually fused in 1875. Marxian ideas spread fast, and the 'red spectre' began to haunt the conservative establishment and the bourgeoisie. In a very short period of time, the impact of industrialization visibly began to transform the social structure in an unprecedented way that produced a new challenge – how to integrate the new classes into the political system.[5]

The efforts in 1848 to create a liberal, constitutional, national German state failed. German nationalism remained a powerful system of ideas nevertheless. It is nationalism, as Ernest Gellner put it in his memorable phrase, that creates nations in the first place. In Germany, this view was supported by a new 'intellectual nationalism', represented by the Prussian school of historiography, which claimed that it had always been Prussia's historical mission to create a German national state.[6] In Bismarck the nationalists had the unforseeable good luck to find a charismatic leader. Bismarck was conservative, but he understood that a 'Greater Prussian' policy could only be achieved with the support of the basically liberal national movement. In 1862 he became Prime Minister and remained the leading figure in German politics for almost thirty years. His impact was enormous. A strong instrument for his power politics was the Prussian army, and when Bismarck used it three times, in 1864, 1866 and 1870, it turned the scales in Prussia's favour.[7]

The result was a political revolution, because for the first time a great power was created in Central Europe. But it was a 'revolution from above', which had an old Prussian tradition. My thesis is that it was only in the 1860s that a new constellation came into existence that, in the long run, led to the creation of a greater Prussian state. There were no economic necessities at that time. Prussia's military strength, good luck, and a charismatic leader enjoying an informal

alliance with the liberal national movement were the factors that determined the authoritarian structure of this new state. It was a monarchy
that for all practical purposes was run by a single person, the Reich
Chancellor, depending solely upon the confidence that the monarch
put in him. There was a powerful bureaucracy that could not be
controlled by Parliament. The Reichstag did not enjoy a parliamentary
system inscribed in the constitution. And there was a strong army
which only took its orders from the new emperor, the Prussian king.

This diagnosis takes me to the *Sonderweg* argument, which tries to
describe and explain the factors that, in the long run, produced
Hitler's dictatorship.[8] There are those who wish to explain this period
using a short-term perspective: the defeat in the First World War,
the Versailles peace treaty, the hyperinflation of the early 1920s are
the things that count. Those who defend the *Sonderweg* argument are
deeply dissatisfied with that narrow explanation. They emphasize
long-term factors, which, in a comparative perspective, help to explain
why in modern German history a specific set of problems created a
unique burden so that Germany was the only civilized and industrialized Western country that succumbed to National Socialism, the most
radical form of Fascism we know of so far.

The followers of this interpretation stressed six problems:

1. There was a specific German ideology that insisted on German
    uniqueness by criticizing Western political culture, turning
    against the basic creeds of liberalism and modern democracy, and
    praising instead the alleged superiority of German monarchies
    and their efficient bureaucracies, German *Innerlichkeit*, and so
    forth.
2. The absence of a successful bourgeois revolution that would have
    enabled the German bourgeoisie to realize its presumably liberal
    political visions.
3. The defeat of liberalism in 1848, during the constitutional conflict
    in the 1860s, and in the critical time when the Empire was
    founded.
4. Germany was perceived as being a 'belated nation', it experienced
    a rather late formation as a national state, which was seen as a
    major source of a traumatically unbalanced political mentality
    that needed the compensation of an extreme nationalism and a
    successful imperialism.
5. The traditional power elites, the nobility, the bureaucracy, the
    officer corps, continued to block successfully the advance of the

rule of Parliament, of liberalism, and of modern democracy. Their influence was disastrous in the long run. The political defence of their privileges created a dangerous tension because in economic and social terms Germany was moving rapidly into modernity.

6. The nobility succeeded, so the argument goes, in 'feudalizing' the upper ranks of the bourgeoisie, which should have defended liberal principles. The army continued to defend its exclusive status.

These basic arguments rest, it seems to me, on a rather simplistic way of thinking. In the process of modernization, traditional and modern elements always combine in a mix, whatever country one analyses. In the German context, however, the representatives of the traditional elements were seen as stunningly vigorous and reckless in their defence of their privileges whereas the representatives of the modern elements were unable to achieve more than a partial political modernization. The thrust of the argument is that these unresolved tensions created the fatal long-term preconditions for the success of, and support for, National Socialism.

These arguments have created a heated debate. The critique of the *Sonderweg* stemmed from a variety of political and scholarly motives, but the empirical and methodological results of the debate can be summarized briefly in the following counterarguments:

1. In very general terms, the German ideology, the *Sonderbewusstsein*, has been confirmed as a general interpretation.
2. The notion of a 'bourgeois' revolution, whenever and wherever that was supposed to have occurred, has been destroyed by modern research.
3. German liberalism was indeed defeated three times, but it promoted a second reform era in the late 1860s and 1870s and it played an important role in city governments until 1918.
4. Recent research tends to deflate the notion of German nationalism's 'belatedness' and stresses in general the political radicalization of nationalism in a comparative perspective.
5. The importance of pre-industrial factors was relativized or even flatly denied, whereas the modernity of German industrial capitalism was stressed repeatedly. It created the problems, it was claimed, that really mattered in the 1920s and early 1930s.
6. The feudalization thesis was convincingly questioned. The common European trend of bourgeois adaptation to the nobility's lifestyle has been underlined. The efficiency of the bureaucracy and the

army were not pre-industrial. In general, it was argued, there were various trends of continuity in modern German history. The dogmatization of *one* cluster, it was claimed, was theoretically and empirically untenable.

Despite some convincing counterarguments of the critics I should like to continue to support the core of the *Sonderweg* arguments. I still see highly specific factors operating within the context of German modernization. The major questions to be posed are the following: (1) In what period of time can we begin to identify these specific factors and in which dimensions can we discover them? (2) When do they begin to cluster effectively? (3) What are the effects? (4) Last but not least, which normative criteria are involved when we criticize their influence?

My basic premises are: (1) 1933 and what followed still need a more convincing explanation; (2) all modernizing Western societies reveal a special mix of traditional and modern elements, but in Germany a rather unique combination formed an especially dangerous syndrome; (3) we need many comparative studies, which we don't yet have. We must therefore at least use a comparative perspective to help clarify some of the problems of the *Sonderweg*.

I shall offer some arguments as to the specific problems that, hopefully, will support my interpretation. It was the era of the German 'Double Revolution' between the early 1840s and the late 1870s that was of crucial importance for this change. The first argument relates to the undeniable importance of certain long-term traditions that were well established before the middle of the nineteenth century and later on turned out to be specifically detrimental. But in spite of their importance they did not possess the capacity, and that remains probably very debatable, to structure decisively the future course of German history. The future remained relatively open despite these conditions. One has to include developments after the 1840s if one wants to understand the *Sonderweg*. The bureaucracy was powerful indeed, but there was an influential liberal wing, and the liberal movement hoped to control it. The army remained strong, but between 1850 and 1862 it had suffered an enormous setback especially in Prussia. The vigorous struggle for a majority in Parliament between 1850 and 1870 demonstrated the powerful urge of the liberal movement to keep up with Western countries. Liberalism was suppressed between 1819 and the 1850s, but the various 'new eras' in some German states afterwards demonstrated how the liberals were willing to fight again and again for political power. The nobility still enjoyed their remarkable influence, but their legal status had been radically changed between Napoleonic times and 1848. The old landowning elite was eventually transformed into a class of agrarian entrepreneurs.

These examples will suffice with regard to these traditions. Evidently, some of the important *Sonderweg* traditions did exert their influence, but a definitive direction had not yet been determined by them.

Which constellation emerged during the period of the 'Double Revolution' that still justifies a defence of the *Sonderweg* argument? I shall offer some arguments.

1. I believe that the political decisions and the configurations of power exerted the most influential impact. The Industrial Revolution changed economic conditions rapidly; the transformation into a class society was accelerated vigorously, and a deep feeling of crisis pervaded the German *ancien régime*. But it was the political challenge of liberalism and of political democracy that produced the most influential results, a succesful response to these challenges. During the crisis of the 1860s Bismarck was able to build up a charismatic régime that lasted for a quarter of a century. During that time Germany was the only European state, *pace* Gladstone, that experienced charismatic leadership for such a long period of time. This had a deep impact upon German political mentality and upon German political culture. For the emerging political culture it meant that antiliberal, antidemocratic, antiparliamentary attitudes were regarded favourably. In terms of the constitutional system it meant a sort of void once the great coordinator was gone.

2. The imperial monarch had a status quite different from that of all other European kings and emperors because he remained the direct commander of the army, controlling the necessary administrative institutions, excluding parliaments (the imperial, the Prussian and those of the other states) and political parties from any control of the army and the navy. I can only think of Japan, which had a comparable semifeudal arrangement until 1945.

3. The army experienced a number of brilliant military victories in three wars within six years, two of them against great powers. These wars gave the military their high status. They formed the basis of a new social militarism that was quite different from the old Prussian one; it surrounded the officer corps with a new splendour.

4. The nobility did experience an unexpected revitalization despite
    its secular decline until the 1860s. Its success story between 1864
    and 1871 meant that noblemen continued to move in the corridors
    of power. They controlled the imperial government, most of the
    federal state governments, the upper bureaucracy, the upper ranks
    of the military, and usually the Upper Houses in most of the
    federal states.

5. The new Germany did get an imperial parliament (the *Reichstag*)
    and in order to defeat the liberal urban voters Bismarck intro-
    duced a democratic suffrage for men older than 25 years of age
    to mobilize the majority of royalist rural voters. The influence of
    Parliament grew in the long run, but it never fought for parlia-
    mentary rule and parliamentary rule has never been granted
    without struggle. In a comparative perspective, no Western
    parliament before 1918 tried so hard to avoid a struggle for
    political hegemony.

6. Liberalism cooperated with the Bismarck government successfully
    but after 1879 it was permanently excluded. Only a successful
    parliamentary system, which would have permitted German
    political society to accept responsibility for solving its own
    problems in the Reichstag, could have compensated those depress-
    ing experiences. But that chance had been lost since the late
    1870s.

7. The authoritarian political structures of the empire tended to
    support the old power elites: first of all the bureaucracy, whose
    influence ranged much wider than that of the French upper
    service and that of the English civil service. Its influence operated
    against the ideal of the citoyen, and its efficient authority in
    everyday life as well as its influence upon political decision-
    making underlines the validity of the *Sonderweg* argument.

8. The utopian vision of a German civil society, as it had been
    developed since the late eighteenth century was realized to a
    remarkable extent in a free market economy, in the realm of law,
    in the educational system, in the field of public opinion, and so
    forth. This is the result of recent research into the history of the
    German *Bürgertum*.[9] In the political arena of the empire, however,
    an authoritarian régime and a powerful bureaucracy were able
    to prevent a decisive influence of the various formations of the
    Bürgertum.

9. Nationalism is, of course, a common political religion everywhere
    in the West and in other parts of the world. But the nature of

nationalism in imperial Germany does show some unique elements. I know that one has to be careful in claiming the word 'unique', but there is the prominent role of militarism, which one does not find in England or in the US; the passionate antisocialism; the dangerous influence of a political and racist antisemitism which in general one does not find within Western nationalism; and the fusion with Lutheranism in an influential 'national protestantism' even stronger than in the US and far more state-oriented, perhaps, than in Sweden. The impact of the Bismarck régime, with its cult of charismatic leadership, also was a core element of this German nationalism.

10. The new imperialism since the 1880s is a common Western experience. But hardly anywhere is the domestic function, the attempt to use imperialist expansion in order to stabilize the basis of legitimacy of the political system, so prominent as in Germany.

11. Power elites tend to fall back on old recipes of success in times of crisis. After three successful wars in the 1860s the Berlin decision makers tried to repeat the performance in 1914. Of course they felt cornered, but the recklessness with which a great war was deliberately accepted in the July crisis of 1914 can hardly be seen in London or Paris, in Vienna or St Petersburg. Was Germany's brinkmanship not also the outgrowth of the political mentality that had been moulded by the wars of unification?

12. The basic dilemma of the German *Sonderweg* remains, I believe, the overlapping of complex and difficult economic, social and political processes of modernization creating enormous strains and tensions during an extremely short time. The most important attempt failed – the reconstruction of the political system and the introduction of what Ralf Dahrendorf has called the 'constitution of liberty' that would have opened the political arena for liberalism and eventually for political democracy.

These value judgements are shot through with normative assumptions about which sort of constitution is most appropriate in the short and in the long run to deal with the social and economic problems of the late nineteenth and twentieth centuries. In the light of our historical experience one can think of many arguments to support the interpretation that a liberal and democratic political system would have been more resilient and better adapted to cope with these problems than the authoritarian régime in imperial Germany. If

Germany was at the crossroads around the middle of the nineteenth century nobody could foresee three successful wars and a charismatic political leader. The era of the 'double revolution' was the turning point, the formative period from which a constellation emerged the political dimensions of which proved to be decisive for the future *Sonderweg*. My arguments do not rest upon the unbroken continuity of detrimental conditions, but they rest upon discontinuity and upon the specific impact of a concrete configuration of forces that emerged from the 'double revolution'.

Notes

1. The *locus classicus* is Eric J. Hobsbawm, *The Age of Revolution*, London 1962. See, however, Friedrich Engels, 'Anti-Dühring' (1878), in *Marx-Engels-Werke*, vol. 20, Berlin 1971, p. 243, and Jacob Burckhardt, *Weltgeschichtliche Betrachtungen* (1868), now only to be used in the critical edition prepared by Peter Ganz, *Über das Studium der Geschichte – der Text der 'Weltgeschichtlichen Betrachtungen'*, Munich 1982, p. 323.

2. For a recent discussion and application of the concept of 'double revolution' to German history in the mid-nineteenth century see Hans-Ulrich Wehler, *Deutsche Gesellschaftsgeschichte*, vol. 2: *Von der Reformära bis zur industriellen und politischen 'Deutschen Doppelrevolution', 1815–1848/49*, 2nd edn, Munich 1989, pp. 585–784, including the relevant literature.

3. As to Central European industrialization, see H.-U. Wehler, *Deutsche Gesellschaftsgeschichte*, vol. 2, pp. 864–67; from a different position Friedrich-Wilhelm Henning, *Deutsche Wirtschafts- und Sozialgeschichte im 19. Jahrhundert*, Paderborn 1996, pp. 323–516, 781–888.

4. See the extensive discussion in Hans-Ulrich Wehler, *Deutsche Gesellschaftsgeschichte*, vol. 3: *Von der 'Deutschen Doppelrevolution' bis zum Beginn des Ersten Weltkrieges, 1849–1914*, Munich 1995, pp. 66–105.

5. As to the nature and impact of German liberalism see H.-U. Wehler, *Deutsche Gesellschaftsgeschichte*, vol. 2, pp. 413–57; vol. 3, pp. 335–43, 866–72; as to Social Democracy, see vol. 3, pp. 348–52, 902–7.

6. The development of German nationalism is presented in Hans-Ulrich Wehler, *Deutsche Gesellschaftsgeschichte*, vol. 1: *Vom Feudalismus des Alten Reiches bis zur Defensiven Modernisierung der Reformära, 1700–1815*, 2nd edn, Munich 1989, pp. 506–30; vol. 2, pp. 394–412; vol. 3, pp. 230–51, 938–65, 1067–85; see Hans-Ulrich Wehler, 'Deutscher Nationalismus', in *idem, Die Geschichte als Gegenwart*, Munich 1995, pp. 127–85.

7. The problems of Bismarck's charismatic rulership and the relevant literature are discussed in H.-U. Wehler, *Deutsche Gesellschaftsgeschichte*, vol. 3, pp. 368–72, 849–54.

8. For a debate of the merits and deficits of the *Sonderweg* argument see
    H.-U. Wehler, *Deutsche Gesellschaftsgeschichte*, vol. 3, pp. 461–86; the
    literature up to 1994: H.-U. Wehler, *Deutsche Gesellschaftsgeschichte*, vol. 3,
    pp. 1381–4. Recent contributions to that evidently endless debate
    include: Jürgen Kocka, 'Nach dem Ende des Sonderwegs', in *Festschrift
    Christoph Kleßmann*, Bonn 1998, pp. 3–10; Heinrich August Winkler, 'Die
    deutsche Abweichung vom Westen. Der Untergang der Weimarer
    Republik im Lichte der Sonderweg-These', in *Festschrift Eberhard Kolb*,
    Berlin 1998, pp. 127–38; G. Steinmetz, 'German Exceptionalism and
    the Origins of Nazism', in Ian Kershaw and M. Lewin (eds), *Stalinism
    and Nazism*, Cambridge 1997, pp. 251–84; S. Baranowski, 'East Elbian
    Landed Elites and Germany's Turn to Fascism: The Sonderweg Contro-
    versy Revisited', in *European History Quarterly* 26, 1996, pp. 209–49; Peter
    Brandt, 'War das Deutsche Kaiserreich reformierbar?' in *Festschrift Helga
    Grebing*, Essen 1995, pp. 192–210; C. Lorenz, 'Beyond Good and Evil?
    The German Empire of 1871 and Modern German Historiography' in
    Journal of Contemporary History 30, 1995, pp. 729–65; R. Collins, 'German-
    Bashing and the Theory of Democratic Modernization', in *Zeitschrift für
    Soziologie* 24, 1995, pp. 3–21; J. D. Stephens, 'The German Path to
    Modern Authoritarianism', in H. E. Chehabi and A. Stepan (eds), *Politics,
    Society, and Democracy*, Boulder, Colorado 1995, pp. 161–81.

9. Recent German research on the *Bürgertum*, mainly done in the *Arbeitskreis
    für moderne Sozialgeschichte* and at the universities of Bielefeld and Frank-
    furt am Main, is succinctly summarized bei Jürgen Kocka, 'Bürgertum
    und Sonderweg' in Peter Lundgreen (ed.), *Bürgertumsforschung*, Göttingen
    2000 (forthcoming). Cf. Hans-Ulrich Wehler, 'A Guide to Future Research
    on the *Kaiserreich*?' in *Central European History* 30, 1997, pp. 541–72, a more
    elaborate German version can be found in *idem*, 'Aufbruch aus der
    Sackgasse? Das Kaiserreich auf dem Prüfstand', in *idem*, *Politik in der
    Geschichte*, Munich 1998, pp. 98–136, 246–58.

WOLFGANG KRUSE

The First World War:
The 'True German Revolution'?

'Since 1789 there has never been a revolution like the
German revolution of 1914.' This used to be a classic topos of German
war ideology during the First World War.[1] In retrospect, the idea that
the outbreak of war released a revolutionary change in the sociopolitical order seems disconcerting and unfounded. It is true that
there is a generally little-appreciated close connection between war
and revolution in modern history.[2] This was especially true in the First
World War, because revolutionary elements played an important role
in the strategies, aims, and above all in the undesirable effects of
the conflict. The war prepared the road for German revolution by
strengthening the class character of society, by producing need and
starvation, by eroding monarchical power and, last but not least, by
the final defeat.[3] However, that the formation of a warring society –
the main target of the November revolution of 1918 – could have been
a revolutionary process itself, is an idea that would scarcely be
entertained by any serious historian today. It entailed no coup. It
brought with it no fundamental reform of the sociopolitical balance
of power – something that was actually reinforced under the banner
of the *Burgfrieden*. It seems quite clear that if you are dealing with
revolution in modern German history, the subject of the First World
War is out of place.

Things look quite different, however, if you change the perspective
and focus on the problem of revolution. In this context, it seems to
me to be important to consider how contemporaries could understand
the war as the motor of a positive sociopolitical process of change –
indeed as a 'German revolution'. The following will therefore largely
be an analysis, at an ideological level, of how the Germans saw
themselves during the First World War. What did it signify when

bourgeois Germany paradoxically dedicated itself to the putative revolutionary overthrow of bourgeois society, something seemingly fulfilled by the war? And in which context can one understand the idea of a revolution directed not against the ruling political structure, but instead one to be carried out by the military monarchy itself? In order to discover the answers to these questions it will first be necessary to examine German world-war ideology more closely in its stages of development, its content, and its social context.

I. The 'August Experience' and the 'Spirit of 1914'

The enthusiasm with which the First World War was greeted in all participating countries has been well described. Less attention has been paid to the widespread and clear limits to this war enthusiasm,[4] so any treatment of the development of a world-war ideology runs the risk of exaggerating an already very one-sided picture. I would therefore like to emphasize that this chapter draws on opinions published in a society dominated by a high level of censorship and propaganda, whereas people's private feelings and statements do not appear here. Even if one may assume a certain social dominance of the ideological topoi,[5] there is a lot to be said for presuming a dichotomy between general public opinion on the one hand, and the enthusiasm preached generally by the spokesmen of the famous German *Bildungsbürgertum,* the educated middle classes, together with the world-war ideology they developed, on the other.

A second and for our subject more important limitation of the notion of war enthusiasm lies in the celebration of the 'August experience', relating less to the fact of war itself and more to the effects that the outbreak of war seemed to entail. Society in the *Kaiserreich* appeared not only to adapt to the conditions of war surprisingly easily, but at the same time to go through an internal process of change – one experienced as a national renewal. In Eric J. Leed's stimulating analysis, enthusiasm for war and the feeling of change were mainly based on an interpretation of mobilization as a carnival-like period of transition – during which governing norms and conditions were temporarily nullified – to a quite different world of war, understood as contrasting totally with civil society.[6] My interpretation also takes up this dynamic of change at the beginning of the war, but sees it in a different perspective and tries to consider the conditions that characterized public consciousness in the transition from peace to war. The most important factor, in this interpretation, is not a long-desired 'redemption by war', based on a widespread German warlike mentality.[7] Most people, even in Germany, were anxious about a major European war, and any analysis of their behaviour has to take this into account. So I first wish to raise the question of the effects that the ever more threatening possibility of war had at the end of July 1914.

As a result of the uncertainty about whether there would be peace or war, of contradictory reports, and martial propaganda, the people became increasingly agitated and uneasy. Indeed, in the major urban centres of public life there arose a heightened 'atmosphere of almost unbearable fear, of endless horror', 'in which', according to a contemporary, 'a horrible end must be viewed with relief'.[8] The oft-remarked feelings of relief and liberation at the beginning of the war therefore had their origin less in a long-developed desire for war and more in its bringing to an end an increasingly unbearable uncertainty. 'Finally! Like a cry of release it runs through the masses' – thus a daily newspaper on the effects of the declaration of a state of siege on the expectant masses in central Berlin. 'No cheering was to be heard, no acclamation, everyone's expression is serious – the horrible tension which bore down upon Berlin, disappeared in a sigh of relief: So it is true!'[9] But this liberating release of tension – and here we find the common source of the enthusiasm for and the ideology of war – soon gained a further depth of meaning and an ideological character in the immediate context of the outbreak of war. Mobilization appeared to release the German *Kaiserreich* from its inner problems. 'We feel as if we've recovered now', 'things are no longer pointless', or 'we've found ourselves, now we are nothing but German'. These were the metaphors of national renewal, presented with increasing enthusiasm.[10] By reverse logic this indicates how oppressive the experience of pre-war society as crisis-prone, meaningless, and alienated must have been. The war seemed to draw a fundamental internal crisis of the *Kaiserreich* to a close.

At the centre of this invocation of national rebirth was the 'August experience' of a rediscovered unity of the German people – to which Emperor Wilhelm II contributed with his famous notion of political *Burgfrieden*, claiming that he no longer recognized political parties, only Germans. 'Now we are', wrote the historian Friedrich Meinecke, 'suddenly over all hurdles, a single, powerful deep-breathing community in life and death.'[11] This national community seemed first to be realized in the socially undifferentiated masses of people that filled the streets, something evidently perceived by many as a national communal experience. 'We ourselves were no longer that which we had long been: Alone', discovered the deeply moved social philosopher Max Scheler. 'The broken vital contact between the levels individual – people – nation – world – God was suddenly restored and the forces swayed more powerfully back and forth than all poetry, philosophy, prayer and cult before could bring to experience.'[12] The jurist Otto von Gierke rejoiced: 'There was no difference in rank, none between better and lesser, richer and poorer, educated and uneducated, employer and employee, old and young (...). In a sudden self-awakening, the German people had come to itself again.'[13] And the philosopher Alois Riehl came to the conclusion: 'Never was a people so united as in those August days, those unforgettable days. A higher life seemed to reveal itself to us. Each of us felt, each of us lived for the whole, and the whole lived in us all. Our more narrow self with its personal interests merged into the great historical self of the nation.'[14]

There is much to be said for seeing in this jubilation not least the enthusiasm of the *Bildungsbürgertum*, who seemingly 'could now communicate again on one level' with the masses.[15] This was doubtless quickly associated with an attempt at enhancing the threatened social position of the writers and professors through an interpretation of the meaning of the war.[16] But at the same time, these interpreters expressed themselves as supporters of diverse social groups and thereby took up general problems of German imperial society, not least with their theme of inner unity. Having complained up to then of the collapse of an inner coherence of the German people caused by the dynamics of industrial capitalistic development of society, and having seen an inner disunity of the *Kaiserreich* in the national, cultural, religious, social and political spheres as a growing threat, it seemed that, finally, the longed-for 'inner' founding of the Empire would be successful, once again as in 1870–71, through 'iron and blood'. A national *Volksgemeinschaft* seemed to take form in military mobilization and to gain organizational permanence through the *Burgfrieden* resolution. 'All the inhibiting, crippling mistrust between the individual ranks and classes, all the discord between parties and arrogance of cliques', rejoiced for example the poet Ernst Dehmel, 'suddenly it was as if it had been made to disappear'.[17] The *Tägliche Rundschau* even described the war as a 'magician and miracleworker', that had finally brought about Germany's inner national unity:

It leads the Guelphs to a glowing declaration of belief in the Empire, it drowns out the curse of Zabern in the roar of jubilation with which the people of the lands of the *Kaiserreich* greet the Prussian troops. It makes the Poles thoughtful and reconsider the theory of the lesser evil, and it achieves that greatest of wonders: it forces the Social Democrats onto the side of their German brothers.[18]

In order to understand how the war became the focal point of national self-discovery, it is important to note the close connection between defining an enemy image and how one sees oneself,[19] but also rather specifically German ideological traditions. Firstly, in Germany war had long been held to have crisis-solving powers – powers that promoted national identity. Only one year before the outbreak of the First World War, the centennial of 1913 had emphatically brought back into public consciousness the memory of the war of liberation against Napoleon, so that the renewed *Volkskrieg* of 1914 could be interpreted as a national awakening in the form of an 'organic politicization of the people' on the model of 1813.[20] Historically closer, however, were the wars of 1864, 1866 and 1870–71 against Denmark, Austria, and France. These had led to a much-praised solution not only to Prussia's constitutional conflict but also to the national problem through the Prussian-dominated founding of the *Kaiserreich,* something celebrated by contemporaries as the second step in the German tradition of 'revolution from above' after the Prussian reforms at the beginning of the century.[21] This national tradition of war, which created a sense of national identity, was easily coupled to the new social Darwinistic ideology of the age of imperialism, and to the martial vitalism of a widespread Nietzsche cult. Against such a striking ideological background, war came to be understood by many as a remedy to the alleged problems of degeneration in modern societies, even before 1914. In his much-read work of 1912, *Germany and the Next War,* for example, the retired head of the German general staff's planning department, Major General Friedrich von Bernhardi, wrote:

War is above all a biological necessity, a regulator in the life of mankind, which cannot be done without, as without it an unhealthy development must arise, excluding every improvement of the species and thus every real culture. (. . .) War is, unlike peace, the greatest expander of power and bringer of life which the history of mankind has known. (. . .) Nothing worse can happen to a talented and powerful people than when it decays into a sedated phaiake-like existence through an unchallenged enjoyment of peace.[22]

In 1914, the idea of the regenerative power of war was connected, in the myth of a national rebirth, to another ideological tradition – the canonizing elevation of the nation, which in the nineteenth century increasingly came to replace secularized Christian value forms and motifs.[23] Social realities of a modern industrial society, however, appeared highly profane in comparison. Especially as regards content, they existed in a very sharp contrast with the nobler values of traditional cultural nationalism and communal attributes of the new *völkisch* ideologies. Urbanization and the development of urban mass societies, the materialism of the market economy and rising social conflict, fundamental democratic mobilization of the masses and the formation of a revolutionary workers' movement, and finally the limited and often unconvincing attempts at bourgeois self-government in the 'talking shop' of the Reichstag – all these were seen by many not as unavoidable components of social and political progress, but instead as part of a process of decay, which would lead to the undermining of all original German, communal forms of social cohesion.[24]

For the cultural pessimists of the pre-war period, the German 'temple' therefore appeared to have lost its 'Holy of Holies' as the result of the development of modern society, as the philosopher Rudolf Eucken adjudged in retrospect.[25] The war, however, allowed an enthusiastic reidentification with an allegedly transformed nation and appeared to give the nation back its halo. 'The words Germany, fatherland, war have magical powers', wrote the young poet Ernst Toller at the beginning of August 1914: 'They float in the air, circle each other, igniting themselves and us.'[26] Even modern technology, often written off as insubstantial, could, for Friedrich Meinecke 'at one stroke gain the great soul of which sensitive artists sometimes dream and in which we can still hardly believe.'[27] The poet Hermann Bahr praised the pseudo-religious 'blessings of war' that had granted the German people in a 'holy war' its 'German Pentecost':

The German essence has appeared to us (. . .) and we can hardly remember how things must have been then, only three weeks ago, as everyone turned against each other with his differences, his uniqueness, his selfishness, as we still lived separately, as we were still parties and not a people. One person did not know the other because he did not know himself. With their unholy desires, everyone had forgotten his true will. Now everyone has found his will again and it has become plain: everyone has only one will. In every German heart there beats the same holy wrath. A holy wrath, a sanctifying wrath, a healing wrath. All German wounds are healed. We are cured. Praised be this war (. . .).[28]

This sacred elevation of the warring nation, then, gained a specific dynamic of transformation through its apocalyptic structural elements, which were especially suitable for transposing the suffering of pre-war society into a war-related celebration of national renewal.[29] Cultural pessimism had produced a number of visions of the end of the world, often related to the threat of the 'great war'. The war, when it came, could therefore be interpreted as both judgement day and renewal, indeed as a world revolution in the form of a secularized apocalypse. 'It is unbelievable, contradicting all predictions and nonetheless of compelling simplicity, that world revolution and judgement day merged into one: the world war', wrote, for example, the industrialist Walther Rathenau.[30] Thus the experience of national renewal could be transferred back to the war and projected outwards. To the 'chosen' German nation was to fall the role of executor; Germans could imagine themselves to be 'fighters against a "world full of the devil", as those who have received the task of fulfilling all exalted prophecies of mankind.'[31] German war ideology thus presents itself as a synthesis of nationalist, pseudo-religious world renewal fantasies, as it was characterized not only by theological but by also quite clearly secular interpretations. 'We wish to carry this crusade to the end in service of the world spirit', argued for example Johann Plenge, 'for our and the world's salvation.'[32]

II. The 'War of Cultures' and the 'Ideas of 1914'

The war was embellished by intellectuals into a 'war of cultures' in which a decision between fundamentally contrasting sociocultural principles was to be made militarily. For Rudolf Borchardt, for example, the war fronts were 'the new schisms of Europe, the new deep and indivisible gap going down to the roots of the occidental ethos, running, like the first one to divide occidental Christianity, through the heart of occidental culture.'[33] This certainly did not refer to the conflict between bolshevism and occidental civilization that Ernst Nolte placed in the centre of his conception of the 'European civil war'.[34] The ideological foundation of this new 'thirty-one years world war'[35] began, in fact, not with the Russian October revolution of 1917, but with the outbreak of war in 1914. At its centre was at first a conflict between Germany and the West. The German 'cultural warriors' embellished the war into a conflict of principle between a 'German culture', understood as sage, profound and vigorous, but also as popular, loyal to the state and conscious of one's duties – on the one hand – and the enemy, a 'Western civilization' written off as flat and decadent, determined by materialistic social structure and political patterns. No less a person than Thomas Mann formulated perhaps the clearest version of this ideological contrast:

> The difference between spirit and politics contains that of culture and civilization, of soul and society, of freedom, and the right to vote, of art and literature; and Germanness, that is culture, soul, freedom, art and not civilization, society, the right to vote and literature.[36]

The German position in the cultural war can doubtless also be explained as a reaction to the claims of the West to be going to war against 'German barbarism' and 'Prussian militarism' in the name of the Enlightenment, democracy, the rights of man and civilization.[37] It was not least against this that invocations of the superior power of German culture and its inseparable connection with militarism were directed. While Western war propaganda, at least at first, generally made a distinction between German culture and German militarism, in Germany this differentiation gave rise to loud protests. 'It is not true that the fight against so-called militarism is not a fight against our culture (...). The German army and the German people are one', one can read in the famed appeal of the Ninety-Three 'To the Cultural World'.[38] And in a declaration signed by more than 3,000 university professors this identification of German culture and militarism gained a clearly offensive tone: 'We believe that for the entire culture of Europe, salvation depends on victory which will be won by German "militarism", by the discipline, the loyalty and self-sacrifice of the united free German people.'[39]

Despite the doubtless dialectic effect in the production of an enemy image and self-image, it would be mistaken to interpret German world-war ideology as primarily a defensive reaction to Western war propaganda. German 'culture warriors' understood themselves rather more as propagandists for the warring nation. 'The time of alienation between culture and politics is past', rejoiced, for example, even such a moderate thinker as Friedrich Meinecke, going on to define the role of culture in war as follows: 'With great noble-mindedness, with that autonomous pathos which Kant preached to us, it takes the hand of the state and becomes a weapon in its hand.'[40] The German understanding of the warring nation and the meaning of its culture was based on national myths developed long before, and was joined together into a unified whole by the impression of national self-discovery and renewal created by the 'August experience'.

It was, however, as contradictory as the existing conflicts of interests that dominated German society. It was based to a great extent on the various social groups projecting their own values and aims onto an allegedly united and purified nation. While on the establishment side, the opposition's profession of support for the ruling order was celebrated, the groups that had up to then been denied acceptance as an integral part of the nation and its political system – from the women's movement to the national and religious minorities to, above all, the Social Democrats – saw in the experience of unity a promise of national recognition and equal treatment.[41] However, the dominant anti-liberal tendency of the world-war ideology gave expression to a troubled relationship with modern industrial capitalistic society, with its accelerated process of change, social conflict, and political emancipation movements. Just as the feeling of national renewal was based on a desire to turn German society's internal conflicts and problems outwards, the anti-Western perception of the enemy arose, above all, from a rejection of core elements of German society itself. These were transferred to the enemy and judged to be consequences of a 'Western' alienation caused by the 'British' industrial revolution and the 'French' political revolution.

While 'signs of decay', long lamented not only in traditional conservative agitation but also in the cultural pessimism of the educated middle classes as well as in the aggressive nationalism of a new bourgeois right, provided the material for an image of 'Western civilization' as the enemy, the German people appeared to return to the traditional virtues of 'German essence', to monarchical authority, cultural inwardness, and national fulfilment of duty within an harmonious social order. If the 'English disease' of liberalism had 'already infected the German national body' before the war,[42] it seemed now as if 'the massive turmoil of the most recent events (. . .) had once again exorcised the demon from the threshold of our nation.'[43] The war thus became a struggle for the defence of a rediscovered 'German essence', which under the banner of a 'German cultural mission' could easily take on an offensive character:

> We plead for the victory of that which we call culture and what we believe we do not alone possess but which we alone in the world conceive and express; a victory over what are for us unnatural principles to which we were bound by our worst instincts, and by our traitors, compromisers, free spirits and others who presented themselves as refined.[44]

The repressive sociopolitical implications of this attempt at finding a national identity that defined itself against the West quickly became clear. 'Arrogance and presumption are at an end, the perspective comes once again from above', commented the Germanophile Swedish constitutionalist Rudolf Kjellén, impressed by the 'spirit of discipline and order' that Werner Sombart, to his great pleasure, saw governing Germany.[45] To this invocation of national unity and community belonged a suppression of social conflict. 'Away with the class war, it must be impossible from now on' – this was the lesson derived from the 'August experience', which then received a more exact form with the labels *Deutsche Gemeinwirtschaft* (German co-operative economy) and national 'war socialism'. To this also belonged the proclamation of a specific 'German idea of freedom', which under critical analysis presented itself as an idealized glossing-over of avoidance of conflict and of submissiveness. The theologian Adolf von Harnack defined it as follows: 'What does freedom mean? To do with pleasure and total devotion and without hindrance that which you should do; to want to do what you must do.'[46]

This 'freedom in a voluntary commitment to the whole, the freedom in a common consciousness and in discipline', as the sociologist of religion Ernst Troeltsch enthused,[47] was seen to be rooted on the one hand in the organic coherence of the German *Volksgemeinschaft*, and on the other it corresponded to a submissiveness to the monarchical authoritarian state. This was understood as the embodiment of reason and morality, so that arising from it was an inner freedom to obey: 'The German is free', adjudged the Hegelian Adolph Lasson, 'because he obeys the law, and the proscriptive law is the expression of reason.'[48] Another justification of 'German constitutionalism', with its strong monarchist prerogatives, had long been developed by historians under the banner of the 'primacy of foreign policy', and the war appeared to give this doctrine emphatic confirmation, as Meinecke emphasized: 'The common social spirit, which has come alive in our state and which secures all our freedom, demands another form of government than the bourgeois class state.'[49]

Even when, especially in the second half of the war, serious conflicts arose between those open to reform – the academic group around Meinecke, Troeltsch and Delbrück pleading for the heralded 'new orientation' of German domestic policy – and a majority supporting the political status quo, the orientation towards German constitutionalism remained, except for Max Weber, a strong unifying force.[50] Those who later became 'republicans of reason' (*Vernunftrepublikaner*) did push for a reform of the Prussian three-class suffrage system, but even here, efforts at reform remained highly questionable as they were coupled with a strengthening of the Prussian upper chamber and the replacement of the national parliamentary suffrage by a plural system with special votes for services to the nation.[51] Above all, during the war the reformers rejected the replacement of monarchical government by a parliamentary ministry as strongly as did their more conservative colleagues. 'A parliamentary system on the Western pattern', Meinecke noted when describing the limits of the 'new orientation', 'is (. . .) not possible'.[52] In place of concrete democratization programmes there appeared a politically diffuse rhetoric of national renewal, in which 'the powerful storm of war' both gave the impression that it would 'do away with the remains of a recent past and bring new ways of life to full bloom, carrying our people far beyond the pseudo-democracy of the Western powers to the signposted true German freedom.'[53]

German world-war ideology in general presented a dichotomy by invoking traditional German cultural values on the one hand and a rhetoric of change, indeed of revolution, on the other. Nonetheless, it would be misleading to dissociate in principle the so-called 'ideas of 1914', with their apparently revolutionary claims to modernity, from traditional features of the 'cultural war' and simply to see it as a 'hurried reaction of German academics to the publicised demands of the Entente (. . .) to convert the German Empire to democracy after destroying its Prussian "militarism"'.[54] Instead, the invocation of national rebirth, trapped in tradition, and the future-oriented proclamation of a national revolution, were combined in an antiliberal understanding of national renewal, which pervaded both doctrines, and in an anti-Western conception of the enemy, which was equally directed at characteristics of German society itself.

However, an important differentiation needs to be made here. For the majority of German war ideologists, the invocation of a 'German' future remained connected – despite the criticisms of the traditions of Western Europe – to a conception of a specifically characterized civil society. The more radical advocates of the 'ideas of 1914' went far beyond this in many respects, and began to sketch clear ideas of a post-bourgeois order, that is a society totally detached from the liberal and emancipatory conceptions of modern civilization. The humane cultural ideal, according to Kjellén, had 'raised too high the worth of life as such as opposed to death'.[83] Werner Sombart put forward the idea of warrior racial breeding, as he wanted to see a new 'race of bolder, more broad-chested, more bright-eyed people grow' in Germany and to place next to these men 'broad-hipped women to bear future warriors'.[84] The focal point of plans for a modern, post-liberal Germany was, however, an ideological reworking of the economic and social organization of the 'home front'. The interpretation of German war society as the starting point of a historically new level of social development, the most extreme forms of which foresaw an anti-liberal and anti-marxist utopia, presents the most remarkable feature of German world-war ideology.

A central role was played here by the term 'organization', which according to Theodor Heuss was at times 'only spoken, written and printed with an exclamation mark'.[55] The 'German secret' of organizational ability – the roots of which were seen on the one hand in the preparedness to fit oneself into society and on the other in the allegedly efficient structure of the bureaucratic authoritarian state – seemed at first to be seen in the supposedly frictionless military mobilization. Troeltsch, for example, saw in the 'overwhelming impression of quiet dutifulness, discipline and competence of the masses' and the 'triumph of material performance' the 'healthy elements of the corporative and organic community's way of thought (. . .) arising in place of an artificial and theoretical social structure'.[56] And Plenge rejoiced: 'There our new spirit is born: the spirit of the strongest combination of all economic and all state forces in a new whole, in which everyone lives with an equal share. The new German state! The ideas of 1914.'[57]

The military formation of economy and society, in particular, was interpreted as a new form of organized people's community (*Volksgemeinschaft*), combining the highly developed corporate organizational structures of modern German capitalism with the bureaucratic and corporate-state traditions of German history, in which a both anti-liberal and anti-marxist solution to the problem of capitalistic class society could be found. The term 'war socialism' as a code for state organization of the war economy was first formulated in the German Social Democrats' attempts to justify their *Burgfrieden* policy by relating it to their own sociopolitical aims.[58] Identifying with the nation appeared to make possible the transfer of what had been up to then specific Social Democratic values onto the warring nation. The German *Kaiserreich* could now be identified with socialism and indeed with revolution, something long related to war in Social Democratic tradition. The spokesman for a right-wing Social Democratic idea of 'social imperialism', Paul Lensch, even recognized the socialist world revolution in the war between 'proletarian' Germany and 'British' world capitalism and argued: 'Thus the age of individualism is coming to an end. A new age and with it a new ideal is arising: the socialized society. And its sword is Germany.'[59]

The interpretation of the war as a force serving the social and democratic aims of the working class movement obviously played an important role in justifying the *Burgfrieden* policy and its content. Above all the idea of the state as agent of socialization had a lasting influence on the development of socialist politics. But ideologically the majority of the SPD did not accept social imperialism with its strong nationalistic, socially oppressive, and politically antidemocratic attributes. Its slogans, however, especially 'war socialism', gained increasing importance, not least outside Social Democracy. Leading economists especially, such as Werner Sombart, Edgar Jaffé, Gerhard von Schultze-Gävernitz, Eduard Heimann, Otto Neurath, and Johann Plenge, took up this idea and developed it further. Germany appeared to have reached a new level of social development through the 'militarization of economic life', a 'state of economic organization, in which all parts of society have merged into an organic unity, everyone in his proper place as a serving member of the community'.[60] Plenge, especially, recognized the new class of managers, which he had already researched in the US before the war, as an agent of this transformation. He saw them as finally having become permanently established with their pervasion of the state and industrial bureaucracy in the war economy. Walther Rathenau and Wichard von Moellendorf were two prominent industrial managers who had joined the leadership of the German war economy. They too were calling for a 'new economy' under the label of a *Deutsche Gemeinwirtschaft*, which 'requires state assistance for its organic amalgamation, to overcome inner frictions and to maximize performance and efficiency'.[61] This appeared to be the final stage of social reconstruction brought about by the formation of a war economy, but ideologically based on the specific German traditions of community, corporate order and bureaucratic state, a combination that Plenge defined as national socialism:

> Because of the necessities of war, the socialist idea struck roots in German economic life, its organization merged in a new spirit, and thus the self-assertion of our nation for humanity gave birth to the idea of 1914, the idea of German organization, the *Volksgenossenschaft* of national socialism.[62]

The basic structures of the war economy, however, remained organized on a private capital basis, as a respectable number of German social scientists discovered – their discoveries gaining little public attention, however. According to Emil Lederer, it entailed less a 'nationalization of the economy' than a 'capitalization of the state'.[63] Accordingly, co-operative and war socialist concepts of the construction of a 'new economy' remained highly vague. Their main idea lay in a military state-organized capitalism, which was to function efficiently on the pattern of a modern Taylorist factory. Otherwise this 'new economy' reflected the traditional German ideas of an organic, corporate social order.[64] Under the regulatory guidance of a state bureaucracy, class conflict between capital and labour was to be overcome in new organizational forms of economic co-operation, the concrete proposals for which, however – 'production co-operatives in which all members interlock organically', 'a national economy combined into a unity', or a 'new German co-operative constitution' – remained very diffuse.[65] The authoritarian and anti-working-class character of these projects of organic, conflictless social construction, which became most clear in the plans of the military high command,[66] could only be superficially covered over by a rhetoric of integration. '"Work together" is the freedom of action! "Fit yourself in" the equality of serving! "Live in the total brotherhood of true socialism"' – these were the new slogans of the 'ideas of 1914' in which Johann Plenge and others saw the German fulfilment and the defeat of the revolutionary ideals of 1789.[67]

In contrasting 1789 and 1914, German world-war ideology gained a historical perspective, according to which higher forms of organized social coherence in the new twentieth century would lead 'youthful' Germany at war to victory over the liberal social forms of the nineteenth century, embodied by her Western opponents. 'A new historical era began for the world and especially for the German people in 1914' – with these words, Meinecke, with the authority of a historian, formulated the widespread belief in the coming of a new age, brought about by war and defined by Germany.[68] 'The great fight is not just between peoples, but between ideologies, and not just between different contemporary schools of thought but between different ages. The World War is a war between 1789 and 1914', wrote Kjellén.[69] And Plenge similarly conceived the war as a world historical conflict between the contrasting principles of 1789 and 1914:

Since 1789 there has been no revolution like the German revolution of 1914. The revolution of the construction and connection of all state powers in the 20th century contrasts to the destructive liberation in the 19th century. This is why there is a certain truth in all this shouting about a new Napoleon. For the second time, an Emperor is marching through the world as leader of his people (. . .). And one may claim that the 'ideas of 1914', the ideas of German organization are as destined for a lasting victory throughout the world as were the ideas of 1789.[70]

III. The Historical Significance of the 'German Revolution' of 1914

When, in 1915, Friedrich Meinecke placed the First World War in the tradition of 'national uprisings' of the German people, the precedents he mentions – the anti-Napoleon war of liberation 1813, the revolution of 1848, and the founding of the Empire, 1870–71 – proved surprisingly similar to the stages of development defined by modern historians of nineteenth-century German history using the term 'revolution' as, for example, presented in this book.[71] The other milestones of the revolutionary dynamic of the twentieth century dealt with here would instead hardly have been defined by Meinecke as national uprisings, with the exception of 1989 and possibly, for a little while, 1933. This illustrates the point that the modern use of the term 'revolution' is altogether more complex than the way disciples of historicism focused it on the national question. Nonetheless, for the 19th century there are important overlaps between the two concepts.

In all the phases mentioned above, both for Meinecke and in the view of modern historians, three factors in particular played an important role, shedding light on the problem of modern German history: war, nation, and social progress. This is also true of the First World War, but here especially progress, which had anyway been to a great extent limited to the area of economy, underwent a fundamental shift in meaning. The dominant sociopolitical doctrines, arising at the time under the banner of the 'triad of power, nationality and culture',[72] could not refer to the progressive tradition of the nineteenth century, the rejection of which gave the 'spirit of 1914' most of its power. German sociopolitical thinking, with its fundamental turning away from Western society, and its refusal to accept social conflict and democratic self-government, had largely broken its previously close connection with the processes of social modernization during the nineteenth century. Instead it now rejected central elements of modern society. The much-trumpeted modernity of the 'ideas of 1914' could accordingly draw on a highly developed and centralized German economy and technological-organizational innovations. However, the proclaimed defeat of the 'ideas of 1789', associated with notions of an organic corporatist order and the authoritarian state, basically fell back on traditionally anti-revolutionary conceptions of society; something political conservatism, trapped in pre-industrial social forms, had long been using as a weapon against the pluralistic conception of modern society.[73]

The paradox, which is becoming clearer here, of a 'political-spiritual self-alienation of the burgher from the real social conditions of his own existence'[74] is rooted above all in the context of the 'German double revolution' in the middle of the nineteenth century.[75] On the one hand, it confronted German society in such a dynamic and complex way with all the forms of disintegration, alienation and social conflict inherent in the development of industrial capitalism, that a multitude of defensive reactions quickly set in and positive identification was doubtless made difficult. Bourgeois Germany increasingly went into society 'like going abroad' and sought its identity above all in the strong class-specific contexts of culture, work and family.[76] On the other hand, the monarchist structure of the new German nation state successfully defended against the onslaught of revolution and democratization, and supported by disturbing propaganda about internal enemies, contributed to the alienation of middle-class Germany. By preventing parliamentary self-government, it also obviated the necessity of becoming involved, responsibly and creatively, in concrete forms of political problem-solving. Instead, a rapidly spreading rejection of modern society in favour of a mythically utopian past arose, the analysis of which presents us with a portrait of a self-alienated 'pathology of cultural criticism'.[77]

This is of course a one-sided perspective on bourgeois self-consciousness in the *Kaiserreich*. Cultural life, especially in Wilhelmine Germany, was heterogeneous, and this was taken by many to be an expression of decadent tendencies.[78] Furthermore, German political thinking also developed a strong identification with the gains of national development and economic modernization. The newly founded *Kaiserreich* with its rapid economic development appeared to represent the idea of youthfulness and seemed to make a justifiable claim to world power.[79] Nevertheless, from the perspective of German world-war ideology there was not only an 'insecurity about the sense and purpose of this increasingly strengthened and unified Nation and its place in the community of Nations'.[80] Bourgeois Germany was deeply in trouble in its domestic affairs, and seemed to require a national renewal. It was the war that lastingly politicized cultural pessimism and created a new forward-looking perspective. However, with the anti-Western thrust of German world-war ideology and its new integration of cultural pessimism, social Darwinism, nationalism, militarism, and industrial managerialism it also led to a strong dominance of conservative attitudes – something that found its clearest expression in the collapse of liberal cultural Protestantism.[81]

Taking an international perspective, some of these findings do not seem very surprising, as Western ideas of war, with their similar frightening chauvinism, also served to support conservative pretensions. But German world-war ideology distinguishes itself, beside its strong anti-liberal character, in two important structural respects. First it was the conception of the enemy as analogous to the problems and fault lines of German society itself that created a special and problematic character. Western propaganda of the struggle of liberal democracy against autocratic militarism was not only more universally defined than the self-referential invocation of German entity. It stood, despite its idealism, much more in harmony with the real developmental tendencies of modern society. German world-war ideology's limited attractiveness, on the other hand, was due not only to its being set, in a superficial sense, 'against the Zeitgeist'.[82] Rather, it was as unattractive as it was problematic because it arose from a rejection of core elements of modern social development in Germany itself and thus gained an unreal, if compulsive character. The West, to exaggerate a little, went to war for its own existing society, but imperial Germany, with its anti-Western enemy image, also fought against the realities of its own industrial society and for a 'German' future conceived in rejection of that society. Consequently, the second problematic peculiarity of German war ideology was its interpretation of the war as a struggle for a historically new, post-bourgeois form of social and political order, indeed as a 'German revolution'.

Through the transfiguration of the ruling monarchical order and its war in 1914, once again an ideological identification with real sociopolitical conditions was created, which seemed to promise a 'German' future without a political upheaval. In 1918, however, this was no longer possible because the war was lost, and the radicalizing dynamic of wartime class society culminated in a real revolution, replacing the monarchy with a democratic constitutional order and placing the emancipatory aims of the proletarian masses on the political agenda. The hope that appeared in the 'ideas of 1914' – that the problems of modern industrial-capitalistic society could be overcome by a specifically German 'revolution' in harmony with the ruling monarchical order – proved to be an illusion. The Prussian-German tradition of a 'revolution from above', at least as ideologically developed in the 'ideas of 1914', had thus been thwarted. The true 'German revolution', however, was still to come, and after the experience of defeat and revolution it could no longer take place with, but only against the ruling order, against Weimar democracy. The result of this 'learning process', first indicated in the development of radical conservatism, but then spreading further out into the bourgeois camp,[85] was the National Socialists' seizure of power, viewed by contemporaries as a 'national uprising', a 'national socialist revolution' and a 'rebirth of the spirit of 1914'.[86]

However much the political form and content of 1914 and 1933 must be differentiated – not least because 1914 entailed an inclusive, but not exclusive, construction of the *Volksgemeinschaft* – the ideological continuities of 'reactionary modernism' do indeed stand out.[87] The form of a *Volksgenossenschaft* of national socialism', which arose in 1933, with its totalitarian domestic social construction and warlike aggression internationally, can indeed be understood as an attempt, drawing on ideology, to solve the crises and problems of modern industrial society through the paradoxes already defined in the 'ideas of 1914' and further developed in the 'conservative revolution' of the 1920s. This was a 'national revolution', reactionary in its ideological foundations, but highly modern in its methods of social organization and in the way it saw itself pointing beyond the conventional liberal conception of modern civilization. 'The German revolution', Robert Ley emphasized in 1935, 'began in those August days, 1914 (. . .)'.[88]

Notes

1. Johann Plenge, *Der Krieg und die Volkswirtschaft*, Münster 1915, pp. 171 f. The best introduction is Reinhard Rürup, 'Der "Geist von 1914" in Deutschland. Kriegsbegeisterung und Ideologisierung des Krieges im Ersten Weltkrieg', in Bernd Hüppauf (ed.), *Ansichten vom Krieg. Vergleichende Studien zum Ersten Weltkrieg in Literatur und Gesellschaft*, Königstein/Ts 1984, pp. 1–30; a more concise version is Reinhard Rürup 'Die Ideologisierung des Krieges: Die "Ideen von 1914"', in Helmut Böhme and Fritz Kallenberg (eds), *Deutschland und der Erste Weltkrieg*, Darmstadt 1987,

pp.121–40. See also Wolfgang J. Mommsen, 'German artists, writers and intellectuals and the meaning of war, 1914–1918', in John Horne (ed.), *State, society and mobilization in Europe during the First World War,* Cambridge 1997, pp. 21–38; for a broader comparative perspective see Wolfgang Kruse and Jeffrey Verhey, 'Zur Erfahrungs- und Kulturgeschichte des Ersten Weltkrieges', in W. Kruse (ed.), *Eine Welt von Feinden. Der Große Krieg 1914–1918,* Frankfurt am Main 1997, pp. 159–95.

2. See Dieter Langewiesche (ed.), *Revolution und Krieg. Zur Dynamik historischen Wandels seit dem 18. Jahrhundert,* Paderborn 1989.

3. See generally Jürgen Kocka, *Klassengesellschaft im Krieg. Deutsche Sozialgeschichte 1914–1918,* Göttingen 1973.

4. See Jean-Jacques Becker, *1914. Comment les français sont entrés dans la guerre,* Paris 1977; Thomas Raithel, *Das 'Wunder' der inneren Einheit. Studien zur deutschen und französischen Öffentlichkeit bei Beginn des Ersten Weltkrieges,* Bonn 1996; Christian Geinitz, *Kriegsfurcht und Kampfbereitschaft. Das Augusterlebnis in Freiburg,* Essen 1998; Jeffrey Verhey, *The Spirit of 1914. Militarism, Myth, and Mobilization in Germany,* Cambridge 2000; Michael Stöcker, *Augusterlebnis 1914 in Darmstadt,* Darmstadt 1994; Wolfgang Kruse, 'Die Kriegsbegeisterung im Deutschen Reich zu Beginn des Ersten Weltkrieges. Entstehungszusammenhänge, Grenzen und ideologische Strukturen', in Gottfried Mergner and Marcel van der Linden (eds), *Kriegsbegeisterung und mentale Kriegsvorbereitung,* Berlin 1991, pp. 73–87.

5. See Klaus Vondung, Deutsche Apokalypse 1914, in K. Vondung (ed.), *Das wilhelminische Bildungsbürgertum. Zur Sozialgeschichte seiner Ideen,* Göttingen 1976, pp. 151–71; for an international comparison see Klaus Vondung (ed.), *Kriegserlebnis. Der Erste Weltkrieg in der symbolischen Deutung und Gestaltung der Nationen,* Göttingen 1980.

6. Eric J. Leed, *No Man's Land. Combat and Identity in World War I,* Cambridge, Mass. 1979.

7. See Roland N. Stromberg, *Redemption by War. The Intellectuals and 1914,* Lawrence 1982; Jost Dülffer and Karl Holl (eds), *Bereit zum Krieg. Kriegsmentalität im wilhelminischen Deutschland,* Göttingen 1986; Thomas Rohkrämer, 'August 1914 – Kriegsmentalität und ihre Voraussetzungen', in Wolfgang Michalka (ed.), *Der Erste Weltkrieg. Wirkung, Wahrnehmung, Analyse,* Munich 1994, pp. 759–77.

8. Karl Grünberg, 'Mobilmachung in Berlin', in Wolfgang Emmerich (ed.), *Proletarische Lebensläufe. Autobiographische Dokumente zur Entstehung der Zweiten Kultur in Deutschland,* vol. 2: *1914 bis 1945,* Reinbek 1975, pp. 94–7.

9. *Tägliche Rundschau,* 31 July 1914, p. 4: 'Aus der Reichshauptstadt. Die Krise in Berlin.'

10. Gustav Roethe, 'Wir Deutschen und der Krieg', in *Deutsche Reden in schwerer Zeit, gehalten von den Professoren an der Universität Berlin,* 3 vols, Berlin 1915, vol. 1, pp. 15–46, here p. 18; Werner Sombart, *Händler und Helden. Patriotische Besinnungen,* Munich 1915, p. 119; Hermann Bahr,

'Das deutsche Wesen ist uns erschienen', in H. Bahr, *Kriegssegen*, Munich 1915, pp. 5–7.

11. Friedrich Meinecke, 'Die deutschen Erhebungen von 1813, 1848, 1870 und 1914', in F. Meinecke, *Die deutsche Erhebung von 1914*, Stuttgart 1914, pp. 9–38, here p. 31. On German historians as political commentators during World War I see Helmut Böhme, 'Die deutsche Geschichtswissenschaft und der Erste Weltkrieg', in H. Böhme and F. Kallenberg (eds), *Deutschland und der Erste Weltkrieg*, pp. 11–74; Christoph Cornelißen, 'Politische Historiker und deutsche Kultur. Die Schriften und Reden von Georg von Below, Hermann Oncken und Gerhard Ritter im Ersten Weltkrieg', in Wolfgang J. Mommsen (ed.), *Krieg und Kultur. Die Rolle der Intellektuellen, Künstler und Schriftsteller im Ersten Weltkrieg*, Munich 1996, pp. 119–42; Stefan Meineke, 'Friedrich Meinecke und der "Krieg der Geister"', in W. J. Mommsen (ed.), *Krieg und Kultur*, pp. 97–118.

12. Max Scheler, *Der Genius des Krieges und der deutsche Krieg*, 3rd edn, Leipzig 1917, p. 2. On German philosophers' interpretations of the war see Hermann Lübbe, 'Die philosophischen Ideen von 1914', in H. Lübbe, *Politische Philosophie in Deutschland. Studien zu ihrer Geschichte*, Munich 1974, pp. 171–236.

13. Otto von Gierke, 'Krieg und Kultur', in *Deutsche Reden in schwerer Zeit*, vol. 1, pp. 75–101, here p. 89. On the theological interpretation of the war see Kurt Hammer, *Deutsche Kriegstheologie 1870–1918*, Munich 1971; Kurt Hammer, 'Der deutsche Protestantismus im Ersten Weltkrieg', in *Francia* 2, 1974, pp. 398–414; Wilhelm Pressel, *Die Kriegspredigt 1914– 1918 in der evangelischen Kirche Deutschlands*, Göttingen 1967; Günter Brackelmann, *Protestantische Kriegstheologie im Ersten Weltkrieg. Reinhold Seeberg als Theologe des deutschen Imperialismus*, Bielefeld 1974; Günter Brackelmann, *Krieg und Gewissen. Otto Baumgarten als Politiker und Theologe im Ersten Weltkrieg*, Göttingen 1991; Heinrich Missalla, *'Gott mit uns'. Die deutsche katholische Kriegspredigt 1914–1918*, Munich 1968; Richard van Dülmen, 'Der deutsche Katholizismus und der Erste Weltkrieg', in *Francia* 2, 1974, pp. 347–76.

14. Alois Riehl, '1813 – Fichte – 1914', in *Deutsche Reden in schwerer Zeit*, vol. 1, pp. 191–210, here p. 207.

15. Thus Eckart Koester, *Literatur und Weltkriegsideologie. Positionen und Begründungszusammenhänge des publizistischen Engagements deutscher Schriftsteller im Ersten Weltkrieg*, Kronberg/Ts. 1977, p. 138, especially in relation to Rainer Maria Rilke; on the writers see also Bernhard Boschert, '"Eine Utopie des Unglücks stieg auf". Zum literarischen und publizistischen Engagement deutscher Schriftsteller für den Ersten Weltkrieg', in Berliner Geschichtswerkstatt (ed.), *August 1914: Ein Volk zieht in den Krieg*, Berlin 1989, pp. 127–35; Helmut Fries, *Die große Katharsis. Der Erste Weltkrieg in der Sicht deutscher Dichter und Gelehrter*, 2 vols, Konstanz 1994– 95; Helmut Fries, 'Deutsche Schriftsteller im Ersten Weltkrieg', in W. Michalka (ed.), *Der Erste Weltkrieg*, pp. 825–48.

16. See K. Vondung, *Deutsche Apokalypse 1914*.

17. Ernst Dehmel, 'Offener Brief an die Kinder', in E. Dehmel, *Zwischen Volk und Menschheit*, Berlin 1919, pp. 9–13.

18. *Tägliche Rundschau*, 5 August 1914, 1st *Beilage:* 'Von Heydebrand bis Scheidemann'.

19. See Michael Jeismann, *Das Vaterland der Feinde. Studien zum nationalen Feindbegriff und Selbstverständnis in Deutschland und Frankreich 1792–1918*, Stuttgart 1992; Konrad Ottenheym and Ernst Horst Schallenberger, *Nation im Kampf. Quellen und Deutungen zum Verständnis des Zeitgeistes während der 1. Phase des Ersten Weltkrieges*, Ratingen 1965.

20. Hermann Oncken, 'Die Ideen von 1913 und die deutsche Gegenwart', in H. Oncken, *Historisch-politische Aufsätze und Reden*, vol. 1, Munich 1914, p. 32; Wolfgang Siemann, 'Krieg und Frieden in historischen Gedenkfeiern des Jahres 1913', in Dieter Düding, Peter Friedemann and Paul Münch (eds), *Öffentliche Festkultur. Politische Feste in Deutschland von der Aufklärung bis zum Ersten Weltkrieg*, Reinbek 1988, pp. 298–320.

21. See Dieter Langewiesche, '"Revolution von oben"? Krieg und Nationalstaatsgründung in Deutschland', in D. Langewiesche (ed.), *Revolution und Krieg*, pp. 117–34.

22. Friedrich von Bernhardi, *Deutschland und der nächste Krieg*, Stuttgart 1912, pp. 11, 21.

23. See Peter Walkenhorst, 'Nationalismus als 'politische Religion'. Zur religiösen Dimension nationalistischer Ideologie im Kaiserreich', in Olaf Blaschke and Frank-Michael Kuhlemann (eds), *Religion im Kaiserreich: Milieus, Mentalitäten, Krisen*, Gütersloh 1996, pp. 503–529.

24. See Helmut Plessner, *Die verspätete Nation. Über die Verführbarkeit bürgerlichen Geistes*, Stuttgart 1959; Fritz Stern, *The Politics of Cultural Despair*, New York 1963; George L. Mosse, *The Crisis of German Ideology. Intellectual Origins of the Third Reich*, New York 1964; Fritz K. Ringer, *The Decline of the German Mandarins*, Cambridge, Mass.1969; Klaus von See, *Die Ideen von 1789 und die Ideen von 1914. Völkisches Denken in Deutschland zwischen Französischer Revolution und Erstem Weltkrieg*, Munich 1980; Robin Lenman, *Die Kunst, die Macht, das Geld. Zur Kulturgeschichte des kaiserlichen Deutschland 1871–1918*, Frankfurt 1994.

25. Rudolf Eucken, *Die geistigen Forderungen der Gegenwart*, Berlin 1917, p. 17.

26. Ernst Toller, *Eine Jugend in Deutschland*, Munich 1978, p. 53.

27. F. Meinecke, *Nationale Erhebungen*, pp. 27f.

28. H. Bahr, *Das deutsche Wesen*, pp. 6 f.

29. See K. Vondung, *Deutsche Apokalypse 1914*; Klaus Vondung, 'Geschichte als Weltgericht. Genesis und Degradation einer Symbolik', in K. Vondung (ed.), *Kriegserlebnis*, pp. 62–84; Wolfgang Kruse, 'Der säkularisierte "Heilige Krieg" des Deutschen Reiches 1914', in *Journal Geschichte* 1989, No 5, pp. 23–33.

30. Walther Rathenau, 'Die neue Wirtschaft', in W. Rathenau, *Gesammelte Schriften in 5 Bänden*, Berlin 1918, vol. 5, pp. 179–261, here p. 259.

31. Paul Natorp, *Der Tag des Deutschen*, Hagen 1915, p. 55.
32. J. Plenge, *Krieg und Volkswirtschaft*, p. 200.
33. Rudolf Borchardt, *Der Krieg und die deutsche Verantwortung*, Berlin 1916, quoted in E. Koester, *Literatur und Weltkriegsideologie*, p. 217.
34. Ernst Nolte, *Der europäische Bürgerkrieg 1917–1945. Nationalsozialismus und Bolschewismus*, Berlin 1987.
35. Eric J. Hobsbawm, *Age of Extremes. The Short Twentieth Century, 1914–1991*, London 1994, p. 22.
36. Thomas Mann, *Betrachtungen eines Unpolitischen*, Berlin 1918, preface, pp. 23 f; for background see Norbert Elias, 'Zur Soziogenese des Gegensatzes von "Kultur" und "Zivilisation" in Deutschland', in N. Elias, *Über den Prozeß der Zivilisation*, Frankfurt am Main 1981, pp. 1–42.
37. See Jürgen von Unger-Sternberg, 'Wie geben wir den Sinnlosen einen Sinn? Zum Gebrauch der Begriffe "deutsche Kultur" und "Militarismus" im Herbst 1914', in W. J. Mommsen (ed.), *Krieg und Kultur*, pp. 77–96.
38. Bernhard vom Brocke, 'Wissenschaft und Militarismus. Der Aufruf der 93 'An die Kulturwelt' und der Zusammenbruch der internationalen Gelehrtenrepublik im Ersten Weltkrieg', in William M. Calder III (ed.), *Wilamowitz nach 50 Jahren*, Darmstadt 1985, pp. 649–719, the appeal p. 718; see further Klaus Böhme (ed.), *Aufrufe und Reden deutscher Professoren im Ersten Weltkrieg*, Stuttgart 1975; Hermann Kellermann (ed.), *Der Krieg der Geister. Auslese deutscher und ausländischer Stimmen zum Weltkriege*, Dresden 1915; Ernst Johann (ed.), *Innenansicht eines Krieges. Deutsche Dokumente 1914–1918*, Munich 1973.
39. 'Erklärung der Hochschullehrer des Deutschen Reiches vom 16.10.1914', printed in B. vom Brocke, *Wissenschaft und Militarismus*, p. 717.
40. Friedrich Meinecke, 'Krieg und Kultur', in F. Meinecke, *Die deutsche Erhebung*, pp. 39–46, here p. 45.
41. See Barbara Greven-Aschoff, *Die bürgerliche Frauenbewegung in Deutschland 1894–1933*, Göttingen 1981; Ernst Zechlin, *Die deutsche Politik und die Juden im Ersten Weltkrieg*, Göttingen 1969; Wolfgang Kruse, *Krieg und nationale Integration. Eine Neuinterpretation des sozialdemokratischen Burgfriedensschlusses 1914/15*, Essen 1993.
42. W. Sombart, *Händler und Helden*, p. 99.
43. Ernst Bertram, 'Wie deuten wir uns?', quoted in E. Koester, *Literatur und Weltkriegsideologie*, p. 155.
44. Rudolf Borchardt, *Der Krieg und die deutsche Selbsteinkehr. Rede gehalten am 5. Dezember 1914 in Heidelberg*, Heidelberg 1915, p. 4.
45. Rudolf Kjellén, *Die Ideen von 1914 – eine weltgeschichtliche Perspektive*, Leipzig 1915, p. 40; W. Sombart, *Händler und Helden*, p. 87.
46. Adolf von Harnack, 'Was wir schon gewonnen haben und was wir noch gewinnen müssen', in *Deutsche Reden in schwerer Zeit*, vol. 1, pp. 147–68, here p. 156; on the tradition see Leonard Krieger, *The German Idea of Freedom*, Boston 1957.

47. Ernst Troeltsch, 'Die Ideen von 1914', in E. Troeltsch, *Deutscher Geist und Westeuropa. Gesammelte kulturphilosophische Aufsätze und Reden,* edited by Hans Baron, Tübingen 1925, pp. 39–58, here pp. 48 f.; see also E. Troeltsch, 'Die deutsche Idee der Freiheit', in E. Troeltsch, *Deutscher Geist und Westeuropa,* p. 80–107.

48. Adolph Lasson, 'Deutsche Art und deutsche Bildung', in *Deutsche Reden in schwerer Zeit,* vol. 1, pp. 103–40, here p. 129.

49. Friedrich Meinecke, 'Die deutsche Freiheit', in *Die deutsche Freiheit. Fünf Vorträge, gehalten im Berliner Abgeordnetenhaus,* Gotha 1917, pp. 14–39, here p. 36; see generally Wolfgang J. Mommsen, 'Die "deutsche Idee von der Freiheit". Die deutsche Historikerschaft und das Modell des monarchischen Konstitutionalismus im Kaiserreich', in *Staatswissenschaften und Staatspraxis* 3, 1992, pp. 30–45.

50. See Wolfgang J. Mommsen, 'Der Geist von 1914. Das Programm eines politischen "Sonderwegs" der Deutschen', in W. J. Mommsen, *Der autoritäre Nationalstaat. Verfassung, Gesellschaft und Kultur im deutschen Kaiserreich,* Frankfurt am Main 1990, pp. 406–21; Klaus Schwabe, *Wissenschaft und Kriegsmoral. Die deutschen Hochschullehrer und die politischen Grundfragen des Ersten Weltkrieges,* Göttingen 1969.

51. See Friedrich Meinecke, 'Die Reform des preußischen Wahlrechts', in F. Meinecke, *Probleme des Weltkrieges,* Berlin 1917, pp. 83–125, here pp. 120 f.; Ernst Troeltsch, 'Der Ansturm der westlichen Demokratie', in *Die deutsche Freiheit,* pp. 79–113, here p. 110.

52. Friedrich Meinecke, 'Grenzen der Neuorientierung', in F. Meinecke, *Probleme des Weltkrieges,* pp. 181–5, here p. 185.

53. Max Sering, 'Staats- und Gesellschaftsauffassung bei den Westmächten und bei uns', in *Die deutsche Freiheit,* pp. 40–78, here p. 77.

54. H. Fries, *Die große Katharsis,* vol. 1, pp. 165 f.

55. Theodor Heuss, 'Abschied von Marx', in *Die Hilfe* 23, 1917, pp. 106–9, here p. 109, here, too, the following quote.

56. E. Troeltsch, 'Ideen von 1914', p. 44.

57. J. Plenge, *Krieg und Volkswirtschaft,* p. 187 f; see also Axel Schildt, 'Ein konservativer Prophet moderner nationaler Integration. Biographische Skizze des streitbaren Soziologen Johann Plenge (1874–1963)', in *Vierteljahrshefte für Zeitgeschichte* 35, 1987, pp. 523–70.

58. See W. Kruse, *Krieg und nationale Integration,* pp. 121–51; Robert Sigel, *Die Lensch-Cunow-Haenisch-Gruppe. Eine Studie zum rechten Flügel der SPD im Ersten Weltkrieg,* Berlin 1976.

59. Paul Lensch, *Die Sozialdemokratie, ihr Ende und ihr Glück,* Leipzig 1916, p. 183.

60. Edgar Jaffé, 'Die Militarisierung unseres Wirtschaftslebens', in *Archiv für Sozialwissenschaft und Sozialpolitik* 40, 1915, pp. 11–47, here p. 45; see Dieter Krüger, 'Kriegssozialismus. Die Auseinandersetzung der Nationalökonomen mit der Kriegswirtschaft 1914–1918', in W. Michalka (ed.), *Der Erste Weltkrieg,* pp. 506–29; Dieter Krüger, *Nationalökonomen im*

wilhelminischen Deutschland, Göttingen 1983; Hans Joas, 'Die Klassiker der Soziologie und der Erste Weltkrieg', in H. Joas and Hermann Steiner (eds), *Machtpolitischer Realismus und pazifistische Utopie. Krieg und Frieden in der Geschichte der Sozialwissenschaften*, Frankfurt am Main 1989, pp. 179–210.

61. W. Rathenau, *Die neue Wirtschaft*, p. 250; see also Walther Rathenau, 'Deutschlands Rohstoffversorgung', in W. Rathenau, *Gesammelte Werke*, vol. 5, pp. 23–58; W. Rathenau, 'Probleme der Friedenswirtschaft', in W. Rathenau, *Gesammelte Werke*, vol. 5, pp. 59–93; Wichard von Moellendorff, *Deutsche Gemeinwirtschaft*, Berlin 1916; generally Friedrich Zunkel, *Industrie und Staatssozialismus. Der Kampf um die Wirtschaftsordnung in Deutschland 1914–1918*, Düsseldorf 1974; Klaus Braun, *Konservatismus und Gemeinwirtschaft. Eine Studie über Wichard u. Moellendorff,* Duisburg 1978; Hans Gotthard Ehlert, *Die wirtschaftliche Zentralbehörde des Deutschen Reiches. Das Problem der 'Gemeinwirtschaft' in Krieg und Frieden*, Wiesbaden 1982; Ernst Schulin, 'Krieg und Modernisierung. Rathenau als philosophierender Industrieorganisator im Ersten Weltkrieg', in Thomas Hughes (ed.), *Ein Mann vieler Eigenschaften. Walther Rathenau und die Kultur der Moderne*, Berlin 1990, pp. 55–69; Wolfgang Kruse, 'Kriegswirtschaft und Gesellschaftsvision. Walther Rathenau und die Organisierung des Kapitalismus', in Hans Wilderotter (ed.), *Die Extreme berühren sich. Walther Rathenau 1867–1922*, Berlin 1993, pp. 151–69; Wolfgang Michalka, 'Kriegsrohstoffbewirtschaftung. Walther Rathenau und die "kommende Wirtschaft"', in W. Michalka (ed.), *Der Erste Weltkrieg*, pp. 485–505.

62. Johann Plenge, *1789 und 1914. Die symbolischen Jahre in der Geschichte des politischen Geistes*, Berlin 1916, p. 82.

63. Emil Lederer, 'Die ökonomischen Umschichtungen im Kriege', in *Archiv für Sozialwissenschaft und Sozialpolitik* 45, 1918, pp. 1–39 and pp. 430–63; Emil Lederer, 'Zur Soziologie des Weltkrieges', in *Archiv für Sozichwissenschaft und Sozialpolitik* 39, 1915, pp. 347–84.

64. See Charles S. Maier, 'Between Taylorism and Technocracy: European Ideologies and the Vision of Industrial Productivity in the 1920s', in *Journal of Contemporary History* 5, No. 2, 1970, pp. 27–61; Richard H. Bowen, *German Theories of the Corporative State. With Special Reference to the Period 1870–1919*, New York 1947.

65. W. Rathenau, *Neue Wirtschaft*, p. 235; W. Sombart, *Händler und Helden*, pp. 75 f.; Johann Plenge, 'Grundlegung der vergleichenden Wirtschaftstheorie', in *Brauns Annalen für soziale Politik und Gesetzgebung* 5, 1917, pp. 39–100 and pp. 492–552, here p. 70.

66. See Martin Kitchen, 'Militarism and the Development of Fascist Ideology. The Political Ideas of Colonel Max Bauer, 1916–1918', in *Central European History* 8, 1975, pp. 199–220.

67. J. Plenge, *1789 und 1914*, p. 90.

68. Friedrich Meinecke, 'Geschichte und öffentliches Leben', in Ernst Jäckh (ed.), *Der große Krieg als Erlebnis und Erfahrung*, vol. 1, Gotha 1916, pp. 18–26, here p. 18.

69. R. Kjellén, *Ideen von 1914*, p. 6.

70. J. Plenge, *Krieg und Volkswirtschaft*, p. 171 f., and J. Plenge, *1789 und 1914*, p. 72.

71. F. Meinecke, 'Die deutschen Erhebungen'.

72. F. Meinecke, 'Probleme des Weltkrieges', in F. Meinecke, *Probleme des Weltkrieges*, Berlin 1917, pp. 35–57, here p. 57.

73. See Martin Greiffenhagen, *Das Dilemma des Konservatismus in Deutschland*, Munich 1971.

74. H. Lübbe, *Ideen von 1914*, p. 212, with special reference to Sombart.

75. See generally Hans-Ulrich Wehler, *Deutsche Gesellschaftsgeschichte*, vol. 3: *Von der 'Deutschen Doppelrevolution' bis zum Beginn des Ersten Weltkrieges*, Munich 1995.

76. See the famous phrase at the beginning of the most important work of the new German social sciences, Ferdinand Tönnies, *Gemeinschaft und Gesellschaft. Grundbegriffe der reinen Soziologie*, Leipzig 1887, p. 3: 'Man goes into society like going abroad.' For recent research see Jürgen Kocka and Alan Mitchel (eds), *Bourgeois Society in Nineteenth-Century Europe*, Oxford 1993.

77. F. Stern, *Politics of Cultural Despair*, p. 1.

78. See W. J. Mommsen, *Bürgerliche Kultur und künstlerische Avantgarde*; Rüdiger vom Bruch, *Wissenschaft, Politik und öffentliche Meinung. Gelehrtenpolitik im Wilhelminischen Deutschland (1890–1914)*, Husum 1980.

79. See Walther Rüegg (ed.), *Kulturkritik und Jugendkult*, Frankfurt am Main 1974; Willibald Karl (ed.), *Jugend, Gesellschaft und Politik im Zeitraum des Ersten Weltkrieges*, Munich 1973.

80. Wolfgang Hardtwig, 'Bürgertum, Staatssymbolik und Staatsbewußtsein 1871–1914', in *Geschichte und Gesellschaft* 16, 1990, pp. 269–95, here p. 295.

81. See Gangolf Hübinger, *Kulturprotestantismus und Politik. Zum Verhältnis von Liberalismus und Protestantismus im wilhelminischen Deutschland*, Tübingen 1994, especially pp. 310 f.

82. J. v. Unger-Sternberg, 'Wie geben wir dem Sinnlosen einen Sinn', p. 85.

83. R. Kjellén, *Ideen von 1914*, p. 16.

84. W. Sombart, *Händler und Helden*, p. 121.

85. See Hans-Jürgen Puhle, *Von der Agrarkrise zum Präfaschismus*, Wiesbaden 1972; Geoff Eley, *Reshaping the German Right. Radical Nationalism and Political Change after Bismarck*, London 1980; Dirk Stegmann, *Die Erben Bismarcks. Parteien und Verbände in der Spätphase des wilhelminischen Deutschland. Sammlungspolitik 1897–1918*, Cologne 1978; Heinz Hagenlücke, *Deutsche Vaterlandspartei. Die nationale Rechte am Ende des Kaiserreiches*, Düsseldorf 1977; Klemens von Klemperer, *Germany's New Conservatism. Its Historical*

Dilemma in the Twentieth Century, Princeton 1957, Armin Mohler, *Die Konservative Revolution in Deutschland 1918–1932*, Darmstadt 1972.

86. For example, at the opening of the newly elected Reichstag on the so-called '*Tag von Potsdam*' (21 March 1933). See J. Verhey, *Spirit of 1914*, p. 224; see also Lothar Kettenacker, 'Sozialpsychologische Aspekte der Führerherrschaft', in Lothar Kettenacker and Gerhard Hirschfeld (eds), *Der 'Führerstaat'. Mythos und Realität. Studien zur Struktur und Politik des Dritten Reiches*, Stuttgart 1981, pp. 98–132.

87. See Jeffrey Herf, *Reactionary Modernism. Technology, Culture, and Politics in Weimar and the Third Reich*, Cambridge 1984; Hans Mommsen, 'National-sozialismus als vorgetäuschte Modernisierung', in H. Mommsen, *Der Nationalsozialismus und die deutsche Gesellschaft*, Reinbek 1991, pp. 405–27.

88. Robert Ley, *Duchbruch der sozialen Ehre*, Munich 1935, p. 71; see generally Timothy W. Mason, *Sozialpolitik im Dritten Reich. Arbeiterklasse und Volksgemeinschaft*, Opladen 1977.

HEINRICH AUGUST WINKLER

Revolution by Consensus?
Germany 1918–19

If one were to list the great revolutions in world history, the German Revolution of 1918–19 would not be among them. It is safe to say that most scholars would agree on this point. However, they would also agree that the more cautious term 'collapse' does not adequately describe the events of 1918 and 1919. The developments of November 1918 were, indeed, revolutionary in nature. The same can be said of the mass strikes in early 1919 and of the bloody fighting in the Ruhr area after the Kapp–Lüttwitz Putsch a year later, which brought a definitive end to the revolutionary period. Where scholars disagree is on how much freedom of action participants in the revolution had, and on what kind of alternative developments were possible. They also disagree on a closely related question: can one, with the benefit of hindsight, call the revolution of 1918–19 a failure?[1]

The assertion that the upheaval of 1918–19 was more than a 'collapse' does not mean that we should abandon this description entirely. Rather, it is important to establish clearly what collapsed and what did not. After the First World War, Max Weber observed that the 'history of the dissolution of the old system of domination, which had been legitimate in Germany up to 1918' showed that the war, on the one hand, 'went far to break down the authority of tradition; and the German defeat, on the other, involved a tremendous loss of prestige for the government. These factors combined with systematic habituation to illegal behaviour, undermined the amenability to discipline both in the army and in industry and thus prepared the way for the overthrow of the older authority.' This sociological finding supports the hypothesis that the German empire had, by the autumn of 1918, to a significant extent forfeited what Weber called the 'most current form of legitimation,' namely the *Legalitätsglauben*.

Weber defined this as a 'belief in legality, the compliance with enactments which are *formally* correct and which have been made in the accustomed manner.'

According to Weber's insightful analysis, three factors caused the collapse of the German empire: the disintegration of established values through the experience of the First World War, the looming military defeat of the Central European powers, and the growth of the black market. All these factors contributed to the failure of the existing economic-political system, which the German emperor embodied. As a result, the German masses held him responsible not only for the duration and catastrophic conclusion of the war but also for their own personal material deprivation. Furthermore, Wilson's 'Fourteen Points' sowed the seeds of hope that Germany would receive a 'just peace' in return for democratizing its political system, so the desire for peace and democracy reinforced each other. A broad majority sought both of these goals in the autumn of 1918. On the eve of 9 November 1918, this majority represented the core of a consensus that, if not all-encompassing, at least crossed both class and confessional lines.

Since Wilhelm II refused to abdicate, it became clear that monarchy had reached its end – not only in Prussia but in all German states. But essential elements of the old system remained in place. This was especially true of the imperial bureaucracy. The 'way in which the old administrative staff continued to function and the way in which its order was simply taken over by the new supreme authorities' was due not only, as Max Weber rightly observed, to the self-interest of the bureaucrats. As he explained: 'The breakdown of administrative organization would, under such conditions, have meant a breakdown of the provision of the whole population, including, of course, the officials themselves, with even the most elementary necessities of life.'

Furthermore, in the 'new administrative staffs' of the Workers' and Soldiers' Councils, which sprang up during the upheaval, Weber recognized a case of 'charismatic leadership' that, nonetheless, did not replace the extant bureaucracy.

It was only by the rise of charismatic leaders against the legal authorities and by the development around them of groups of charismatic followers, that it was possible to take power away from the old authorities. It was furthermore only through the maintenance of the old bureaucratic organization that power once achieved could be retained. Previous to this situation every revolution which has been attempted under modern conditions has failed completely because of the indispensability of trained officials and of the lack of its own organized staff.[2]

With these remarks, Max Weber voiced a paradoxical thesis with implications for more than just the revolution of 1918–19, namely that the maintenance of a high degree of administrative continuity was both a necessary condition for, and a limitation on, the revolution. Weber was not alone: one of his more extraordinary contemporaries, Eduard Bernstein, also entertained very similar notions. In a book written in 1922 (and nowadays almost completely forgotten), the father of Social Democratic revisionism named two reasons why this revolution was so mild in character: the degree of both industrialization and democratization in Germany. According to Bernstein, the more complex the society, the more difficult it becomes to effect radical change within a short period of time. In addition, by 1918 Germany already had a long tradition of widespread political participation. As a result, one could only call for an enlargement, not a limitation, of existing political liberties.[3]

An expansion of existing freedoms meant three things in 1918: firstly, the elimination of the three-class voting system in Prussia and its replacement with universal suffrage; secondly, the extension to women of the general men's voting rights which Bismarck had already established in 1866 for elections to the Parliament, or Reichstag, of the North German Confederation; and thirdly, the introduction of a government which would be politically responsible to the parliament. Theoretically, these goals had already been obtained on 9 November 1918. The alterations to the imperial constitution of 28 October 1918 had instituted the principle of government responsibility to the parliament. 'In principle,' the majority parties in the Reichstag – those being the Majority Socialists, the Catholic Center Party and the left-liberal Progressive People's Party – had already effected the desired changes to voting rights through an accord on 8 November. However, the arbitrary actions of the emperor, the naval leaders and the army in the days after the October constitutional changes made clear that the new parliamentary system existed only on paper, and the accord of 8 November came too late to change the course of events.

The revolution from below broke out because the revolution from above, in the guise of the October constitutional reform, had failed. A military counter-revolution had doomed the revolution from above; the turning-point came when the naval command ordered the High Seas fleet to sail for England on 30 October. The refusal of German sailors to execute this order marked the beginning of the revolution from below. On 1 November, the rebellion reached the city of Kiel. Workers joined with sailors. By 6 November, the revolutionary masses had gained control over six north German cities. The first crown to topple was that of the Bavarian king on 7 November. Two days later, in Berlin, Majority Socialist Philipp Scheidemann announced the birth of the German Republic.

Only ten weeks after the end of the German monarchy, Germans went to the polls to elect a national constituent assembly. The decision to elect a constituent assembly as soon as possible had its origins in the logic of German constitutional development. The Social Democrats, before 1914 the most energetic advocates of a democratization in Germany, would have lost political credibility if they had wavered in this task. The MSPD, or Majority Socialists – who had approved war credits for the empire up to the bitter end and had even, in October 1918, taken part in the first parliamentary imperial government in the Cabinet of Prince Max von Baden – consistently strove for an election date in January 1919. The moderate leaders of the USPD, or Independent Social Democrats – who had broken off from the Social Democratic Party in 1916–17 over the issue of war credits and who, since 10 November, had been working together with the Majority Socialists on the revolutionary Council of People's Deputies – sought a later date, such as April or May 1919. They wanted to use the intervening time to secure democracy with precautionary administrative and economic measures and improve the chances for the advancement of socialism. However, at the first Congress of Workers' and Soldiers' Councils, the Majority Socialists emerged victorious. A wide majority voted to hold the elections to the National Constituent Assembly on 19 January 1919.

There were many reasons for this decision. The longer the elections were delayed, the greater the risk of violent upheaval. In light of this danger, the sovereignty of the electorate had to be established as soon as possible. However, even within the short time period remaining to the Council of People's Deputies, reforms along the lines of those sought by the USPD could have been implemented. These reforms could have included steps towards democratizing the bureaucracy, creating a military service loyal to the republic, establishing public oversight of economic power, even turning the coal industry into public property. In the opinion of the MSPD, however, such far-reaching measures required a democratic mandate, and the voters had not yet delivered such a mandate. The Majority Socialists also underestimated the danger that the political right, embodied primarily by senior military officers, posed to the new Republic.

Instead, the MSPD members who served as People's Deputies assigned absolute priority to solving the most pressing problems of the transition period. They sought to hold the empire together, provide for an orderly return of the Western Army to the homeland, get the economy moving again, avoid a German descent into general chaos and 'Russian conditions' and, above all else, set the stage for free elections as quickly as possible. The extent to which the Deputies succeeded in these tasks represents a remarkable achievement. They did not view themselves as the founders of a democracy, however. Rather, they perceived of their actions in the manner described by Friedrich Ebert, the Chairman of the Council of People's Deputies, in his report to the National Assembly on 6 February 1919: 'We were in the fullest sense of the word the liquidators of the old regime.'[4]

The policies of the Majority Socialists in the revolutionary transition period between November 1918 and January 1919 comprise one of the most controversial chapters of modern German history. In the former West Germany, Kiel historian Karl Dietrich Erdmann's 1955 analysis of their policies dominated all others for a decade. According to Erdmann, in 1918–19 there was a choice between two clear alternatives. Either there could be 'a social revolution in alliance with the forces striving for a proletarian revolution, or a parliamentary republic in alliance with the conservative forces, such as the old officer corps'.[5]

In the middle of the 1960s, however, another explanation gained ground. Younger historians, such as Eberhard Kolb, Peter von Oertzen and Reinhard Rürup advanced arguments similar to those published in 1935 by the independent Marxist Arthur Rosenberg. They, like Rosenberg, argued that the alternative to the 'Weimar solution' did not in fact lie in a pact with the Communists, because they did not have sufficient popular support in the months after the war. Rather, the central task at the time was the execution of far-reaching changes in power relations. The true alternative was cooperation with the Workers' and Soldiers' Councils, most of whom were inclined towards the Social Democrats. With them, the Majority Socialists could have pushed through such changes if they had really wanted to do so.[6]

In the further development of the scholarly debate, the revisionists' central argument continued to gain adherents. The ruling Social Democrats had more room to manoeuvre than they thought. As a result, with more political decisiveness, they could have changed more and preserved less. Cooperation with the functionaries of the old regime was unavoidable; but the Social Democrats should have asserted their claim to political leadership more convincingly. In contrast, the current assessment of the Councils ranks them as much less important than previously assumed. The Councils could have helped push through an active reform policy, but, as long as they identified themselves with Social Democracy, they could not be regarded as an independent power factor. In other words, the German Workers' and Soldiers' Councils should not be overestimated and described as the founders of a 'third way' between a parliamentary system and a more direct democracy, or *Basisdemokratie*. It is apparent that this was never true of the minority that sought a ruling system consisting exclusively of councils. Whatever 'charisma' the Council leaders may have had – Max Weber believed that some of them possessed this quality – it disappeared extraordinarily quickly.

Another argument now viewed with much scepticism is the idea that 'preventive intervention' in the weeks after the November collapse would have secured the later survival of the Weimar Republic. Even if bureaucrats and judges who were openly hostile to the new Republic had been removed from their offices – as would have been not only possible but also desirable – the rest of the bureaucracy and judiciary would still have remained. Whoever declared political war against them or indeed against the 'bourgeoisie' in general would have been endorsing civil war. This is precisely what the Communists did. Democrats of all stripes could not do so, because they sought a parliamentary democracy and viewed a willingness to cooperate with the moderate forces in the working class and the bourgeoisie as a necessary precondition.

A Marxist pre-war Social Democracy would not have been willing to make a 'class compromise' of this nature, because it would have contradicted the dogma of class conflict. But if the fight over war credits had not destroyed the unity of the Social Democratic Party, the entry of the Social Democrats into a coalition Cabinet would have done so. It must be said, however, that the dividing line in the latter case would not have been identical to the split that actually occurred between the MSPD and USPD. The division of the 'Marxist' workers' movement was therefore, as paradoxical as it may sound, both a heavy burden on the first German democracy – and a necessary precondition for it.

The political cooperation between the Majority Social Democrats and the bourgeois parties of the middle, which had its origins in the war, survived the events of 9 November 1918. 'Bourgeois' state secretaries operated as the actual leaders of political departments, theoretically under the supervision of the Council of People's Deputies. However, as exercised by the 'associate delegates' from the socialist parties, this supervision was often little more than a formality.

Friedrich Ebert and his political friends were convinced that their party would need to call on the cooperation of moderate forces within the bourgeoisie in any case, even if the MSPD and USPD were to secure a majority in the elections for the National Constituent Assembly. The two workers' parties did not have sufficient professional and administrative experience among them to ensure effective functioning of the government. Calling for the construction of a democracy through exclusion of the *Bürgertum* was a luxury that only those who called for a 'dictatorship of the proletariat' could allow themselves.

Hiding behind the 'dictatorship of the proletariat', however, was often another form of political control, as the Russian example showed: the dictatorship of an *avant garde* of professional revolutionaries over the proletariat and population as a whole. When the Bolsheviks put an end to the freely elected constituent assembly in January 1918, they showed the world what a minority that combined the 'right consciousness' with a desire for power could achieve. The German adherents of the Bolsheviks were much weaker than their Russian exemplars, but were still fascinated with the concept of imitating Lenin's example. When Karl Liebknecht, leader of the newly founded Communist Party of Germany or KPD, called on 5 January 1919, for an end to the reign of Ebert and Scheidemann, it served as a signal to his followers to hinder the elections for the National Constituent Assembly. The People's Deputies *had* to suppress this revolt, which history remembers under the dubious name of 'Spartacus uprising', by force of arms. Otherwise they would have become accomplices to a Putsch and would have been responsible for starting a civil war. This civil war would, in turn, almost inevitably, have caused the Allies to intervene and would have touched off a new European war.

The responsibility for the excess bloodiness of the suppression of the January uprising rests with the Council of People's Deputies, which after 28 December 1918 consisted solely of Majority Social Democrats. One member in particular is to blame: Gustav Noske, *Volksbeauftragter* in charge of military questions since 29 December. Right-leaning free corps, or *Freikorps*, committed the acts of violence. The Peoples' Deputies had called for the formation of the *Freikorps*, because they felt that the few formations loyal to the republic were too weak to defend it. Among the errors of the Social Democratic Party in the weeks immediately following 9 November 1918, the failure to challenge the old military order ranks as one of the most serious. Ebert seems to have trusted the loyalty of the army chiefs of staff unconditionally and he ignored the early, and sensible, calls for reform from the Soldiers' Councils.

But one cannot blame the leaders alone; the fault also lies with their followers. Only a few workers were prepared to use weapons in a fight against rebels from their own class: The *Freikorps* filled a vacuum which was a product of both political decisions and a widespread social democratic mentality. A deep-rooted anti-militarism merged with a sense of class solidarity that crossed party lines: it was to these sentiments that the Social Democratic *Vorwärts* had appealed when it called on 10 November for *Kein Bruderkampf*, or 'no war between brothers'.

The period of the revolutionary interregnum ended with elections for the National Constituent Assembly, on 19 January 1919. Despite clear gains by the MSPD, the two Social Democratic Parties together failed to receive an absolute majority, garnering instead only 45.5 per cent of the vote. The Majority Socialists, the Centre Party and the German Democratic Party, the successor to the Progressive People's Party, joined together to form the 'Weimar Coalition', thus perpetuating a model of political cooperation that had first appeared in wartime. The election results did not allow for the construction of an anticapitalist majority. Despite this, the position of the MSPD would still have been strong enough to allow for the nationalization of the pitcoal mining industry, as the experts of the recently appointed Socialization Commission proposed. What was missing was not the strength, but rather the will: the Party did not recognize the political urgency of such a step.

Apart from the military, there remained two components of the imperial power elite that opposed any kind of democratization: those with large land holdings east of the Elbe River and the heavy industrialists. There was no movement in support of confiscating and redistributing the large agrarian holdings in 1918–19 to threaten the landowners, but the industrialists faced broad social support for the socialization of the mining industry. This support intensified in the second half of December 1918, and in January 1919; indeed, the second phase of the German revolution began with the strikes in the Ruhr and central German regions at the beginning of 1919. In contrast to the first phase, this phase did not enjoy widespread support capable of crossing party lines. The social basis for this revolutionary movement consisted instead of a group far more proletarian and more radical than had been the case in the first weeks after the overthrow of the monarchy. The socialization movement sought far-reaching changes in the nature of property relations in several key regions. Their demands went far beyond a mere nationalization of industry. Rather, factory councils or *Betriebsräte* were to become the basis for a new 'economic democracy'. However, the manner in which movement leaders envisioned the division between the power of the workers and the power of the state varied widely.

The radicalization of early 1919 was a consequence of dissatisfaction with the first phase of the revolution. Neither the existing social relations nor the power structures had changed much. Part of the working class now sought to effect the changes themselves, in complete disregard for the results of the parliamentary elections. But the concrete achievements of this extraparliamentary movement remained limited. Property relations stayed the way they were. Involvement of the workers in industrial decision-making increased only slightly and never fulfilled the expectations of the Majority Social Democrats, let alone of the radical left. Wherever local extremists attempted to overthrow the status quo, the Freikorps and regular military troops halted them with excessive violence; indeed, the radical left's disregard for the will of the majority put wind in the sails of the right. The right, however, fought not only the left, but also the alleged source of the left's strength: democracy. The clearest examples of this are the long-term effects of the two Munich Council Republics in April 1919, one anarchistic and the other communist. It is no coincidence that Munich later became the birthplace of one of the most extreme right-wing anti-democratic movements. The trauma of the experience of the Council Republics sowed the seeds that Adolf Hitler reaped.

The second phase of the German revolution ended with the overthrow of the Second Munich Council Republic on 3 May 1919. Disagreement over basic issues of political and social order had characterized this phase. One could say, with only a small grain of salt, that an excess of consensus in the first period had created an excess of dissent in the second. The result of the 'Stinnes–Legien agreement' of 15 November 1918 (named after a leading industrialist and the chairman of the executive organ of the socialist trade unions) supports this notion. The 'Stinnes–Legien agreement' from the first phase had established the *Zentralarbeitsgemeinschaft* (ZAG), a joint board of labour and business organizations.

In this agreement, employer and employee associations agreed to an organized form of cooperation that recognized the parity of capital and labour. They further formally recognized each other as negotiating partners and agreed to introduce the eight-hour working day. It must be noted, however, that the employers viewed this concession as temporary, unless this new policy were to be implemented in other countries as well. At first, the 'Stinnes–Legien agreement' seemed to be a triumph for the unions. However, this arrangement served as a kind of insurance for the employers against the threat of nationalization. The socialization movement for this reason challenged the unions, who for their part viewed the *Betriebsräte* as dangerous competitors. The overly close cooperation between the established representatives of capital and labour proved to be counterproductive: the social conflict that was building up flowed into new and more revolutionary channels.

With hindsight we can now say that the revolution entered a new phase in May 1919: the phase of latency. The debate over the acceptance or refusal of the Treaty of Versailles took centre stage instead. If the National Constituent Assembly had said 'no', the consequences would have been dramatic. About the ultimate result there can be no doubt: the Allies would have occupied Germany.

By accepting the peace treaty, Germany saved itself from this fate. However, the country could not make peace with itself about the treaty, because all questions of war guilt had been almost systematically suppressed. The decision of the democratic leaders (including the Social Democrats) to avoid any discussion of the question of war guilt – to which documents from the imperial period increasingly testified – meant that they could not fight the so-called *Kriegsunschuldlegende*, or concept that Germany was being wrongly blamed for starting the war. Nor could they fight its twin, the so-called *Dolchstoß* or stab-in-the-back myth. According to this legend, Germany's defeat in the First World War was due not to the failure of the army – which remained 'unbeaten in the field' – but rather to its betrayal by Marxist forces on the home front. Under these conditions, there could be no moral break with the Empire.

After summer 1919, a certain political calm seemed to settle on Germany. The signing of the Versailles Treaty on 28 June and the ratification of the Weimar Constitution on 31 July established both the foreign and domestic framework of the new republic. But appearances deceived. In the military and among the large East Elbean landowners there existed strong sentiment in favour of revising both the peace treaty 'dictated' to Germany by the war's victors and the constitutional basis for the republic. The resentment boiled over into rebellion with the Kapp-Lüttwitz Putsch of March 1920. Named after its leaders, Wolfgang Kapp, a former high-ranking official from East Prussia, and Walther von Lüttwitz, the commanding General of Berlin, this rebellion was the first major upheaval provoked by the right. Lacking the support of the bureaucracy and the population, however, it failed. Workers and their political parties answered this Putsch with a general strike, which contributed to its sorry defeat, but which also inspired an extreme left-wing upheaval in the Ruhr region.

The revolt on the Ruhr was the largest proletarian uprising in German history and also the last of the mass movements that had begun with wildcat strikes in 1917.[7] The revolution had emerged from its phase of latency, thanks to the Kapp–Lüttwitz *coup d'état*, but it met with the same failure that had greeted the counter-revolution. Massive popular support lasted only until the defeat of the coup and the capitulation of Kapp and Lüttwitz. Attempts on the part of the Social Democratic unions in 1920 to achieve finally what they and the Majority Social Democratic Party had failed to do in late 1918 did not succeed. At first, Social Democratic workers took part in the Ruhr uprising, but the true leaders were the left-wing communists and anarchists. Under their leadership, the rebels became divided and isolated. The real victor of this third and last revolutionary phase was the military. With the defeat of the Red Ruhr Army, it became the most important body for enforcing public order.

One of the first lessons of this period is that, on the national level, the basic decisions of the first phase could no longer be corrected. The first phase, which was characterized by relatively widespread consensus over the necessity for peace and democracy, was far less 'revolutionary' in its aims and means than the following periods. However, the first phase was more 'formative', in the sense that it created the framework for the Weimar Republic. The second and third phases were characterized by social protest against what growing numbers of workers viewed as the failings of the first period. But those protests never commanded a majority in the population as a whole.

The majority showed what it wanted in elections: first in the vote for the National Constituent Assembly on 19 January 1919; and then in the Reichstag elections a year later, on 6 June 1920. In 1919, the parties that later formed the Weimar Coalition attained a two-thirds majority; in 1920, they did not even attain an absolute majority. The true winners were the Independent Social Democrats on the left and Stresemann's German People's Party and the royalist German National People's Party on the right. This meant that, from 1920 on,

governments seeking to rule on the basis of a parliamentary majority
had to include parties which had voted against the Weimar Constitution in July 1919. The chances for a political stabilization of the
Weimar Republic diminished dramatically.

What had happened in November 1918 was, above all else, a change
in the form of state. This new form survived not only the Kapp–
Lüttwitz Putsch, the disasters of 1923, and the election of Imperial
Field Marshal Paul von Hindenburg to the presidency in April 1925,
but also to a certain extent the 'Third Reich' as well, since Hitler
never once thought of reinstating the monarchy. Among friends Hitler
even spoke thankfully of the proclamation of a German republic: he
credited the Social Democrats with having spared him the trouble
that Mussolini experienced with 'his' king.[8] The change of regime in
1918 represented, if not a complete, at least a significant alteration
in the make-up of the elite. The aristocracy had dominated the
political elite of the Empire, in particular its executive. In contrast,
the republic found its rulers mainly among the bourgeoisie, the petty
bourgeoisie, and the workers. Senior government bureaucrats and
military officers remained members of the power elite, even if the
numbers of military officers did fall in accordance with the terms of
the Versailles Treaty. Both before and after 1918, business leaders
were also part of the power elite. East Elbian Junkers at first lost
their privilege of 'direct access' to the source of political power after
the overthrow of the monarchy.[9] Not until 1925, when the election of
Hindenburg essentially produced a conservative 'refounding' of the
republic, did the Prussian landowners manage to restore some of their
lost influence.

A societal revolution did not happen in 1918–19. It hardly could
have happened. The empire had collapsed, both militarily and politically, but the social fabric had survived the rigours of the war. Neither
the moral crisis that Max Weber described as the 'systematic habituation to illegal behaviour' nor the material relations that had caused
it ended with the war. Black marketeering, shady dealing, and
profiteering all appeared as part of 'war socialism' and more or less
continued to exist until the beginning of 1924. After 1918, as the
German currency, one of the most important indicators of the orderli-
ness of societal relations, declined in value, the moral crisis increased
in intensity. The inflation had begun in 1914, thanks to the mis-
managed financing of the war. It worsened after 1918, thanks to
the employment of the currency first as a means to achieve social
contentment and then to undercut the demands of the Allies for

reparations. In this regard, as in others, the war did not really end until 1923–4. The most important effect of the currency devaluation was its social and psychological impact. Those members of the middle classes who lost both savings and the money invested in war bonds also lost their ability to trust the state.[10]

The republic that emerged from the revolution of 1918–19 never truly possessed what Max Weber held to be the essential characteristic of a state as a political institution: the '*monopoly* of the *legitimate* use of physical force in the enforcement of its order'. During the war, this monopoly had decomposed; as Weber rightly observed, the war had brought about the widespread distribution of weapons, and this created one of the preconditions of the revolution of 1918/19.[11] The delivery of *Reichswehr* weaponry to not only the *Freikorps* but also to citizens' militias, in part a reaction to what was seen as the forced, one-sided disarmament of Germany, created a militarization of public life. The consequences of this militarization lasted longer than the upheavals in the five years following the armistice. In the years thereafter, paramilitary associations of all political stripes hindered the formation of a 'civil society'.[12]

The Weimar parliamentary system remained burdened by its own birth: it came into existence in conjunction with the military defeat of Germany. Because of this, enemies of the new democracy could insultingly call the new republic 'un-German'. Memory of the authoritarian imperial state influenced supporters of the republic as well. Again and again, they behaved as if the most important political divide ran between the government and the parliament, as it had during the period of monarchical constitutionalism, and not between the governing majority and the opposition, as the logic of parliamentary democracy required. Many crises resulted from the fact that no government could rely on 'its' majority in parliament for support. This undermined further the already weak belief in the legitimacy of democratic rule.

Another source of conflict was built into the Weimar constitution itself. Its authors, fearing a kind of 'parliamentary absolutism', had written a 'reserve constitution' along with the 'normal constitution'. According to the reserve constitution, in an emergency – exactly what that meant remained unclear – the president could take over the lawmaking function of the parliament. As the people would have directly elected him, there could be no doubt about his democratic legitimacy. In essence, the president would become a kind of provisional dictator. After parliamentary rule definitively failed in 1930, power transferred as a matter of course from the parliament to the president. The true beneficiaries of the progressive loss of parliamentary power were the National Socialists. Now they could appeal both to widespread dissatisfaction with the parliamentary system, which had become little more than a farce, *and* they could appeal to the citizen's right of participation in the political process. This right had existed since the introduction of universal manhood suffrage in Bismarck's time, but now it had become nearly meaningless.

Hitler thus profited from the same contradiction in the modernization process that resulted in the restrained nature of the revolution of 1918–19: the democratization of voting rights took place quite early, but the democratization of the governing system took place much later. This contradiction did not preordain that Hitler would come to power as a result of the German crisis of state. But it does explain why this result was possible.

In the end, must we regard the revolution of 1918-19 as a failure? The answer seems to be yes; but its direct and indirect accomplishments suggest otherwise, because they survive until today. There is a republic, women have the right to vote, and collective bargaining rights for organized labour and unemployment benefits still exist. Without question, the Weimar parliamentary system was a failure. However, it provided Germans with a valuable opportunity to become familiar with democracy on both the national and state level, and this in turn helped them to draw conclusions from its collapse. If, after 1949, 'Bonn' did not become 'Weimar' it is due in no small part to the fact that Bonn could learn from the example of Weimar. Reunited Germany is once again what Weimar used to be: a democratic German nation state. In contrast with Weimar, the new Berlin republic is not a naive democracy. It has the chance to learn not only from the lessons of Weimar, but also from the years of successful democratic experience in Bonn. Both chapters – Weimar and Bonn – combine to form a solid foundation of historical experience. On the basis of this double foundation, the united German state can preserve and develop its democracy.

Notes

1.   In order to keep the critical apparatus as brief as possible, I would like to direct readers to three of my works that explain the revolution in far more detail than I can here: *Die Sozialdemokratie und die Revolution von 1918–19*, Berlin 1980; *Von der Revolution zur Stabilisierung: Arbeiter und*

Arbeiterbewegung in der Weimarer Republik 1918–1924, Berlin 1985; *Weimar 1918–1933: Die Geschichte der ersten deutschen Republik*, Munich 1994.

2. Translator's note: English translations of the Weber quotations are taken from Max Weber, *Economy and Society. An Outline of Interpretive Sociology*, edited by Günther Roth and Claus Wittlich, vol. 1, Berkeley 1978. English page numbers are listed in brackets after the German page numbers. Max Weber, *Wirtschaft und Gesellschaft. Studienausgabe*, ed. by Johannes Winckelmann, vol. 1, Cologne 1964, p. 197 (p. 37) (part 1, chapter 3, paragraph 13); p. 27 (p. 265) (part 1, chapter 1, paragraph 7).

3. Eduard Bernstein, *Die deutsche Revolution von 1918/19. Geschichte der Entstehung und ersten Arbeitsperiode der deutschen Republik*, ed. and introduced by Heinrich August Winkler, annotated by Teresa Löwe, Bonn 1998, pp. 237 ff.

4. Gerhard A. Ritter and Susanne Miller (eds), *Die deutsche Revolution 1918– 1919. Dokumente*, Hamburg 1975, pp. 208 ff.

5. Karl Dietrich Erdmann, 'Die Geschichte der Weimarer Republik als Problem der Wissenschaft', in *Vierteljahrshefte für Zeitgeschichte*, 3, 1955, pp. 1–19. Quotation is taken from p. 7.

6. Arthur Rosenberg, *Entstehung und Geschichte der Weimarer Republik*, ed. and introduced by Kurt Kersten, Frankfurt am Main 1983; Eberhard Kolb, *Die Arbeiterräte in der deutschen Innenpolitik 1918–1919*, Düsseldorf 1962; Peter von Oertzen, *Betriebsräte in der Novemberrevolution*, Düsseldorf 1963; Reinhard Rürup, *Probleme der Revolution in Deutschland 1918–19*, Wiesbaden 1968.

7. Gerald D. Feldman, Eberhard Kolb, Reinhard Rürup, 'Die Massenbewegungen der Arbeiterschaft in Deutschland am Ende des Ersten Weltkrieges', in *Politische Vierteljahresschrift* 13, 1972, pp. 84–105; Wolfgang J. Mommsen, 'Die deutsche Revolution 1918–1920. Politische Revolution und soziale Protestbewegung', in *Geschichte und Gesellschaft* 4, 1978, pp. 362–91.

8. Rainer Zitelmann, *Hitler: Selbstverständnis eines Revolutionärs*, Stuttgart 1990, pp. 51ff.

9. Carl Schmitt, *Gespräch über die Macht und den Zugang zum Machthaber*, Pfullingen 1954.

10. Gerald D. Feldman, *The Great Disorder: Politics, Economics and Society in the German Inflation, 1914–1924*, Oxford 1993; Richard Bessel, *Germany after the First World War*, Oxford 1993.

11. M. Weber, *Wirtschaft*, vol. 1, p. 39 (p. 54) (part 1, chapter 1, paragraph 17), p. 197 (p. 37).

12. Norbert Elias, 'Die Zersetzung des staatlichen Gewaltmonopols in der Weimarer Republik', in N. Elias, *Studien über die Deutschen. Machtkämpfe und Habitusentwicklung im 19. und 20. Jahrhundert*, Frankfurt am Main 1989, pp. 282–94; James M. Diehl, *Paramilitary Politics in Weimar Germany*, Bloomington 1977; Bernd Weisbrod, 'Gewalt in der Politik. Zur politischen Kultur in Deutschland zwischen den beiden Weltkriegen', in *Geschichte in Wissenschaft und Unterricht* 43, 1992, pp. 391–405.

HANS MOMMSEN

The Nazi Regime: Revolution or Counterrevolution?

Did the Nazi regime intend to produce a social revolution and did it push Germany into modernity? The debate over this issue started in St Antony's College, Oxford. David Schoenbaum's dissertation on *Hitler's Social Revolution* gave birth to the topic,[1] and Ralf Dahrendorf's *Society and Democracy in Germany* provided a larger theoretical framework.[2] Thereafter the topic attracted more than twenty-five years of intensive research, and was raised in different contexts. During the hegemony of the theory of totalitarian dictatorship, belief in the basically revolutionary character of the National Socialist dictatorship lost some ground, but it was revitalized by Karl Dietrich Bracher's theory of 'legal revolutions'[3] and by Ernst Nolte, who drew a close parallel between the Nazi seizure of power and the Russian October Revolution.[4]

The comparison between 1933 and 1917 implies that the seizure of power was a well-prepared revolutionary act and Adolf Hitler was, therefore, a successful revolutionary. While Hugh Trevor-Roper, in his pioneering study on *The Last Days of Hitler,* avoided this conclusion and cast some doubt on Hitler's revolutionary qualities,[5] Joachim C. Fest did not hesitate to locate Hitler's role in world history closer to 'the great revolutionaries' on the left than to their counter-revolutionary opponents on the right. Fest admits, however, that Hitler's revolution was less intentional than those of Lenin or Robespierre, and he refers in this context to Dahrendorf's main thesis – that the social revolution that he attributes to the Third Reich was associated more with the indirect repercussions than with the explicit intentions of Hitler's policy and was sealed by his ultimate defeat. Nonetheless, Fest situates Hitler's rule in the context of the general process of social revolution in Germany, identifying it with its jacobinistic phase and calling it 'the German phenomenon of revolution' (*'die deutsche Erscheinung der Revolution'*).[6] In conjunction with this, he is inclined to attribute to Hitler *'historische Größe'*, whereas Jacob Burckhardt possibly would have classified the dictator among the 'ruthless and ruinous destroyers' (*'kräftige Ruinierer'*).[7]

These and other outstanding interpretations of the Nazi dictatorship contain a mixture of a personalistic approach and a more structuralist approach. Dahrendorf is inclined to regard Hitler primarily as the instrument of the overdue social modernization of Germany, more recent Hitler-centred interpretations, such as those presented by Rainer Zitelmann and Michael Prinz, display him as a deliberate modernizer of Germany and hence as an often misunderstood revolutionary who combined both political and social revolution.[8] Paradoxically, they refer to Dahrendorf's early arguments by accentuating the thesis that modernization could either lead to democratic or to totalitarian mentalities, to the *'Staatsbürger* and the *Genosse'*.[9]

Historians who are inclined to underline the rather anti-modern traits of Nazi politics and ideology – such as Henry Turner, who spoke of an 'utopian anti-modernism', and Jeffrey Herf, who coined the term 'reactionary modernism'[10] – and those who take the viewpoint of former socialist writers like Franz Neumann or Ernst Fraenkel, regard the assumption of a genuinely modernizing function of the regime to be highly questionable. To describe National Socialism as a historical companion of Lenin, who at least had a clear-cut programme for Russia's modernization, seems to overestimate Hitler's intellectual capacity and political leadership. Similarly, conclusions of this kind overlook the genuinely fascist character of National Socialism.

One should start from Juan Linz's description of the fascist movements, including National Socialism, as 'late-comers on the political scene' – essentially determined by their anti-marxist and their anti-liberal orientation, but distinguished from similar *völkisch* groups in the Wilhelmine period by the very fact that they were post-revolutionary protest movements that received their impetus by mobilizing the anti-bolshevik and anti-marxist prejudices of wide strata of the population.[11] Insofar, the Nazi movement had a specific counterrevolutionary origin, as it never had any chance of winning over large segments of the working classes. The originally significant left wing under Otto Strasser's leadership, which saw itself as a friend of the Soviet Union and wanted to form an essentially socialist party, left the NSDAP during the *Kampfzeit*.[12]

Without its counter-revolutionary impetus, which was directed towards the elimination of the results of the November revolution and, simultaneously, promised to overcome the latter's shortcoming of not having been a true national revolution, the success of the NSDAP after September 1930 would not have been possible. Hitler's strategy of avoiding making a choice between a pro-socialist and a pro-capitalist course was part of it.

Actually, Hitler and the leading party functionaries – and most contemporaries including the representatives of the later resistance movement – were deeply affected by the trauma of the November revolution.[13] Until the very end of the regime, the fear that a second 9 November might occur determined National Socialist domestic policy. Outstanding examples are the reluctant implementation of total mobilization for war or Himmler's instalment as Reich Minister for the Interior after Mussolini's fall in 1943.[14] The resisters thought along similar lines and justified the intended overthrow of the regime primarily by arguing that a new 9 November, leading to the complete internal bolshevization of Germany, had to be prevented at all costs.[15] Only in this rather counter-revolutionary respect, however, does the assumption of Horst Möller, that the National Socialist seizure of power formed the climax of a revolutionary period that started in 1918 and ended in 1945, have some plausibility.[16]

If the term 'revolutionary' is used with the rather general meaning of disrupting the legal framework of an existing community, Hitler and his followers, who did not pay any attention to juridical and institutional categories, but after the abortive putsch of November 1923 could not afford any open conflict with the republican authorities and especially with the army, fit this rather formal category. But there is no significant difference from other right-wing politicians either. If the notion of being 'revolutionary' alludes to Hitler's willpower, the explicit 'cult of the will' as it has been shown by J. P. Stern,[17] may be called 'revolutionary' and the same is true with respect to his deliberate use of violence in politics for propagandistic reasons.

In all this, the NSDAP is not much distinguished from either national-conservatives or the *völkisch* right-wing groups. Its peculiar appearance and its main source of strength relied on its specifically fascist character, and this refers to its organizational pattern as well as to its perception of politics. Since the works of Nyomarkay,[18] Tyrell,[19] Noakes[20] and others, it is unquestionable that the combination of factionalism and charisma, of actionism and leadership cult, resulted in a peculiar political form that turned the lack of programmatic coherence into a maximum of propagandistic flexibility. This enabled the party to mobilize primarily the non-modern sectors of German society and to appeal to resentments, prejudices and hatred in that constituency. The Nazi ideology provided only a few fixed points, and the Party leadership avoided programmatic options that could narrow the party's space for action. Hence, the movement could focus all its energies on propagandistic issues and did not dissipate its impetus by reconciling different streams of opinion among its members. Conversely, the party tried to give itself the appearance of an united revolutionary movement, representing a fundamental alternative to the existing Weimar parties. Hitler's attempt to dissociate the NSDAP from the competing political parties of Weimar proved to be quite successful during the election campaigns after 1930 but failed in the November 1932 elections, where the party deliberately kept a distance from the parties of the 'national opposition', a policy that did not gain support from its bourgeois constituency.[21]

As far as the contents of the Nazi *Weltanschauung* are concerned, they did not significantly differ from the concepts of the right-wing bourgeois parties, even with respect to racial anti-Semitism, which was strong in the DNVP as well.[22] What was different, was the impetus, the weight of sheer organizational power, the impact of complete recklessness used against the political enemy and the principle of not reflecting on the long-term consequences of its short-term tactical steps.[23] The Nazi ideology was anything but a contingent philosophy, and Hitler used to refer to it by stressing the rather vague notion of the 'National Socialist idea', which he regarded as the true unifying formula. Hitler's memorandum justifying the dissolution of Gregor Strasser's party apparatus in December 1932 shows this tendency very clearly.[24]

Thus, the uniquely fascist feature of the Party and its propaganda appear to be the crucial element that distinguished the Nazi movement from competing forces, while its *Weltanschauung* comprised a great variety of frequently conflicting political targets and ideas serving changing propagandistic needs in a chameleon-like fashion.[25] Unquestionably, the Nazi protest movement belongs within the general context of the anti-liberal and anti-enlightenment main stream of contemporary German and central European political thought. Part of this was the 'conservative revolution', and the rather vague perspective of a fundamental reform of society and state as predicted by authors like Spengler and Möller van den Bruck. They provided the intellectual climate in which National Socialism could become a mass movement and could find the sympathies of important segments of the educated classes.[26] But unlike the nationalistic writers on the bourgeois right who longed for a transformation by an all-encompassing reform, National Socialism tried to achieve this by all means and, above all, by continuous political mobilization and the formation of a socially heterogeneous mass movement.[27]

Historians like Karl Dietrich Bracher viewed this totalitarian approach as the specific revolutionary element in Nazi politics. By coining the term 'a legal revolution' to describe the peculiar characteristic of the Nazi seizure of power (as well as comparable contemporary revolutions), which avoided the techniques and means of earlier revolutionary upheavals and by subsuming the October revolution and that of January 1933 under the notion of a 'seizure of power of a new type', thereby referring to the specifically unrevolutionary (pseudo-legal) technique of the *Machtübernahme*, he tried to verify his proposition.[28]

Actually, the so-called legal road to power was heavily challenged, and not only by the Stormtroopers. Even Hitler himself thought of violent alternatives to the pseudo-legal tactics that, however, ultimately proved to be successful.

The use of violence against political opponents, Jews and other excluded groups as well as the politics of synchronization (*Gleichschaltung*) do not deserve the adjective 'revolutionary' and were still covered by a fictitious legality. Although Hitler carried out a constitutional revolution, he was not, even then, ready to leave the shield of formal legality. Hitler's refusal to agree to Frick's proposition in 1937 of replacing the rule by the Enabling Law by proclaiming a new and hence revolutionary constitution of the Great German Reich was significant in this respect. Surprisingly, he rejected Frick's proposal with the argument that he wanted to avoid any violation of the Enabling Law that could be regarded as a revolutionary step.[29] Hitler's decision to separate the offices of the president and of the chancellor after his death was similar. Formally, the Weimar constitution was still valid when the Third Reich collapsed.

This shows that Hitler, especially, was extremely reluctant to replace the former governmental system in any institutionalized form. This was due to his personal inclination to avoid anything that would commit him to given rules or institutions. Hence he broke repeated promises to install a leadership council or a similar representative body for which originally the Senate Hall in the Brown House in Munich had been built.[30] One can argue that Hitler wished to keep future options open. Hence, he supported something like a 'permanent revolution', knowing very well that any institutional and political consolidation would destroy the very foundations of his rule.

If one analyses the possible direction of this policy of avoiding any institutionalization of the political system, one becomes aware of the genuinely atavistic features of the way the regime developed. Hitler's obvious predilection for the emergence of a new leadership type under the lawless conditions of the occupied Russian and Ukrainian territories, his belief in hardness as moral qualification, his unlimited support of the principle of *Menschenführung* and, therefore, an extreme personalization of politics, makes clear the inevitable destination of the regime.[31] It is just misleading to connect this complete decay of the body politic with the notion of 'revolution'. The inherent process of self-destruction of the National Socialist regime makes it impossible to anticipate its future under the fictitious assumption of its eventual military victory.

In this context it is of some interest to note to what extent National Socialism used the term revolutionary to describe its own position. Only in the period from 1920 to 1922 would Hitler use the term 'revolutionary' in order to describe the aims of the national opposition, but this was put in the context of a 'Germanic revolution'. Then the use of the term 'revolutionary' as self-description disappeared and did not come into regular use again before January 1933, when Goebbels shrewdly presented the conquest of power by the NSDAP through the formation of the 'Cabinet of national concentration' on 30 January 1933 as a 'national uprising' or as a 'national revolution'.[32] Goebbels thereby tried to gain the support of still-reluctant parts of the 'national opposition'. The approach of presenting National Socialism as the symbol of Germany's newly won internal unity proved to be particularly successful in drawing former opponents in the Catholic population into the national camp.[33] Simultaneously, it took up the myth of the national revolution that had failed in 1919, and thus created an intellectual bridge to the ideas of 1914.

As far as this writer is aware, the term 'revolutionary' was used as a positive concept only by the pseudo-socialist left wing, which was eventually suppressed with the dissolution of the *Nationalsozialistische Betriebszellenorganisation* (NSBO). Moreover, the term was used in connection with the November 1923 putsch. Then, the propaganda referred to the 'national' or 'Germanic' revolution, and also to the 'German revolution' to announce the projected march on Berlin.

During the crucial election campaigns after September 1930, however, Hitler avoided the term revolution and replaced it by claiming that the Nazi party would provide a new secular start and fundamental reform. The notion, that it fought for the 'victory of a Weltanschauung, not just the victory of one party' among others, was directed against the national-conservative right and tried to neutralize its damaging attacks on the NSDAP because it had revealed its party character by refusing to join the camp of the 'national opposition'.[34]

After January 1933, however, Hitler did not hesitate to take up the term 'revolution' in order to describe the fundamental change that was obtained by the seizure of power. He spoke of the 'well disciplined National Socialist revolution' to calm bourgeois fears in order to obtain the middle parties' support for the passing of the Enabling Law.[35] He would praise it as the 'revolution of the revolutions',[36] the 'greatest revolution of all time' (*aller Zeiten*).[37] The meaning of this term can be understood from Hitler's utterance to Sefton Delmer who interviewed him, while the Reichstag building was still burning: 'You witness now the start of a new great epoch in German history.'[38] Later on the dictator will talk of a 'true revolution of historical dimensions'.[39]

This did not prevent Hitler from calling for the end of revolutionary acts after the summer 1933 and from demanding that 'the revolution has to be channelled into the bed of a sound evolutionary development', as he told the *Reichsstatthalter* at that time,[40] although he used the term 'national socialist revolution' later on repeatedly.[41] Symptomatic was Rudolf Hess's speech foreshadowing the June 1934 massacre, in which he depicted Hitler as the greatest strategist and revolutionary, a point obviously directed against Ernst Röhm's internal criticism and pseudo-revolutionary language.[42]

Except for the conservative opponents of Hitler who, like Ludwig Beck, spoke of the Nazis as 'brown Bolsheviks',[43] contemporaries would perceive Nazi politics as a mixture of revolutionary and counter-revolutionary elements. This fits in with the contemporary semantics of the term 'revolution' with respect to National Socialism. Even if Hitler sometimes called himself a 'revolutionary' he lacked the ability to replace the tradition he had destroyed by anything like a lasting and positive new order.[44] In general, both Hitler and Nazi propaganda generally used the term 'revolutionary' in a rather sweeping and contradictory fashion. Thus, there is no semantic access to the hypothesis that National Socialism was basically a revolutionary phenomenon.

Interestingly, the revolutionary discourse of the NSDAP that disappeared in the middle of the 1930s, returned in the last months of the regime. Hitler's utterance in May 1944 that 'we are not at the end of this revolution, but in a way only in the first year of it' and that 'it would take hours' for him 'to explain it further',[45] belonged to this pseudo-revolutionary discourse revived by the party radicals of the last hour. This late utterance must be perceived in conjunction with the desperate attempts to overcome the critical military situation that emerged after the lost battle of Stalingrad.

Despite Goebbels's and Speer's late attempts to reorganize the governmental system and restore authority at the top, Hitler supported the increasing informality of the political decision-making process and the steady undermining of hitherto functioning public institutions by ever more informal new commissariats. Hitler's personal mentality, but also the structure of the Party leadership, which was essentially created in December 1932, prevented any long-term stabilization of the political system.[46] Conversely, its creeping dissolution led to a situation in which any control of the diverging administrative bodies as well as the regional Party organizations became virtually impossible. Even Goebbels, who since July 1944 in his new function as 'Reich Commissioner for the Total War Effort' tried to turn the clock back, failed completely. Instead, the process of self-destruction accelerated even more.

The battle of Stalingrad marked the beginning of an unstoppable decay of the regime, which was accompanied by unremitting attempts by Martin Bormann as leader of the Party chancellery and Robert Ley as Reich organization leader, to regenerate the NSDAP as a political force and to complete the creeping process of Party domination. After Stalingrad, the NSDAP returned to its demand that it should function as the true bearer of the National Socialist idea and, simultaneously, take over public responsibility under the pretext that this was a precondition for maintaining the war effort and inducing the people to fight to the last man. It is symptomatic that, during these months, the Party increasingly returned to the myths of the *Kampfzeit* and renewed its belief in its invincibility, that had allegedly been proved by the example of 9 November 1923, when the movement underwent a terrible defeat that ultimately led to its victory.

In conjunction with the idealization of the spirit of the *Kampfzeit* the fiction emerged that only the compromises that the Party had accepted in 1933–34, leaving the old elites with decisive influence in state and society, were responsible for the military crisis and the weakening of the public determination to hold out. The struggle for the total mobilization of the German people appeared to be the foremost task of the NSDAP, and the Party increased its pressure on the municipal and regional administrations. Symptomatic of these attempts of the party to regain lost ground was the self-reproach of not having completed the takeover of the state apparatus in 1933–34 and of having accepted a compromise with the old elites. Unremittingly, the movement regretted its failure to achieve racial as well as political homogeneity, and the military crisis and the signs of sinking public morale were attributed to this. Consequently, the expanding reign of terror was now directed against the German population at large and especially against potential opponents of the 'National Socialist idea'.[47]

Symptomatic of the Party's intensified ambition to expand its power and of the increasing usurpation of governmental prerogatives by the Nazi Party was the introduction of the National Socialist leadership officer[48] and the establishment of the *Deutscher Volkssturm*, whose units were to be led by Party functionaries.[49] The proclamation of the establishment of this last militia stood in the context of a general propagandistic offensive that idealized the *Kampfzeit* of the NSDAP, symbolizing its ability to overcome even severe crisis, as in November 1923, and appealing to the myth of the wars of liberation in 1813. The latter was reflected in the UFA colour film, *Kolberg*, by Veit Harlan, which was first shown on 30 January 1945 in the already encircled fortress La Rochelle. The film praised the people's community and tried to show that out of a national sacrifice the national rebirth might occur.[50] In conjunction with historical reminiscences of this kind, Himmler could address the *Volkssturm* in his proclamation on 18 October 1944, the anniversary of the Battle of the Nations at Leipzig, as a 'revolutionary people's movement' and could even draw the parallel to the Prussian *Landwehr*.[51]

The vision of a revolutionary upsurge of the German people was far from reality. In contrast with 1813, there was no positive vision for which the Germans could fight, apart from preventing the occupation of their country by the Soviet army, whose retaliation they had to fear for the crimes they had committed in Russia. There was not the slightest revolutionary element within this policy, which was leading towards complete destruction, accompanied by Wagnerian overtones of self-sacrifice. Hence the fact that the regime returned to its original pseudo-revolutionary language could not disguise its purely destructive nature.

The completion of the blocked Nazi revolution of 1933 was supposed to lead to the establishment of a true people's community and the radical extinction of any alien elements, a concept that this time was not restricted to racial aliens but was directed against actual or potential opponents of the National Socialist idea. To this extent, the Party returned to its propagandistic origins, and it participated even more in Goebbels's cult of the will, which was pressed upon Hitler. Under the illusionary assumption that fanaticism was more important than actual military strength, Bormann and Goebbels conceived the *Deutsche Volkssturm* as the true people's community and as a 'holy people's army', which would finally replace the rotten *Wehrmacht*.

The fanaticism of the last hour, which prevented the Third Reich from stopping a war that was definitely lost, represented in some respects what could be called the revolutionary element within National Socialism, which coincided with its self-perception as primarily a propagandistic mobilization without any clear-cut programmatic target. The chameleon-like characteristics of National Socialist propaganda were symptomatic of a political strategy relying on the mobilization of the non-synchronic disparate segments of society.

The mainly propagandistic exploitation of the notion of revolution by the Nazi regime has not prevented some historians from depicting Hitler's historical role and the long-term repercussions of his politics as revolutionary. Interpretations of this kind culminated in Rainer Zitelmann's Hitler biography, in which the dictator appears as a fairly reasonable politician who pursued a mainly rational political programme that basically consisted of a social revolution leading towards modernity.[52] Like his predecessors, Zitelmann has difficulties in proving the revolutionary nature of Hitler's political course, and uses a variety of somewhat conflicting arguments in this context. On the one hand, he claims that Hitler enforced the primacy of politics versus economics as a 'revolutionary' act, but that is hardly convincing, setting aside the fact that there was no basic change in Germany's mainly capitalist structure despite elements of a command economy.[53] By arguing in this way, Zitelmann adopts the typical formalizations of political values in Nazi propaganda, which tend to equate the terms 'fanatical' with 'revolutionary', while usually preferring the term 'fanaticist'.

On the other hand, Zitelmann tries to strengthen his argument by claiming that Hitler and the Nazi movement never intended to restore the past and that they ultimately destroyed the social and institutional remnants of imperial Germany. In this respect he can rely heavily on Martin Broszat's thesis of the specific anti-traditional policy of the regime, in which he discerns remarkable modernizing elements.[54] Broszat, while correctly stressing the anti-traditional traits of Nazi politics, overestimated the modernizing impetus of the regime, having in mind predominantly its anti-Catholic and anti-bourgeois tendencies.[55] In this respect Broszat overlooks the otherwise well-recognized fact that the achievements of the regime did not surpass its purely destructive and parasitic nature and did not create any stable social and institutional structure in order to replace the traditional order.

The debate over the alleged Nazi improvements in social policy starts from shaky foundations. Although Robert Ley's extravagant reform schemes show certain similarities to the Beveridge plan, they remained totally unrealized and were largely utopian fictions, because social strategies of this kind presupposed the continuous economic exploitation of the non-Germanic peoples.[56] Despite this plain fact, Michael Prinz and Rainer Zitelmann are inclined to embrace the allegedly positive aspects of National Socialist social policy, underlining its function for the modernization of German society by abolishing former class and status divisions.[57] In order to underpin the theory of Hitler's social revolution they put considerable weight on the regime's progressive social security strategies, although they mainly remained speculative and excluded the non-productive part of the populace.

Both authors, however, go even further and maintain that, far from being oriented toward pre-industrial and pre-democratic social and political values, Hitler and the regime were outspoken protagonists of modernity in all its dimensions.[58] The typical mixture of modern means and atavistic targets that characterized the Nazi regime is thereby consigned to oblivion, although the neofeudal tendencies in occupied Soviet territory are well known.[59] Moreover, Zitelmann's assumption that Hitler was unrestrictedly favouring modernization cannot be reconciled with David Schoenbaum's correct observation that the real outcome of National Socialist strategies contradicted its original programmatic intention and that there was a constant replacement of 'revolutionary means' and 'targets', although his thesis of a 'twofold revolution' is less convincing.[60]

Many of the visionary targets of Hitler and his followers consisted of a strange combination of romantic reminiscences and arbitrary projections, and while in general National Socialism was anti-traditional, basic elements of modernization, especially the necessity of increasing participation, were missing.[61] That the National Socialist regime adapted modern means in many respects does not imply that it was able or willing to form a modern society in any real sense of the word. This was hardly compatible with the unrestricted leadership principle, the rejection of bureaucratic procedures, and the feudalization of power as a predominant trend, not only in the occupied territories but in the Reich as well. As Matzerath and Volkmann have convincingly pointed out, National Socialism envisioned an utopian third way, avoiding any choice between socialism or capitalism.[62] Sometimes this specific ambivalence has been mistakenly identified as a revolutionary technique. As far as any application of the modernization theory to the genuine political structure of National Socialism is legitimate at all, it produces rather negative results.[63]

Another argument to prove the specific revolutionary quality of the Hitler regime refers to the realm of foreign policy and equates 'objectless expansion' with revolutionary aggression.[64] This view has been rejected by Andreas Hillgruber, who underlined the continuity of German foreign policy from the Empire to the Third Reich, although he otherwise supported the intentionalist interpretation and emphasized the racial elements in Hitler's foreign policy.[65]

But it appears to be difficult to call the reckless expansion and use of terroristic violence, as well as the deliberate destruction of subjugated people, including the genocide against the European Jews and large parts of the Slavic people in eastern and Central eastern Europe, revolutionary. The complete disregard of, and contempt for, historical rights and the voluntary destruction of existing historical structures may be called revolutionary. But if one associates with it the ability to establish new and lasting political institutions, and this is the positive connotation of the term 'revolution', its use is incompatible with the ruinous and self-destructive features of the regime. Moreover, one should avoid taking account of the futuristic projections by the regime, such as Speer's architectural projects or Himmler's vision of the Great Germanic Empire, and one should focus on the actual outcomes, which meant devastation all over Europe.

Some historians, especially Anglo-Saxon scholars like Daniel Goldhagen, use the term 'revolution' in order to describe the racial policies of the regime as an attempt to create a 'new body social' and the 'inculcation in the Germans of a new ethos'.[66] There is no dispute about the fact that Heinrich Himmler's bottomless resettlement policy in Eastern Europe, together with the death of the European Jews as well as many millions of other people, mainly of Slavic nationality, was historically unique and of world historical dimensions. Of Himmler's scheme, however, the destructive and criminal dimension

– the murder of more than five million Jewish people – was implemented, while the general programme fell to pieces, as Götz Aly has shown impressively enough.[67] To describe the targets of Nazi racial and settlement policy as 'revolutionary' seems to me to invest this destructive course of the regime with a constructive component, even though it was abortive from the start and would not have resulted in any qualitative social change. If Goldhagen claims an inherent 'revolutionary transformation of society', he fails to state to what goal it would lead, while it consummated itself in pure destruction.[68] It led, however, to self-destruction, which should not be regarded as a revolutionary process, because at the end stood, not a qualitative change of the social fabric or the political structure, but decay and dissolution.[69]

The research debate has returned to the issue that had been presented thirty years ago by Ralf Dahrendorf – the relative ability of the regime to achieve a modernization of Germany's crisis-ridden society and the degree to which fundamental social change under the impact of the war events can be attributed to a deliberate policy of the regime.[70] But the assumption that the extended use of modern means necessarily implied the formation of a new society, as Zitelmann and Prinz suggest, is dubious. Both authors tend to interpret the regime's intentions in isolation from their actual repercussions, which in the final balance were anything but positive.[71]

There is no question that the Nazis did use those aspects of modernization that appeared to be advantageous for them, a point that can be demonstrated, for instance, with respect to propaganda by the early use of film, radio, and even airplanes for election campaigning.[72] Moreover, the regime used the impulses of the Weimar rationalization movement for its own ends, but they remained restricted to certain industries.[73] Nazi propaganda also mobilized the contemporary belief in technological progress, but the impact of rationalization and technological progress was largely restricted to a few armament sectors that were not significant for the economy at large. In general, the measurable output of technological change declined, especially in comparison with Western industrial societies.[74]

The myth of Nazi modernization culminates in the observation that the regime eliminated the inherited social class divisions in German society, as far as the psychological dimensions were concerned, while there was no relevant change in the general social stratification.[75] The inherited tension between blue and white collar workers was even strengthened by output-oriented wage regulations favoured by the

German Labour Front (DAF).[76] Hence, the amount of equalization through Nazi social policy was insignificant, but new social barriers of race and political conviction were created. The old aristocracy lost its social privileges but, particularly after the failure of the plot of 20 July 1944, the ascending SS elites would have replaced it, as is demonstrated by Himmler's readiness to supply landed estates in the east to the ascending party meritocracy.[77]

The extent to which a social revolution originated under the Nazi regime, therefore, deserves closer investigation. Although, as Schoenbaum has already pointed out, the Third Reich formed an open society providing extended chances for upward social mobility, this was limited because of the enforced decline of private consumption and a one-sided allocation of economic resources.[78] In general, the incentives for rationalization and modernization were limited even in the sector of the armament industries and despite the fact that the regime functioned on the basis of uncontrolled deficit spending. The example of the Volkswagen factory shows clearly that all attempts to achieve an intensive rationalization of production were doomed to fail because of the lack of economic coordination and long-term planning and of reliability of economic decision-making during the war years.[79] Even in those sectors where one would expect a considerable increase in rationalization and modernization, the inbuilt antagonistic elements of the system suffocated almost all incentives in this respect.[80] Hence it is difficult to assess the effective results of the Nazi social revolution, except those due to the implications of the Allied air offensive and the huge migration of refugees before and after 1945.

The Nazi movement drew its strength from the continuous attempt to appear different from all competing political parties and groups, and it deliberately avoided any programmatic commitments. This strategy was continued during the regime phase. Hence, the regime was characterized by the very inability to replace destroyed structures by more than preliminary formations. From this viewpoint the question whether National Socialism was revolutionary or counter-revolutionary has to be answered by the observation that, although there existed competing ideological wings and the pseudo-socialist element gained increasing influence during the late war years, its atavistic elements came increasingly to the fore, connected with unrestricted use of terror and violence in order to force reality into the procrustean bed of the 'national socialist idea'.

As a genuinely parasitic structure consuming its own foundations, the Nazi regime appears as a tumour-like deviation from the course of politics in the twentieth century, which, relying on the strength of the inherited state apparatus as well as the deep pro-authoritarian mentality of the German elites, could temporarily exert an unforeseen reign of terror, violence and inhumanity, but possessed neither the ability for self-reproduction nor that of paving the way to modernity in any positive sense.

Notes

1. David Schoenbaum, *Hitler's Social Revolution. Class and Social Status in Germany*, Oxford 1966; new edition: *Die braune Revolution. Eine Sozialgeschichte des Dritten Reiches*, Munich 1968.
2. Ralf Dahrendorf, *Gesellschaft und Demokratie in Deutschland*, Munich 1965.
3. Karl Dietrich Bracher, *Zeit der Ideologien. Eine Geschichte des politischen Denkens des 20. Jahrhunderts*, Stuttgart 1982, pp. 171, 179; cf. Karl Dietrich Bracher, *Zeitgeschichtliche Kontroversen. Um Faschismus, Totalitarismus und Demokratie*, Munich 1976, pp. 62 ff.
4. Ernst Nolte, *Der Europäische Bürgerkrieg. Nationalsozialismus und Bolschewismus*, Berlin 1987; see also Ernst Nolte, *Das Vergehen der Vergangenheit. Antwort an meine Kritiker*, Berlin 1987.
5. Hugh R. Trevor-Roper, *The Last Days of Hitler*, 3rd edn, London 1958, pp. 260 f.
6. Joachim C. Fest, *Hitler. Eine Biographie*, Berlin 1973, p. 1035.
7. J. C. Fest, *Hitler*, pp. 24 f.; Jacob Burckhardt, *Weltgeschichtliche Betrachtungen*, chapter 5, where Burckhardt distinguishes the great historical individuals representing the process of cultural transformation from '*die großen kräftigen Ruinierer*'.
8. Michael Prinz and Rainer Zitelmann (eds), *Nationalsozialismus und Modernisierung*, Darmstadt 1991, p. ix; R. Zitelmann, 'Die totalitäre Seite der Moderne', ibidem, p. 13; cf. Rainer Zitelmann, *Hitler. Selbstverständnis eines Revolutionärs*, 4th edn, Stuttgart 1991, pp. 495 f.
9. R. Dahrendorf, *Gesellschaft und Demokratie*, Munich 1965, p. 448.
10. Henry A. Turner, 'Faschismus und Modernisierung', in H. A. Turner, *Faschismus und Kapitalismus in Deutschland*, Göttingen 1982, pp. 157–82; Jeffrey Herf, *Reactionary Modernism. Technology, Culture, and Politics in Weimar and the Third Reich*, Cambridge, Mass. 1990, pp. 11 ff.
11. Juan J. Linz, 'Some Notes Toward a Comparative Study of Fascism in Sociological Historical Perspective', in Walter Laqueur (ed.), *Fascism. A Reader's Guide. Analyses, Interpretations, Bibliography*, Berkeley 1976, pp. 4 ff.
12. Cf. Peter D. Stachura, 'Der Fall Strasser. Gregor Strasser, Hitler, and National Socialism 1930–1932', in: P. D. Stachura (ed.), *The Shaping of the Nazi State*, London 1978, pp. 88–130.

13. See Timothy W. Mason, 'The Legacy of 1918 for National Socialism', in Anthony Nicholls and Erich Matthias (eds), *German Democracy and the Triumph of Hitler,* London 1971, pp. 215–39.

14. Cf. Dieter Rebentisch, *Führerstaat und Verwaltung im Zweiten Weltkrieg. Verfassungsentwicklung und Verwaltungspolitik,* Stuttgart 1989, pp. 499 f.

15. Hans Mommsen, 'The German Resistance against Hitler and the Restoration of Politics', in *Journal of Modern History* 64 (suppl.), 1992, pp. 123 f.

16. Horst Möller, 'Die nationalsozialistische Machtergreifung. Revolution oder Konterrevolution?', in *Vierteljahrshefte für Zeitgeschichte* 31, 1983, pp. 251 ff.

17. J. P. Stern, *Hitler. The Führer and the People,* London 1975; German edition: *Hitler, der Führer und das Volk,* Munich 1978, pp. 78 ff.

18. Joseph Nyomarkay, *Charisma and Factionalism in the Nazi Party,* Minneapolis 1967, pp. 145 f.

19. Albrecht Tyrell, *Vom 'Trommler' zum 'Führer'. Der Wandel von Hitlers Selbstverständnis zwischen 1919 und 1924,* Munich 1975, pp. 43 f., 60 ff.

20. Jeremy Noakes, *The Nazi Party in Lower Saxony 1921–1930,* Oxford 1971, pp. 250 f.

21. Cf. Thomas Childers, 'The Limits of National Socialist Mobilisation: The Elections of 6 November 1932 and the Fragmentation of the Nazi Constituency', in T. Childers (ed.), *The Formation of the Nazi Constituency, 1919–1933,* London 1986, pp. 243 ff.

22. Cf. Donald L. Niewyk, *The Jews in Weimar Germany,* Manchester 1980, pp. 49 ff.

23. Gerhard Paul, *Aufstand der Bilder. Die NS-Propaganda vor 1933,* Bonn 1990, p. 239; cf. Detlef Grieswelle, *Propaganda der Friedlosigkeit. Eine Studie zu Hitlers Rhetorik 1920–1933,* Stuttgart 1972.

24. Denkschrift über die inneren Gründe für die Verfügungen zur Herstellung einer erhöhten Schlagkraft der Bewegung, 15 December 1932 (Bundesarchiv Berlin, NS 22/110). Cf. Udo Kissenkoetter, *Gregor Strasser und die NSDAP,* Stuttgart 1978, pp. 162 f.

25. Cf. Martin Broszat, 'Soziale Motivation und Führer-Bindung des Nationalsozialismus', in M. Broszat (ed.), *Nach Hitler. Der schwierige Umgang mit unserer Geschichte,* Munich 1988, p. 28.

26. Cf. Joachim Petzold, *Wegbereiter des deutschen Faschismus. Die Jungkonservativen in der Weimarer Republik,* Cologne 1978, pp. 218 ff., 351 f.; Yuji Ishida, *Jungkonservative in der Weimarer Republik. Der Ring-Kreis 1928–1933,* Frankfurt am Main 1988, pp. 242 ff.; Stefan Breuer, *Anatomie der Konservativen Revolution,* Darmstadt 1993, pp. 190 ff.

27. Cf. A. Tyrell, *Vom 'Trommler' zum 'Führer',* p. 53.

28. K. D. Bracher, *Zeitgeschichtliche Kontroversen,* p. 91.

29. Cf. Günter Neliba, *Wilhelm Frick. Der Legalist des Unrechtsstaates,* Paderborn 1992, pp. 155 f.; Martin Broszat, *Der Staat Hitlers,* 11th edn, Munich 1989, pp. 360 ff.

30. M. Broszat, *Der Staat Hitlers*, pp. 360 f.

31. Karl Teppe and Dieter Rebentisch, *Verwaltung contra Menschenführung im Staat Hitlers. Studien zum politisch-administrativen System*, Göttingen 1986, pp. 24 f.

32. Cf. R. Zitelmann, *Hitler*, pp. 82 f.

33. Cf. Georg Denzler and Volker Fabricius, *Christen und Nationalsozialisten*, vol. 1, Frankfurt am Main 1993, pp. 66 f.

34. Hans Mommsen, 'Government Without Parties. Conservative Plans for Constitutional Revision at the End of the Weimar Republic, in James Retallack (ed.), *Between Reform, Reaction and Resistance. Studies in the History of German Conservatism from 1789 to 1945*, Providence 1993, pp. 355 ff.

35. Speech in the *Reichstag* on 23 March 1933, in Max Domarus (ed.), *Hitler. Reden und Proklamationen 1932–1945*, vol. 1, part 1, Munich, 1963, p. 237; cf. R. Zitelmann, *Hitler*, pp. 92 f.

36. Speech in the *Reichstag* on 30 January, 1937, in M. Domarus, *Hitler*, vol. 1, part 2, p. 665.

37. Memorial Speech on 8 November 1940, quoted in R. Zitelmann, *Hitler*, p. 104; cf. Speech in the *Reichstag* on 20 February 1938, in M. Domarus, *Hitler*, vol. 1, part 2, p. 796; cf. R. Zitelmann, *Hitler*, p. 95.

38. Sefton Delmer, *Die Deutschen und ich*, Hamburg 1963, p. 191; cf. Fritz Tobias, *Der Reichstagsbrand. Legende und Wirklichkeit*, Rastatt 1962, pp. 112 f.

39. R. Zitelmann, *Hitler*, p. 104 and M. Domarus, *Hitler*, vol. 2, part 2, p. 1658.

40. 'Reichsstatthalterkonferenz, July 6, 1933', in *Die Regierung Hitler, Teil I: 1933/34* (= *Akten der Reichskanzlei, Regierung Hitler 1933–1938*), Boppard 1983, No. 180, pp. 630 f. Cf. 'Amtliche Mitteilung vom 6. Juli 1933 über eine Erklärung Adolf Hitlers vor den Reichsstatthaltern', in Herbert Michaelis and Ernst Schraepler (eds), *Ursachen und Folgen. Vom deutschen Zusammenbruch 1918 und 1945 bis zur staatlichen Neuordnung Deutschlands in der Gegenwart*, vol. 9, Berlin 1964, pp. 233 f.

41. Cf. R. Zitelmann, *Hitler*, pp. 93 ff.

42. Speech by Rudolf Hess, 25 June 1934, quoted in Karl Dietrich Bracher, Wolfgang Sauer and Gerhard Schulz, *Die Nationalsozialistische Machtergreifung*, Cologne 1974, pp. 285 f.

43. Cf. H. Mommsen, 'The German Resistance against Hitler and the Restoration of Politics', pp. 119 f.; cf. Hans Mommsen, 'Gesellschaftsbild und Verfassungspläne des deutschen Widerstandes', in H. Mommsen, *Der Nationalsozialismus und die deutsche Gesellschaft*, Reinbek 1991, pp. 250 f.

44. Cf. Hans Mommsen, 'Hitler's position in the Nazi System', in H. Mommsen, *From Weimar to Auschwitz*, Princeton 1991, pp. 185 ff.

45. Hans-Heinrich Wilhelm (ed.), 'Hitlers Ansprache vor Generalen und Offizieren am 26. Mai 1944', in *Militärgeschichtliche Mitteilungen* 20, 1976, p. 159.

46. Jeremy Noakes, *Government, Party and People in Nazi Germany*, Exeter 1980,
     p. 15; Hans Mommsen, 'Die NSDAP als faschistische Partei', in *Festschrift
     für Walter Euchner*, Göttingen 1994, pp. 262 f.
47. Klaus-Dietmar Henke, *Die amerikanische Besetzung Deutschlands*, Munich
     1995, pp. 846 f.
48. Arne and W. G. Zoepf, *Wehrmacht zwischen Tradition und Ideologie. Die NS-
     Führungsoffiziere im Zweiten Weltkrieg*, Frankfurt am Main 1988.
49. Hans Mommsen, 'Die Rückkehr zu den Ursprüngen – Betrachtungen
     zur inneren Auflösung des Dritten Reiches nach der Niederlage von
     Stalingrad', in Michael Grüttner, Rüdiger Hachtmann and Heinz-
     Gerhard Haupt (eds), *Geschichte und Eimanzipation, Festschrift für Reinhard
     Rürup*, Frankfurt am Main 1999, pp. 418–34.
50. Erwin Leiser, *Deutschland erwache. Propaganda im Film des Dritten Reiches*,
     3rd edn, Hamburg 1989, pp. 111 ff.
51. Franz W. Seidler, *Deutscher Volkssturm. Das letzte Aufgebot 1944/45*, Munich
     1989, p. 383.
52. R. Zitelmann, *Hitler*, p. 495 and passim; cf. Rainer Zitelmann, 'National-
     sozialismus und Moderne. Eine Zwischenbilanz', in Werner Süß (ed.),
     Übergänge. Zeitgeschichte zwischen Utopie und Machbarkeit, Berlin 1990, pp.
     195–223.
53. R. Zitelmann, *Hitler*, p. 493; cf. Avraham Barkai, *Das Wirtschaftssystem
     des Nationalsozialismus. Der historische und ideologische Hintergrund 1933–1936*,
     Cologne 1977, pp. 21 f.
54. Martin Broszat, 'Plädoyer für eine Historisierung des Nationalsozia-
     lismus', in M. Broszat, *Nach Hitler*, pp. 275 ff.: National Socialism
     represents *'ein Stück nachgeholter sozialer bürgerlicher Revolution, wenn auch
     mit stark rückwärts gewandter Ideologie'* (p. 276).
55. Cf. Martin Broszat, 'Resistenz und Widerstand', in M. Broszat, Elke
     Fröhlich and Anton Grossmann (eds), *Bayern in der NS-Zeit. Herrschaft
     und Gesellschaft im Konflikt*, part IV, Munich 1981, pp. 702 f.
56. Cf. Marie-Luise Recker, *Nationalsozialistische Sozialpolitik im Zweiten Welt-
     krieg*, Munich 1985, pp. 126 ff., 299 f.; M. Broszat, 'Plädoyer', pp. 279 f.
57. Michael Prinz, *Vom neuen Mittelstand zum Volksgenossen. Die Entwicklung
     des sozialen Status der Angestellten von der Weimarer Republik bis zum Ende der
     NS-Zeit*, Munich 1986, pp. 334 f.; Michael Prinz, 'Die soziale Funktion
     moderner Elemente in der Gesellschaftspolitik des Nationalsozialismus',
     in M. Prinz and R. Zitelmann (eds), *Nationalsozialismus und Modernisierung*,
     pp. 308 f., 316 f.
58. R. Zitelmann, *Hitler*, pp. 349 ff.; M. Prinz, 'Die soziale Funktion', in M.
     Prinz and R. Zitelmann (eds), *Nationalsozialismus*, pp. 318 f.; see also
     the new editorial in the 2nd edition (Darmstadt 1995).
59. Robert Koehl, 'Feudal Aspects of National Socialism', in Henry A. Turner
     (ed.), *Nazism in the Third Reich*, New York 1972, pp. 160 ff.
60. See my postscript to David Schoenbaum, *Die Braune Revolution. Eine
     Sozialgeschichte des Dritten Reiches*, Cologne 1980, pp. 352 ff.

61. Jens Alber, 'Nationalsozialismus und Modernisierung', in *Kölner Zeitschrift für Soziologie* 41, 1989, pp. 346–65.

62. Horst Matzerath and Heinrich Volkmann, 'Modernisierungstheorie und Nationalsozialismus', in Jürgen Kocka (ed.), *Theorien in der Praxis des Historikers*, Göttingen 1977, p. 99; Jeremy Noakes, 'Nazism and Revolution', in Noel O'Sullivan (ed.), *Revolutionary Theory and Political Reality*, Brighton 1982, p. 87.

63. Cf. Hans Mommsen, 'Noch einmal: Nationalsozialismus und Modernisierung', in *Geschichte und Gesellschaft* 21, 1995, pp. 391–402; Christof Dipper, 'Modernisierung und Nationalsozialismus', in *Neue Politische Literatur* 36, 1991, pp. 450–6.

64. Klaus Hildebrand, *The Foreign Policy of the Third Reich*, London 1973, pp. 145 f.; Hans-Adolf Jacobsen, *Nationalsozialistische Außenpolitik 1933–38*, Frankfurt am Main 1968, pp. 319 ff.

65. Andreas Hillgruber, 'Kontinuität und Diskontinuität in der deutschen Außenpolitik von Bismarck bis Hitler', in A. Hillgruber, *Großmachtpolitik und Militarismus im 20. Jahrhundert*, Düsseldorf 1974, pp. 11–36.

66. Daniel J. Goldhagen, *Hitler's Willing Executioners. Ordinary Germans and the Holocaust*, New York 1996, pp. 456 f. Goldhagen speaks of 'the most brutal and barbarous revolution of modern western history for those who would be excluded from the new Germany and Europe . . .'

67. Götz Aly, *'Endlösung'. Völkerverschiebung und der Mord an den europäischen Juden*, Frankfurt am Main 1995, pp. 399 f.

68. D. J. Goldhagen, *Hitler's Willing Executioners*, p. 458.

69. J. Noakes, 'Nazism and Revolution', p. 95, states: 'Nazism was rooted in crisis, and its whole system of politics was geared in effect, to the maintenance of crisis as a permanent state.'

70. R. Dahrendorf, *Gesellschaft und Demokratie*, pp. 432 f. Dahrendorf ascertains, however, that the social revolution effectuated by National Socialism had been a somewhat unintended, although necessary result of its reign.

71. Cf. H. A. Turner, *Faschismus und Anti-Modernismus*, pp. 157–82; J. Herf, *Reactionary Modernism*, pp. 219 f.

72. Cf. G. Paul, *Aufstand der Bilder*, pp. 187 ff., 204 f.; Karl-Heinz Ludwig, *Technik und Ingenieure im Dritten Reich*, Düsseldorf 1974, pp. 89 f.

73. Cf. Rüdiger Hachtmann, *Industriearbeit im 'Dritten Reich'. Untersuchungen zu den Lohn- und Arbeitsbedingungen in Deutschland 1933 bis 1945*, Göttingen 1989, pp. 75 ff., 78; Wolfgang Zollitsch, *Arbeiter zwischen Weltwirtschaftskrise und Nationalsozialismus*, Göttingen 1990, pp. 33 ff.

74. Alan Milward, *Die deutsche Kriegswirtschaft 1939–1945*, Stuttgart 1966, pp. 92 ff.

75. D. Schoenbaum, *Hitler's Social Revolution*, pp. 65 f., 206 f.; cf. the criticism by J. Noakes, 'Nazism and Revolution', p. 91, with respect to Schoenbaum's overdrawn distinction between social reality and its subjective impression.

76. Tilla Siegel, *Leistung und Lohn in der Nationalsozialistischen 'Ordnung der Arbeit'*, Opladen 1989, pp. 165 ff.

77. Cf. Rolf-Dieter Müller, *Hitlers Ostkrieg und die deutsche Siedlungspolitik*, Frankfurt am Main 1991, pp. 28 f.

78. J. Noakes, 'Nazism and Revolution', p. 83.

79. Hans Mommsen and Manfred Grieger, *Das Volkswagenwerk und seine Arbeiter im Dritten Reich*, Düsseldorf 1996.

80. Christoph Buchheim, 'Zur Natur des Wirtschaftsaufschwunges in der NS-Zeit', in *Zerrissene Zwischenkriegszeit. Wirtschaftshistorische Beiträge. Knut Borchardt zum 65. Geburtstag*, Baden-Baden 1994, pp. 97–119, who argues, that the Nazi dirigistic policy prevented a rapid expansion of the German economy during the 1930s.

PETER BRANDT

Germany after 1945:
Revolution by Defeat?

Among historians, it is generally agreed that the military collapse of 1945 presents one of the sharpest breaks in modern German history – even if foreign, constitutional, economic and social historical discontinuities did not necessarily occur at the same time. The Wehrmacht's unconditional surrender on 7 and 8 May 1945 was not simply the capitulation of an army – an occurrence common throughout history, as for example in Napoleon's capitulations of 1814 and 1815. On 9 May 1945, the new rulers, the victorious powers, abrogated, at least *de jure*, all German sovereignty in order to achieve their goal of completely destroying National Socialism and the conditions of its resurrection. As for the demands of unconditional surrender, President Roosevelt had to draw on the example of the American Civil War, 1861–65, to find a historical parallel.[1]

A depiction of the end of the Second World War as an 'unparalleled revolution',[2] basically refers to social side effects and consequences of defeat during the time span between the onset of 'total warfare' and the beginning of economic normalization. It conveys the tectonic dislocation of society that was associated with the breakdown of Germany: a chaotic rupture of the state and its economic unity together with an enormous displacement of population. An influential collection of essays that elaborates on these theses, brought out by the Institut für Zeitgeschichte in 1988, is entitled *From Stalingrad to Monetary Reform*.[3]

The obvious continuities, extending beyond the period directly after the war, do not necessarily disprove our basic assumption of a break. As with all such breaks, even the most severe, one can invariably find significant continuities. The history that a society has accumulated always has its effects in a new period of that society's development.

This holds true not only for mentalities, labour resources, levels of technology, material resources, and to a great extent for the distribution of property (with the exception of the communist-led revolutions of the twentieth century). Thus, for example, there can be no doubt today that while feudalism in France as an agrarian mode of production had already disappeared to a great extent by 1789, the power of aristocratic and non-aristocratic estate owners in the countryside, though no longer feudal, generally survived the disruptions of the 1790s.[4] Nonetheless, there are still good reasons for insisting on the world-historical significance of the Great Revolution, including the Napoleonic wars.

In this essay, I would like to approach an answer to the question posed in the title in a number of sections. First, I would like to raise the question of signs of a revolution from below and of revolutionary structural reforms. Second, after a short look at the Soviet occupation zone, I would like to examine those changes brought about by defeat and by the military government in the period directly after the war, which set the foundations for a new political start. A third section will focus on economy and society in the Western zones and the consolidated Federal Republic from the point of view of that which distinguished them from their predecessors. Finally, I would like to comment on whether one can understand the break I have examined as a revolution.

I. Revolution from Below?

There was no revolution – understood as an overthrow of the old order brought on by a broad mass of people – in Germany in 1945, not even a defeated or failed revolution. Throughout occupied Europe, from the time of the turning point in the war, the collapse of National Socialist rule was accompanied by a rise of antifascist popular movements with social-revolutionary tendencies. After liberation, these generated a transformation in the political climate in favour of democratic structural reforms, bringing in their wake impressive electoral successes for the left.[5]

In Germany, on the other hand, mass support for National Socialism declined only slowly and intermittently as military defeat began to appear inexorable after 1943. Even as the total hopelessness of a continuation of the war became obvious in the first months of 1945, sabotage of Hitler's orders of destruction, or efforts to undermine the country's defence occurred at best only at a local level. National Socialism's self-destructive dynamic, which tended towards the collapse of state and society, together with territorial fragmentation brought about by the war, diminished the ability of all social groups, including the elites, to act as long as National Socialist rule continued. The conspirators of 20 July 1944, an ideologically and socially broad coalition, were quite well aware that if their coup were to succeed, they would then need to create popular support. Responsible for the widespread feeling among Germans of a lack of alternatives and of hopelessness were, apart from a growing awareness – even if incomplete and vague – of German war crimes, the demands for unconditional surrender and the Allies' conduct of the war, namely the bombardment of urban residential areas. There were, however, also deeper causes, which lay in the character of the National Socialist system of rule. National Socialism was capable of actively mobilizing a large part of the German population, and unquestionably of maintaining the loyalty of the majority, even if it is not true to assume, as is often the case at the moment, an almost complete agreement between government and the people.[6]

In the resistance and among political exiles of the left, it came to be recognized increasingly, as the war continued, that Germany would have to be conquered by the Allied armies if the brown dictatorship were to be overthrown. At the time, there were still hopes of the victors allowing, and perhaps even supporting, a 'dependent revolution'.[7] The programmes of the various communist and social-democratic/socialist groups in exile and in the resistance showed remarkable similarities during the war: all presupposed the necessity of founding a new German democracy through a deep intervention in its social structure, as had not been the case with the Weimar Republic. Although not directly seen as socialist, the new order was to break with the power of National Socialism and the dominant aristocratic-bureaucratic classes as well as with the influence of major finance, in particular heavy industry. Establishing a parliamentary form of government was subordinate in time to this aim, and models were sketched containing quite authoritarian elements, while at the same time assuming a substantial participation of grass root workers' committees in such a 'democratic revolution',[8] as it was sometimes called. That democratic socialists understood this differently from communists is of secondary importance here.

The aim of a socially well-established 'democratic revolution' was based on a plausible analysis of the development of bourgeois society in Germany. Because the monarchical state of the nineteenth century adopted the economic desires of the bourgeoisie in that it – like the agrarian aristocracy – adapted to capitalism, the old elites were able to retain political and, in part, social leadership. The subjugation of the bourgeoisie under this leadership allowed its leading representatives, namely the major industrialists, to integrate themselves into the system – with ever greater influence in the long term. In comparison, the compromise with a reformist labour movement on which the Weimar Republic was based appeared forced and unfavourable. A democratic revolution in Germany could only have been carried through against the bourgeois camp, and that meant that it was only possible through action by the workers – who then, of necessity, would have presented their own interests and goals, and called into question the bourgeois framework (which is exactly what happened in 1918–19). A radical surmounting of those powers and structures, which worked against the development of a liberal, civil society, without damaging its capitalist basis, was in practice not possible as an autochthonic process in this century. Had the coup of 20 July 1944 been successful, it would have led to Germany's remaining much closer to the traditions of pre-1933: either in the form of a conservative constitutional state or – in the wake of a second wave of coups defined by the Social Democrats – in the form of a type of authoritarian democracy with strong anti-capitalist elements.

In fact, following the occupation of the German Reich, a number of local antifascist committees were set up, and in some cases these organizations achieved a membership of some thousands. Most, however, were small, local *ad hoc* groups, representing a reaction of the surviving cadres of the old labour movement to the collapse of society. In the four occupation zones in Germany there were hundreds of such 'Antifas', as the Americans called them, even in small towns. They directed their energies primarily towards survival through communal self-help, worked for the removal of 'Nazis', and often saw themselves as forerunners of a united socialist party or as a popular movement of the left, supplanting old-style parties. The American Marxist economist Paul Sweezy, working for the Office of Strategic Services (OSS) in Bremen in 1945, saw in the Antifas 'a genuine revival of revolutionary working class activity'.[9]

The existence of Antifa committees certainly provides an argument against contemporary observers' generalizations about the Germans' complete 'political apathy' after the end of the war. It can also be argued that the Antifas' potential, and their democratic grass roots, could well have played a more significant role in restructuring society and reconstituting the labour movement in Germany than was in fact the case. Their influence often extended far beyond the original circle of initiators. However, they were not the expression of a revolutionary mass movement – unlike the workers' and soldiers' councils of 1918–19, which arose out of a true popular uprising against the continuation of the war.[10] The clearest indication of their relative feebleness was the ease with which they were broken up by either the occupation powers themselves, or the administration under their orders, most of them indeed in the spring and summer of 1945. Held by the victors to be dysfunctional for the maintenance of law and order, the Antifas were regarded at the same time as politically independent and difficult to control, and for the Western Allies often as crypto-communists as well.

'Revolution will not be tolerated', a British officer informed workers' representatives from the Gelsenkirchen Bergwerks AG on 15 April, 1945.[11] Nonetheless, provisional works councils, chosen by elections in the autumn of 1945, left behind greater traces than the local antifascist committees. During the first years, works council activities oscillated within an unusual ambivalence between an orientation either towards conflict or towards consensus, as was generally typical for the labour movement in this period. Directly after the end of the war, it was the provisional works councils that often ensured the makeshift repair of factories and improvised a restarting of production under their direct control (when management was absent). While often finding themselves in a sort of forced alliance with company management in a defence against Allied plans for dismantling plants and other restrictive economic measures, they were at the same time able to enforce a certain level of worker participation in the large companies – something which, in everyday practice, often went far beyond later legal regulation. The works councils held a restoration of management power in the factories, and in society in general, to be out of the question – not only due to the extent of material destruction (greatly overestimated in relation to industrial plants), but also because of the political and moral discrediting of capitalism, the continued existence of a controlled economy, and a partial suspension of property rights in some key areas of the economy.[12]

In the Soviet occupation zone, works councils achieved the greatest influence. They accelerated the expropriation of industrial plants, but were then broken up as the last autonomous representation of the workers in the wake of further sovietization in 1948.[13] In the West, the strong position of the works councils, which in the period of a divided and non-monied economy had fulfilled indispensable functions for the support of employees (although limited mostly to factory level), evaporated as well. In 1951 it was the trade unions that were able to defend the right of co-decision in the mining and iron and steel industries as their achievement of the postwar years. The British had introduced it in 1947 in the iron and steel industry, after private employers had conceded it to the unions. Co-decision (*Mitbestimmung*) created the nucleus of economic consensus structures in an area that had been characterized by social and political confrontations before 1933.[14] In this, the trade unions saw a 'revolutionary act'.[15] In fact, their ideas of a new order, intended to give the labour movement and its organizations a central role in the German economy and politics, failed. Equally, an internal organizational model of a centralized, unified trade union favoured by some of the leadership and membership also failed – not least owing to the objections of the Western occupation powers. Disquiet about communist influence was only one motive among many. There was also concern about a predominance of authoritarian bureaucratic structures in the labour movement and therefore an insistence on a decentralized evolution from below.[16]

In 1948 and 1949, the strategic concepts of Social Democracy – embodied in the charismatic SPD leader Kurt Schumacher – failed as well. Schumacher believed in the possibility of the Social Democrats becoming the determining power in elections by distinguishing themselves clearly from both the bourgeois parties and the Communists, and in this way achieving a democratic republic based on a socialist economic order. He held private capitalist reconstruction to be impossible to implement economically, socially and politically and, as he assumed the Western Allies had a major interest in ensuring a more secure foundation for German democracy than had been the case in the Weimar Republic, he hoped for a certain benevolence towards SPD policies despite its active defence of the national interests of the German people.[17] Viewed from a contemporary perspective, this assumption appeared well founded. An analysis produced by the US Department of State at the end of 1945 assumed 'that no German government will in future be able to stay in power independently and democratically if they have not at least nationalized key industries and the banking system'.[18] The anticapitalism of the period, which is even evidenced in the CDU/CSU, also contained within it populist 'antiplutocratic' reinforcement from right-wing ideologies.

The failure of Schumacher's concept of a parliamentary socialism tolerated by the West became noticeable at the latest in 1948 when, by and at the instigation of the main Western power, the US, a number of socialization and co-decision laws passed in the Western German Provinces were suspended. 'Time is on our side', stated General Clay in October 1947.[19] The role of opposition that the SPD had held since 1947 in the Economic Council (a sort of pre-parliament in the British-American *Bizone*) was confirmed by the result of the first Federal parliamentary elections in August 1949. From the beginning, the SPD had no realistic chance of winning a majority on its own. A look at the results of elections held in the provinces in 1946–47 shows that this could not even have been achieved by absorbing Communist voters.[20] In retrospect, one can say that a reordering of society, carried through by a – at times quite successful – reattachment to an old-style labour movement, had definitely failed by 1952 (with the trade unions' defeat in the conflict over the factory constitution law) and 1953 (with the second general election, which brought the CDU/CSU a triumphal electoral victory). At the same time, the revolt of 17 June 1953 saw the collapse in East Germany of the last great outburst of traditional workers' protest, which had to a great extent oriented itself politically towards the West German SPD.[21]

Not only socialists were able to find grounds around the mid 1950s for believing that – despite a liberal constitution – an 'authoritarian state for the defence of property' (Kurt Schumacher) had been established as a consequence of the re-consolidation of capitalism and thus of bourgeois influence in West Germany. The class structure was only temporarily eclipsed in 1945 and was overlayered by new polarizations arising from the conditions of the time, such as those between city and country, natives and refugees, black marketeers, property owners and the impoverished, those with access to foodstuffs and those without such access, those with National Socialist backgrounds and those without. Not only the conservative climate of opinion, but also the extensive re-consolidation of the leading elites' position in state and society justifies the assumption of a 'restoration', whereby in some areas there had been a considerable re-enlistment of former NSDAP members.

Helmut Schelsky, one of the leading sociologists of postwar Germany, expressed the view in 1955 that 'the feeling of being surrounded by restorative tendencies [is] doubtless the dominant social impression of our West German situation'. For Schelsky, restoration was above all a reaction of 'private and public planning and cautiousness' to real changes to the old social structure through National Socialism, war, the collapse and occupation.[22]

II. The Sociopolitical Significance of the Break of 1945

Nonetheless, the results of the Second World War for German society remain formative. This is most obvious in the eastern zone, later the GDR, where conquest by the Red Army, as in Eastern Europe generally, led to a change in political system and a radical social upheaval along the lines of the Stalinist Soviet Union. Here it is of secondary importance whether the USSR consciously intended the sovietization of Eastern Europe and the division of Germany from the beginning or not. In contrast to the official interpretation of local communists, the transformation process exceeded a bourgeois-democratic reformation as early as 1945–46 and included, at first *de facto,* and then *de jure,* the expropriation of capital. Such moves, however, were not necessarily unpopular in the West at the time, nor were a range of other measures justified by antifascist motives. The poor image of the Eastern zone, arising soon after the war's end, originated mainly due to assaults on German women by members of the Red Army, massive reparations taken by the USSR, and the power politics of the German communists; all these appeared to confirm to a certain extent the anti-bolshevist propaganda of the Nazi government. In the eastern zone in 1948, in the wake of the attempt to overcome the reconstruction crisis of 1947 through an increase in individual productivity, and parallel to preparations for the founding of the Federal Republic, the transformation into a system of Party rule and state-run economy of a Soviet type had progressed so far as to be irreversible without a fundamental change of direction in the Kremlin. It was only out of consideration for the German question that the SED leadership delayed the official beginning of the 'construction of socialism' until the summer of 1952.[23]

While political and sociopolitical upheaval in East Germany was pushed through incomparably more radically than in the West, economic and socioeconomic developments there showed numerous retarding elements in the long run. With all the changes in forms of ownership, the GDR remained to a great extent a traditional industrial society, something that also found its expression in the persistence of older habits and attitudes pointed out by some observers. The model of the 'construction of socialism' along Soviet Communist lines betokened a concentration on heavy and commodity industries and a relative detachment from world markets. Where social changes did lead in the same 'modernizing' direction as in the Federal Republic, they took effect more slowly and less effectively. Alternative initiatives and diverging conditions, as for example the high level of employment and training among women, were not able to mobilize GDR society sufficiently to correct its fundamental disadvantages, low productivity and a lack of innovation.[24]

The restructuring of society in the Soviet zone had its effect on the Western zones, and not solely due to the simple fact of a division of Germany and the related achievement of an anticommunist consensus in the West. As a result of the division of Germany, a much more homogeneous state, culturally and socially, arose in West Germany than was the case with the Reich – despite the influx of 15 million refugees and exiles. In the medium term, the wave of refugees brought with them a considerable confessional and social interfusion and encouraged the breaking up of clearly separated sociocultural milieus.[25]

Most important was the complete loss of power by the old Prussian protestant dominant class with its strong aristocratic elements through the destruction of the army, the disbanding of the Prussian state as well as the Reich and, above all, through the expropriation of estates east of the Elbe. The latter took place, on the one hand, because the entire German population from the provinces east of the Oder and Neiße – which were to a great extent given to Poland – was driven out, and on the other because all agricultural estates of more than 100 hectares in the Soviet zone were broken up, a measure also motivated by Communist policy *vis-à-vis* their allies. As a result, organized antidemocratic conservatism lost one of its main pillars, and Germany's economy a heavy burden. For a land reform in the West, where it was also planned, the radical implementation of a redivision of land in the East meant some difficulties, but this reform had in any case less importance in the West because of the limited social importance of the estate owners. As a result of this 'deprussification', liberal and Catholic groups in the West gained greater room for political development. Through the newly founded non-denominational Christian CDU/CSU, the Rhenish-Catholic element under Konrad Adenauer was even able to take over the leadership of the bourgeois bloc for the first time, something that was made possible as Catholics, due to the division of Germany, were no longer a minority. Catholicism had shown itself to be fairly resistant to National Socialism before 1933. Apart from the deep shock that the catastrophic end of the German Reich caused many members of the bourgeoisie, faced with the need to adapt to a materially superior opponent, this shift also contributed to nationalist and antidemocratic tendencies, including those to the right of the middle, no longer being able to gain decisive influence in the party landscape.

The founding of the Union was the most important reform in the German party system; on the left, an attachment to the period before 1933 predominated at first. But here, too, important changes occurred: first through the SPD's absorption, to a great extent, of potential Communist voters with the onset of the Cold War. The SPD became thus, *de facto*, the united party of the labour movement in West Germany. An accelerated disintegration of the proletarian milieu in the late 1950s as well as the competition mechanism of the newly installed parliamentary form of government, raised the SPD to the second largest 'people's party' (next to the CDU/CSU). The dominance of these 'people's parties', from 1960 much closer together, had a determining influence on the unusual stability of the West German party system, the fundamental structures of which were set by the Allies and German politicians together and were upheld, together with administrative regulations and laws, through the politically insecure first phase. Here too, of central importance, beyond all interventions and regulations, was the trauma of National Socialism.[26]

The dissolution of the unified German state meant all the more a break with the past as the economic ties and communication links between west and east had for centuries been closer than those between north and south. Unlike in the plans for the division of Germany considered by some of the Allies during the war, there were hardly any historical precedents for a border between the eastern zone and the western zones, later the inner-German border.

'The core of Germany is Prussia', declared Churchill in September 1943 in the House of Commons.[27] Prussia's dissolution and the establishment of, in part, quite new Provinces did indeed create the conditions for a much more balanced federal state development. In contrast to opinions widely held among the Allies, federalism belonged to the autochthonic, but certainly not to the clearly progressive and liberal traditions in Germany. Instead, reactionary – often clerically coloured – monarchical and corporate state movements expressed themselves in strong federalist and regional particularistic terms, especially in Bavaria.[28] Only as a result of Allied pressure and the resistance of German democratic forces, namely the Schumacher SPD – supported *de facto* by the British – was a broadly accepted and functional constitutional solution to the federal problem achieved.[29]

The breakup of major business enterprises and cartels in banking, in steel and chemicals, effected by the Western Allies – also as an alternative to socialization – had, unlike the expropriation of eastern estates, a delaying effect. However, together with an increased world-market orientation, it contributed to German management becoming more open to liberal economic thinking. The sociopolitical changes described above were more important for founding West Germany's democracy than the constitutional consequences, which were a result of the Weimar Republic's failure.

A few legends have come into being, describing what the Allies agreed to call 'denazification'.[30] This included a banning of all National Socialist organizations, internment of more than 300,000, not always important, National Socialist office holders and the sentencing of the main National Socialist criminals by allied courts. Above all, it meant the removal of National Socialists from all leading positions, not only in state and local government, but also in social institutions and the economy. In the Soviet zone this was applied most rigorously, thus contributing to an almost complete change in elites. However, the discrimination against nominal NSDAP members was stopped after a chaotic early phase.[31]

In the US zone (and to a lesser extent in the other Western zones, where things proceeded more pragmatically) one must distinguish a first phase, where the military government itself dismissed former National Socialists, especially in the administration, and even in the private economy, from a second phase, which began in 1946. During the first phase a radical change of elites occurred, generally only temporarily, down to the level of village mayor. By the end of July 1945, about 70,000 people held to be National Socialist activists were dismissed from their positions in the US zone. By the end of March 1946 the figure was 337,000. However, the denazification policies of the American military government soon collided with its other goal of rejuvenating material life, especially the economy, by maintaining a regulated German administration.

With the Law for Liberation from National Socialism and Militarism, passed by the German prime ministers of the US zone on 5 March 1946, the decision was transferred to German *Spruchkammern*, which, in a court-like process – on the basis of an automatic classification according to given categories of culpability – were to establish

individual guilt and responsibility. In the course of 1947, Provinces in
the French and British zones took up this procedure.

Denazification policies suffered because the examination process
extended to the entire population and because its actual goals were
inadequately defined. They also included both a political cleansing
of personnel and measures for punishment. Furthermore, American
intentions never coincided with those of the Germans (both from the
left and, for mostly other reasons, from the right) who were charged
with implementing the process from 1946. From 1945 to 1950 the
authorities located in the three Western zones approximately 3.7
million cases, from which nearly 1.3 million were not processed further
because of various amnesties (for example, for reasons of youth), 1.2
million were 'exonerated' (category V), 1 million were seen as
'followers' (nominal Nazis, category IV), 150,000 as 'lesser offenders'
(category III), 23,000 as 'offenders' (activists, category II) and 1667
as 'major offenders' (war criminals, category I). In the end, mainly
higher and middle civil servants as well as upper management were
actually most affected by the measures of denazification.[32]

As, after some delay, the serious cases came to court, the US pushed
for a quick ending to denazification – a policy that, although generally
popular at its onset, had increasingly fallen into disfavour – in view
of the upcoming founding of the Federal Republic. The final and most
extensive wave of rehabilitation was brought in by the German
Parliament in 1951 with the Law for Article 131 of the Constitution,
which was almost unanimously approved. This law returned a large
number of already 'denazified' civil servants, who had not yet been
reinstated, to positions to which they were entitled according to a
normal civil servant career structure. German contemporaries of
nearly all colours viewed denazification as a grand failure. Most of
those affected were either exonerated immediately or rehabilitated
later. Nonetheless, the upper and middle administrative civil servants
were publicly humiliated and their confidence was shaken, deeply and
long term, through temporary layoffs and sometimes even internment. Even as late as 1953, British military police were active in
removing elements grouped around prominent National Socialists in
the conservative liberal FDP in North Rhine-Westfalia.[33] Apart from
that, denazification measures did at least serve to remove to a great
extent leading National Socialists, in the more narrow sense, from
political life in the Western zones and the Federal Republic and to
give new, democratic leaders a head start. Not only the leadership of
the Social Democrats and the trade unions, but also the majority of

Adenauer's first cabinet had experienced the collapse of the Weimar Republic as politicians and were marked by opposition in the broader sense to the Hitler dictatorship.

For this reason, the overall effects of denazification are today viewed less critically by historians than before.[34] Doubts may still be raised about the hybrid *Spruchkammer* procedure's efficiency and adequacy. Despite all the disagreement about the extent of personnel cleansing measures and social structure reforms, there was a consensus among Germans, based on a shared experience of life under the totalitarian dictatorship: a distinction was made between 'respectable' and 'unrespectable' Nazis whereby the latter seemed to be concentrated in the areas of the repression apparatus and National Socialist organizations. Moreover, actions against 'stirrup holders' and those main beneficiaries from the traditional elite (such as von Papen, Krupp and Schacht) could depend on broad support. On the other hand, Germans were prepared to show a great deal of understanding for the daily opportunism of contemporaries and the 'misled idealism' of many National Socialists. This, however, does not alter the fact that the majority of the population's rejection of National Socialism as government and as ideology was complete and irreversible. For those who trusted Hitler even up to the final phase of the war, the illusions of National Socialism were broken in the winter and spring of 1945 as the violent terror of the desperados at the head of the German Reich was directed more and more against the German population itself. This shock, reinforced by the less than heroic behaviour of many National Socialist officials and by the generally relatively humane behaviour of the Western victorious powers, disillusioned even the most indoctrinated youths. Allied fears of a dogged national resistance movement and partisan actions ('*Werwolf*') proved completely unfounded. The specific form of the war's end allowed – unlike in 1918 – no room for a *Dolchstoßlegende* and removed the odium of treason from cooperation with the victorious powers from the outset.[35]

The positive side of denazification was 'reeducation' with its goal of reorienting the German people 'towards democracy and peace'.[36] Less tangible, related measures gained high priority, especially in relation to the founding of the Bonn government and also from the financial point of view. Here too, the American military government led the way, including to a greater extent non-government organizations such as trade unions, Churches and private foundations. For example, the setting up of residential officers at the local level in the

US zone served to care for social groups such as youths and to accelerate the spread of Western, democratic thinking.[37]

III. The Economic and Social Basis of the Bonn Republic

The chance was taken. As the Western Allies began to press for the founding of a West German state in spring and summer 1948 and the Parliamentary Council went to work, concepts for a democratic, parliamentary and federal state were already in place, having been tested at least partially in the Provinces. In the provincial parliaments and councils of Hamburg and Bremen, a basic consensus emerged on questions concerning the shape of a democratic state, founded on general considerations, experiences and compromises – despite social and political disagreements. Their negative model was the failed democracy of Weimar. A more optimistic point of view came to be shared only with the passing of time and after the first signs of success, making it possible to look upon the rupture of 1945 with a positive attitude.

A few years ago, Hans Mommsen quite rightly noted critically that conservative, authoritarian and elite elements of German political thought were still present in the first postwar years – and not only on the right of the political spectrum.[38] Many felt themselves confirmed in their scepticism towards mass democracy and a party state by the experience of National Socialism. The dictatorial views of some socialists have already been mentioned. Moreover, especially determined opponents of Hitler from different backgrounds at first favoured variants of a 'third way' between the Soviet Union and the US, as was true of East German politicians – for example the Christian Democrat Jakob Kaiser.[39] In the view of these individuals, Germany – and this always means all Germany – should be a 'bridge between East and West', not only in foreign policy orientation but also in its sociopolitical order. Concepts of this sort without exception referred to the problem of Germany's position in the middle of Europe without such views necessarily having been fed by anti-parliamentary and anti-Western resentments. In view of all these reservations and traditions of German thought it is remarkable how quickly and clearly an orientation towards the West, namely the constitutional order of a parliamentary democracy, gained support in Germany outside the Soviet area of influence. Apart from general force of circumstances –

occupation and the beginning of the Cold War – instruction and targeted intervention by the victorious Western powers contributed to the fact that West Germany's democratic constitutional order was no longer authoritarian.

Despite the shape of a 'conservative democracy', as the second German republic presented itself, Richard Löwenthal commented in 1974 that state and society 'were something totally new, not only in contrast to the collapsed Hitler dictatorship, but also in contrast to the Weimar Republic and Imperial Germany'.[40] Löwenthal emphasizes, above all, a change in attitude among property-owning upper classes and leading civil servants. Unlike in the Weimar Republic, they stuck to the democratic rules in the Bonn republic as naturally as corresponding groups in England or the US. This is also unquestionably true of the self-employed intelligentsia. It therefore becomes clear that the tradition of German special consciousness, the bourgeoisie distancing itself from the West,[41] came to an end after 1945. Little indication exists that – without a convulsive turn of events – this tradition could have been taken up again by the relevant forces. This is all the more significant as the mentality of the population as a whole has also been transformed in the past decades from an authoritarian orientation – not to be confused with pro-Nazi sympathies – to much more democratic values. The virulence of authoritarian patterns of continuity was frozen, as it were, after 1945, in an apolitical reconstruction alliance until, really only since the 1960s, social change brought forth noticeable transformations. In general, one can say that authoritarian and even National Socialist apologetic attitudes in the population weakened more slowly than reservations about representative democracy as a form of government.[42] The 'transformation of values', which made itself felt in the entire West European-North American cultural area, was especially dramatic in the Federal Republic. Certainly, for Germany since the early 1950s – despite repeated prophecies of doom – one cannot see any greater danger for democracy, based on election results as well as opinion research, than in comparable countries.

This change in attitude was based on the development of the economy and its social consequences. Without exaggeration it may be said that the life of the majority of the population was transformed more quickly and more fundamentally between the mid-1950s and the mid-1970s than in the previous 60 years. Here I refer above all to mass consumption of new utility goods and services. Without overcoming a capitalist mode of production, consumption united the

vast majority of society more than before, and – this being decisive –
on a much higher level. Only the enormous economic growth of the
1950s created the preconditions for expanded social politics without
a greater struggle over questions of distribution. Apart from a housing
programme, mainly oriented towards needs, and the equalization of
burdens for refugees, it was basically the improvement of pensions
in relation to wages that created political stability in West Germany.
Sociopolitical regulation was made even more necessary by the war's
destructive consequences. The pension reform of 1957 emphasized,
moreover, a qualitative change in the function of social policy from
assistance of last resort to preservation of status.[43] At the beginning
of the 1950s, average real income, especially that of the workers, was
still quite modest; only towards the end of the decade did the rapid
development of the material standard of living reach the lower half
of society.

Never before had the German economy experienced such a long
period of such rapid economic development, lasting from 1948 to at
least 1973. Between 1950 and 1975, real domestic product per capita
in the Federal Republic tripled. The growth of average private
consumption, which had risen only slightly in the first half of the
century, followed this trend. During these 25 years after 1950 a rapid
structural change occurred, characterized by a decline in the agrarian
sector, an expansion of services, an extraordinary increase in the
educational sector, and above all by a growth in exports as well as
changes in trade relationships now dominated by an exchange of
finished goods among industrial nations.[44]

Willingness to compromise on both sides in pay conflicts, as well
as apprenticeship courses aiming at a high level of training, afforded
German products a good position on the world market despite
relatively high pay levels, at least until recently. Indeed, in the early
years, German industry's chances were given a boost by relatively low
pay levels that existed at the time. The West German combination
of competitiveness abroad and a general high level of pay reflects
the effect of a characteristic range of institutions. Included here is
the implementation of the principle of industrial associations in the
trade union movement in the first postwar years, that – unlike, for
example, Great Britain – concentrated the interests of professional
organizations and rationalized labour relations. The West German
model was based on a historical compromise between a liberal
capitalism, introduced after the Second World War, and two different
forces – Social Democracy and Christian Democracy – balancing each

other, as well as between specific German traditions and different versions of modern liberalism and socialism, and naturally between capital and labour. This compromise, supported by a relatively broad political and social consensus, was made possible by a simultaneous weakening or elimination of the radical wings of the labour movement and the national conservative, authoritarian faction of the bourgeoisie.

Economic development in other Western industrial nations tended to be quite similar. The unexpected economic growth was called an 'economic miracle' – and not only in Germany. Therefore sound scepticism is required when dealing with an explanation of German economic development as very specific. If we put together economic reconstruction and the emergence of consumer capitalism with the new arrangement of international trade relations – which is essential in this case – the connection is clear.

To contemporary Germans the negative aspects of Western Allied German policy appeared to predominate in the first two or three postwar years. They missed a comprehensive, constructive concept. Although this judgement was quite one-sided – for example the significance of the Morgenthau plan was greatly overestimated – it did have a realistic core, and that not only in view of the awful living conditions of the majority of the population in this period: the lack of housing and food. In fact, the policies of the Western Allies during and just after the war involved a postponement of decisions in the period of complete four-power control of Germany. In practice, the Western Allies', that is the American, German policy seemed indecisive and contradictory for this reason. Postponement was, however, quite rational in terms of their own global aims and interests, in the framework of which Germany played a very important, but not decisive role, as long as the cohesion of the anti-Hitler coalition was given priority. From the middle of 1947 rejection of 'Potsdam' by the British and Americans, already promoted by the British Foreign Office, was recognizable as a new policy. The Germans placed great hopes in the Marshall Plan, even before the currency and economic reform in the summer of 1948 seemingly normalized supplies of food and other necessities at one stroke. In fact, expansion had clearly begun before with a reopening of the traffic network and an increase in productivity in the coalmines. However, in the experience of the West Germans, the currency reform came to be seen as a deep break between the period of great need of the late war and early postwar period and the beginning of the recovery.[45]

The United States' aims, as set by their policy makers during the war, and implemented politically in the years thereafter, were to construct a unitary and liberal capitalist world market, following the principle of reducing trade and payment barriers, multilateralism and currency convertability – in contrast to the protectionism and the formation of economic blocs in the interwar period. This would never have been achieved without the hegemony of the US and thus without its military victory, especially not in combination with an anchoring of representative democratic government forms in Western Europe, including West Germany. The decision to form a separate German state out of the three Western zones occurred in the wake of a formation of an Atlantic alliance against the Stalinist Soviet Union. The axiomatic decision that preceded measures such as the Marshall Plan to unite West German territory, thereby making use of a recon- struction of Western Europe aiming at integration – as it was not believed to be manageable otherwise – had not only to do with the nascent Cold War but also with a long-term American strategy. Reintegration of West Germany in the world economy began with the three Western military governments joining the OEEC, prior to the founding of the Federal Republic. All this meant that those German politicians whose concepts were most compatible with the aims of the US had the best chances of gaining the upper hand in the decisive period of 1947–48, especially in view of the worsening East– West conflict. In economic and social policy, this person was the neo- liberal Ludwig Erhard, protagonist of a 'social market economy', and in foreign and security policy Konrad Adenauer. They supported unconditional opening to and integration with the West and broke, not with the aim of German influence in the world, but with the old attempt to find an independent role as a major power.[46] Even during the final days of the National Socialist government, a learning process began in the circles of German heavy industry, including even SS intelligence, whereby Erhard took on an important role. Rejecting autarkic and *Großraum* concepts, they sought instead a re-orientation towards international economic relations which took into consideration the special weight of the US and the separation of economy and state.[47]

The strong economic and political ties between the Federal Republic and the developing Western community are difficult to imagine without Germany's defeat in 1945. Equally it is clear that the repres- sion of anticapitalist and radical democratic tendencies in the labour movement was another requirement of at least this variant of liberali- zation in Germany. Of course German Social Democrats were not anti-Western, even before 1960 (in matters of the constitution and political culture, they were clearly more pro-Western than other parties). In the 1940s and 1950s, however, they were, because of all-German and sociopolitical reservations, not prepared to accept the foundations set by the US and the Adenauer government.[48]

In view of the desire of most planners and administrators of American policy, for all their differences, for a liberal and democratic, but still capitalist Germany along Anglo-American lines, it becomes perfectly understandable that the military government discouraged and, where necessary, stopped socialist efforts, while at the same time supporting the advocates of such efforts, namely the Social Democrats. Indeed, sometimes they went even beyond this when it was felt that allegedly anachronistic privileges strongly anchored in the German past should be eradicated, such as in the educational system and in the civil service. With certain reservations, this was also true of the British – who, despite a Labour government in London, became more and more financially dependent on their main ally – and the French, who for the same reason had to give up their traditional policy of seeking to weaken Germany territorially and thus to control it.

Recent academic work determinedly emphasizes the reforming efforts of the Allies and a resistance by German forces that even went as far as obstruction. Restructuring radio as a public institution, especially at the insistence of the British, and the American process of press censorship are as much a part of this context as are the generally unsuccessful attempts to remove restrictive trade legislation, to standardize the social insurance system further and to democratize the school system. However, the greatest impact was placed on the controversy that continued up to 1952 about a reform of the civil service, in the course of which, in the spring of 1949, the Allied law was imposed but was never applied by the new Federal Republic.[49]

This law of 1949 included some important elements of the Anglo-American views of German professional civil servants as undemocratic, ineffective and overprivileged. Its principal aim was to turn public servants into employees who did not enjoy life tenure, who had specific job descriptions, and who should gain their positions through open competition and not through career structure. The reform failed because of the interests of affected groups – they had a strong lobby among German parliamentarians – and also because, as in some other areas of Allied and German reforms – supporters presented differing and sometimes even contrasting concepts and thus obstructed each other.

Bourgeois society in Germany was not simply consolidated from outside but was also structured anew in a way that had not been seen in German history up to then. The starting point of the 'Westernization' of Germany was not the assumption of power by autonomous bourgeois forces – and the political success of the bourgeoisie. On the contrary. Under the liberalizing dictatorship of the Western occupation powers, German political and social factors were dependent on the Western Allies, especially the Americans. Their existence overlaid and distorted power structures of German society for a certain period. Although they could not simply ignore those factors, even at the beginning of the occupation period, the Allies were always influential at the political level.

IV. The Defeat as Revolution?

I do not wish to begin a long discussion of terminology here, but would like to emphasize that the almost careless use of the term 'revolution'[50] does not appear useful, when every relatively rapid change, every sort of break is termed 'revolutionary' up to a 'reading revolution' and the like. In general, I have great doubts about the applicability of the term 'revolution' to economic and social processes of change that are not directly related to destructive political processes. I even have some misgivings about the first 'Industrial Revolution', although this term has become generally accepted. Under 'revolution' I understand a not always but generally violent, relatively sudden overthrow of the political system, which is not always but generally supported by mass movements, and which is as a rule connected with a change of elites. If the overthrow of the state leads to a break with one social order in favour of another, one can speak of a 'social revolution', for example in Russia after 1917. My attempt at a definition allows the secondary forms 'revolution from above' and 'external revolution', that is, through conquest in war. Classic examples of an 'external revolution' in more recent German history would be the revolutionary and hegemonic wars of France around 1800 and – in relation to my subject today – the military actions of the USSR on German territory in the winter and spring of 1945, which initiated a political and social upheaval as a 'dependent revolution' of local communists and their allies. In East Germany one can limit this 'external revolution' in general to the second half of the 1940s. Spontaneous mass action and mass actions in general played no significant part, as the question of power had been decided in May 1945.

Much more difficult is an answer to the question of revolution through military defeat in relation to West Germany. But first a few remarks on the thesis emanating from Ralf Dahrendorf and David Schoenbaum that National Socialism had already, if unintentionally, caused a modernizing 'social revolution', in which the old German class society, still pervaded by the remains of the estates, was overcome, and thus the way for postwar development made free.[51] The transformation of the officer corps, which – especially after the turning point of the war – changed its social composition and its attitude towards a kind of National Socialist popular army, can serve as an example for a modernization introduced by National Socialism. Even if there were considerable drawing on older traditions during the formation of the federal army, the policies of inner leadership and the pragmatism of leading officers prevented a relapse into predemocratic behaviour.[52]

With all due respect for the above named authors, the 'social revolution' of National Socialism appears to me to be an example of just that sort of inexact use of the term 'revolution' among historians and sociologists which I have already criticized. One cannot argue with the fact that in the Third Reich the 'modernization' of German society continued and indeed accelerated in some areas. Even the Weimar Republic and indeed Wilhelmine Germany saw some dramatic, partial modernization processes, often underestimated by historians of the Nazi era. For those specific characteristics of postwar development such as mass consumption of, for example, automobiles, social insurance and social mobility, similar phenomena in the middle and late 1930s, even quantitatively, are only precursors. Models of modernization processes, including abandonment of the countryside, and an increase in the tertiary sector, show there would not have been any significant acceleration in the 1930s and 1940s.[53] The criterion of revolution depends entirely on the extent to which relevant social changes were actually related to a political change of regime.[54] Thus one cannot attribute war-related changes directly to National Socialism.

Especially in view of a surmounting of pre-bourgeois influences in German society, Dahrendorf's thesis does not convince me. The suppression of the attempted coup of 20 July 1944 did not mark the decisive blow against Prussian aristocracy. Rather, this date only accelerated the loss of importance of the agrarian aristocracy, the first signs of which could be seen even before the First World War, and which was carried further by the overthrow of the monarchy and the National Socialist takeover within the ruling power bloc. This group was, in fact, finally eliminated as a factor of power only as a consequence of total defeat at war.

Thus we are back to 1945 and the postwar period. I will just sum up the main points. Even if, in the 1950s, it looked as if capitalism and bourgeois order had only been reconstructed in the Federal Republic, using the old personnel and even some specific traditions such as that of the professional civil service, the continuation of the Bonn experiment made it possible to recognize how deep the break of 1945 was. There can be no doubt that the completeness of the Allied victory and the explicitness of the political foundations laid for West Germany in the years from 1947 onward were very influential for the Federal Republic's success. In fact, however, the massive changes in society and attitudes of the 1950s and 1960s were due rather more to developments, which – with certain displacements in relation to periodization and speed of the process – appeared in all developed capitalist countries of North America and Europe and even in some cases beyond that. Intervention in German society by the victors of the Second World War was thus possibly a necessary, but in no way sufficient, condition for the more recent social changes of the past decades, which have created a new, 'Westernized' Germany. In order to provide an answer to the question posed above, I would emphasize the national and historical importance of the break in 1945, but plead for moderation in the use of the term 'revolution' for West Germany. Unlike East Germany, West Germany did not experience any social upheaval as a direct consequence of a revolution initiated from outside, by the victorious powers. The closest one can come would be to define the change of government in the spring of 1945, in the wake of the Western Allies' advances, as a political revolution. Social development in West Germany, including the radical reforms mentioned above, were, however, not simply the result of this revolutionary change of government in a limited sense. It occurred as a result of the military overthrow of National Socialism, the conservative modernization of the 1950s with its, in part, counter-reformist elements, the long economic boom, not only in Germany, since the late 1940s and, not least, the restructuring of the international economy and state order in the Western hemisphere. The question raised in the title cannot be answered with 'yes' or 'no', and that, indeed, was not the aim of this chapter. It was for me rather a matter of setting out the problem that has to be discussed.

Notes

1. Alfred Vagts, 'Unconditional Surrender vor und nach 1943', in *Vierteljahrs-hefte für Zeitgeschichte* 7, 1959, pp. 280–309, here p. 293. The academic literature on the problem raised has almost exploded since 1985. An introduction to the problem is provided by the following general works and collections of essays: Christoph Kleßmann, *Die doppelte Staatsgründung. Deutsche Geschichte 1945–1955*, Göttingen 1982; Christoph Kleßmann, *Zwei Staaten – eine Nation. Deutsche Geschichte 1955–1970*, Göttingen 1988; Rudolf Morsey, *Die Bundesrepublik Deutschland. Entstehung und Entwicklung bis 1969*, Munich 1987; Karl Dietrich Bracher, Wolfgang Jäger and Werner Link (eds), *Republik im Wandel 1969–1982 (Gechichte der Bundesrepublik Deutschland*, vol. 5, part 1 and 2), Stuttgart 1986–87; Wolfgang Benz (ed.), *Die Bundesrepublik Deutschland. Geschichte in drei Bänden*, Frankfurt am Main 1983; Mary Fulbrook, *The Divided Nation. A History of Germany 1918–1990*, Oxford 1992; William Paterson and Gordon Smith (eds), *Perspectives on a Stable State*, London 1981; Werner Conze and M. Rainer Lepsius (eds), *Sozialgeschichte der Bundesrepublik Deutschland. Beiträge zum Kontinuitäts-problem*, 2nd edn, Stuttgart 1995; Ludolf Herbst (ed.), *Westdeutschland 1945–1955. Unterwerfung, Kontrolle, Integration*, Munich 1986; Martin Broszat (ed.), *Zäsuren nach 1945. Essays zur Periodisierung der deutschen Nachkriegs-geschichte*, Munich 1990; Hans-Erich Volkmann (ed.), *Ende des Dritten Reichs – Ende des Zweiten Weltkriegs. Eine perspektivische Rückschau*, Munich 1995; Heinrich Oberreuter and Jürgen Weber (eds), *Freundliche Feinde? Die Alliierten und die Demokratiegründung in Deutschland*, Munich 1996.

2. Thus in reference to Helmut Schelsky in the introduction to Martin Broszat, Klaus-Dietmar Henke and Hans Woller (eds), *Von Stalingrad zur Währungsreform. Zur Sozialgeschichte des Umbruchs in Deutschland*, Munich 1988, p. XXV.

3. A critical review by Heinrich August Winkler, 'Sozialer Umbruch zwischen Stalingrad und Währungsreform', in *Geschichte und Gesellschaft* 16, 1990, pp. 403–9.

4. Robert Forster, 'The French Revolution and the "New Elite" 1800–1850', in Jaroslaw Pelensky (ed.), *The American and European Revolution, 1776–1848*, Iowa City 1980, p. 186.

5. Winfried Loth, *Die Teilung der Welt. Geschichte des Kalten Krieges 1941–1955*, 5th edn, Munich 1987; Julius Braunthal, *Geschichte der Internationale*, vol. 3, Hannover 1971.

6. On the character of the National Socialist government and developments 1943–45 see Peter Reichel, *Der schöne Schein des Dritten Reiches. Faszination und Gewalt des Faschismus*, Munich 1992; Ian Kershaw, *The Hitler Myth. Image and Reality in the Third Reich*, Oxford 1987; Hans Mommsen (ed.), *Herrschaftsalltag im Dritten Reich. Studien und Texte*, Düsseldorf 1988; Hans Mommsen, *Der Nationalsozialismus und die deutsche Gesellschaft. Ausgewählte*

152 *Peter Brandt*

Aufsätze, Reinbek 1991; Martin Broszat, *Der Staat Hitlers. Grundlegung und Entwicklung seiner inneren Verfassung,* Munich 1978. On 20 July 1944 and the conspiracy: Peter Hoffmann, *Widerstand, Staatsstreich, Attentat. Der Kampf der Opposition gegen Hitler,* Munich 1969; Peter Hoffmann, *Widerstand gegen Hitler und das Attentat vom 20. Juli 1944,* 4th edn, Konstanz 1994; Peter Steinbach, *Widerstand im Widerstreit. Der Widerstand gegen den Nationalsozialismus in der Erinnerung der Deutschen,* Paderborn 1994. Sabotage of Hitler's scorched-earth orders and moves to undermine the defence in spring 1945: Gitta Sereny, *Albert Speer. Das Ringen mit der Wahrheit und das deutsche Trauma,* Munich 1995; Norbert Haase, 'Desertion – Kriegsdienstverweigerung – Widerstand', in Peter Steinbach and Johannes Tuchel (eds), *Widerstand gegen den Nationalsozialismus,* Berlin 1994, pp. 526–36.

7. Paul Hagen, *Germany after Hitler,* New York 1994.

8. Thus, for example, the wording of the brochure *Zur Nachkriegspolitik deutscher Sozialisten,* Stockholm 1944. This paper was produced by members of the left-wing socialist SAPD (Socialist Workers Party of Germany) which reattached itself to the SPD in Swedish exile in 1944. On the development of the programmes of resistance and exile in expectation of the end of the war see in summary: Peter Brandt, 'Die Arbeiterbewegung. Deutsche Nachkriegskonzeptioneu und ihre Perspektiven unter alliierter Besatzung', in *Journal für Geschichte* 3, 1985, pp. 35–43.

9. Paul M. Sweezy, *The Present as History. Essays and Reviews of Capitalism and Socialism,* New York 1953, p. 249. On the Antifa movement in general see: Lutz Niethammer, Ulrich Borsdorf and Peter Brandt (eds), *Arbeiterinitiative 1945. Antifaschistische Ausschüsse und Reorganisation der Arbeiterbewegung in Deutschland,* Wuppertal 1975. For Bremen see Peter Brandt, *Antifaschismus und Arbeiterbewegung. Aufbau – Ausprägung – Politik in Bremen 1945/46,* Hamburg 1976.

10. Jürgen Kocka, *Klassengesellschaft im Krieg. Deutsche Sozialgeschichte 1914–1918,* 2nd edn, Göttingen 1978; Ulrich Kluge, *Die deutsche Revolution 1918/19. Staat, Politik und Gesellschaft zwischen Weltkrieg und Kapp-Putsch,* Frankfurt am Main 1985; Reinhard Rürup, 'Demokratische Revolution und "dritter Weg". Die deutsche Revolution von 1918/19 in der neueren wisenschaftlichen Diskussion', in *Geschichte und Gesellschaft* 9, 1983, pp. 278–301.

11. Quoted in L. Niethammer, U. Borsdorf and P. Brandt (eds), *Arbeiterinitiative,* p. 301.

12. Christoph Kleßmann, 'Betriebsräte und Gewerkschaften in Deutschland 1945–1952', in Heinrich August Winkler (ed.), *Politische Weichenstellungen im Nachkriegsdeutschland 1945–1953,* Göttingen 1979, pp. 44–73; Peter Brandt, 'Betriebsräte, Neuordnungsdiskussion und betriebliche Mitbestimmung 1945–1948. Das Beispiel Bremen', in *Internationale wissenschaftliche Korrespondenz zur Geschichte der deutschen Arbeiterbewegung*

20, 1984, pp. 156–202; Michael Fichter, 'Aufbau und Neuordnung: Betriebsräte zwischen Klassensolidarität und Betriebsloyalität', in Martin Rüther (ed.), *Zwischen Zusammenbruch und Wirtschaftswunder. Betriebstätigkeit und Arbeiterverhalten in Köln 1945–1952*, Bonn 1991.

13. Siegfried Suckut, *Die Betriebsrätebewegung in der sowjetisch besetzten Zone Deutschlands (1945–1948). Zur Entwicklung und Bedeutung von Arbeiterinitiative, betrieblicher Mitbestimmung und Selbstbestimmung bis zur Revision des programmatischen Konzepts der KPD/SED vom 'besonderen deutschen Weg zum Sozialismus'*, Frankfurt am Main 1982.

14. Horst Thum, *Mitbestimmung in der Montanindustrie. Der Mythos vom Sieg der Gewerkschaften*, Stuttgart 1982; Gabriele Müller-List, *Das Gesetz über die Mitbestimmung der Arbeitnehmer in den Aufsichtsräten und Vorständen der Unternehmen des Bergbaus und der Eisen und Stahl erzeugenden Industrie vom 21. Mai 1951*, Düsseldorf 1984; Norbert Ranft, *Vom Objekt zum Subjekt. Montanmitbestimmung, Sozialklima und Strukturwandel im Bergbau seit 1945*, Cologne 1988.

15. Walther Pahl, 'Mitbestimmung in der Montanindustrie nach dem Gesetz vom 10.4.1951', in *Gewerkschaftliche Monatshefte*, 1951, pp. 225–7, here p. 226.

16. Michael Fichter, *Besatzungsmacht und Gewerkschaften. Zur Entwicklung und Anwendung der US-Gewerkschaftspolitik in Deutschland 1944–1948*, Opladen 1982; Siegfried Mielke, 'Der Wiederaufbau der Gewerkschaften: Legenden und Wirklichkeit', in H.A. Winkler (ed.), *Politische Weichenstellungen*, pp. 74–87.

17. Willy Albrecht (ed.), *Kurt Schumacher. Reden-Schriften-Korrespondenzen*, Bonn 1985; Kurt Klotzbach, *Der Weg zur Staatspartei. Programmatik, praktische Politik und Organisation der deutschen Sozialdemokratie 1945 bis 1965*, Bonn 1982; Ernst Ulrich Huster, *Die Politik der SPD 1945–1950*, Frankfurt am Main 1978.

18. 'Field Intelligence Studies from the OSS mission for Germany', in Ulrich Borsdorf and Lutz Niethammer (eds), *Zwischen Befreiung und Besatzung. Analysen des US-Geheimdienstes über Positionen und Strukturen deutscher Politik 1945*, Wuppertal 1976, pp. 275–311, here p. 311 (retranslation from the German).

19. Quoted in John Gimbel, *The Origins of the Marshall Plan*, Stanford 1976, p. 216. On the security policies of the Western Powers in Germany see also Rolf Steininger, 'Reform und Realität. Ruhrfrage und Sozialisierung in der anglo-amerikanischen Deutschlandpolitik 1947/48', in *Vierteljahrshefte für Zeitgeschichte* 27, 1979, pp. 167–240; John H. Backer, *Die deutschen Jahre des General Clay. Der Weg zur Bundesrepublik 1945–1949*, Munich 1983; Otmar N. Haberl and Lutz Niethammer (eds), *Der Marshall-Plan und die europäische Linke*, Frankfurt am Main 1986; Werner Link, 'Der Marshall-Plan und Deutschland', in *Aus Politik und Zeitgeschichte. Beilage zur Wochenzeitung 'Das Parlament'*, No. 50, 13 December 1980, pp. 3–18, as well as the works named in footnotes 45 and 46.

20. A comparison of voter distribution in the sum of the provincial parliamentary elections in the Western zones 1946/47 with voter distribution in the first Federal election of 1949 produces the following figures; SPD 35 per cent and 29.2 per cent, KPD 9.4 per cent and 5.7 per cent, CDU/CSU 37.6 per cent and 31 per cent, FDP 9.3 per cent and 11.9 per cent. While the two parties of the left lost votes, the relative loss of the CDU/CSU was overcompensated for by gains by the FDP and smaller bourgeois parties (12.9 per cent).

21. Arnulf Baring, *Uprising in East Germany*, Ithaca 1972; Axel Bust-Bartels, *Herrschaft und Widerstand in den DDR-Betrieben*, Frankfurt am Main 1980; Ilse Spittmann and Friedrich Wilhelm Fricke (eds), *17. Juni 1953. Arbeiteraufstand in der DDR*, Cologne 1982.

22. Helmut Schelsky, 'Über das Restaurative in unserer Zeit' (1955), in H. Schelsky, *Auf der Suche nach Wirklichkeit. Gesammelte Aufsätze*, Düsseldorf 1965, pp. 405–14, here pp. 405 f.

23. Harold Hurwitz, *Demokratie und Antikommunismus in Berlin nach 1945*, vol. 1: *Die politische Kultur der Bevölkerung und der Neubeginn konservativer Politik*, Cologne 1983; Dietrich Staritz, *Die Gründung der DDR. Von der sowjetischen Besatzungsherrschaft zum sozialistischen Staat*, Munich 1984; Hermann Weber, *DDR – Grundriß der Geschichte. Die abgeschlossene Geschichte der DDR 1945–1990*, new edition, Hannover 1991; Hartmut Mehringer (ed.), *Von der SBZ zur DDR. Studien zum Herrschaftssystem in der Sowjetischen Besatzungszone und in der Deutschen Demokratischen Republik*, Munich 1995.

24. Werner Weidenfeld and Hartmut Zimmermann (eds), *Deutschland-Handbuch. Eine doppelte Bilanz 1949–1989*, Bonn 1989; Hans Joas and Martin Kohl (eds), *Der Zusammenbruch der DDR. Soziologische Analysen*, Frankfurt am Main 1993.

25. Wolfgang Benz (ed.), *Die Vertreibung der Deutschen aus dem Osten. Ursachen, Ereignisse, Folgen*, Frankfurt am Main 1985; Rainer Schulze and Doris von der Brelie-Lewien (eds), *Flüchtlinge und Vertriebene in der westdeutschen Nachkriegsgeschichte*, Hildesheim 1987; Paul Erker, 'Revolution des Dorfes? Ländliche Bevölkerung zwischen Flüchtlingszustrom und landwirtschaftlichem Strukturwandel', in M. Broszat, K.-D. Henke and H. Woller (eds), *Von Stalingrad*, pp. 37–425.

26. Alf Mintzel and Heinrich Oberreuter (eds), *Parteien in der Bundesrepublik Deutschland*, Bonn 1990; Helga Grebing, 'Die Parteien', in W. Benz (ed.), *Die Bundesrepublik Deutschland*, vol. 1, pp. 126–91; Hans Otto Kleimann, *Die Geschichte der CDU 1945–1982*, Stuttgart 1993; Felix Becker, *Kleine Geschichte der CDU*, Stuttgart 1995; Dietrich Staritz (ed.), *Das Parteiensystem der Bundesrepublik. Geschichte – Entstehung – Entwicklung*, 2nd edn, Opladen 1980; K. Klotzbach, *Der Weg zur Staatspartei*; Geoffrey Pridham, *Christian Democracy in Western Germany. The CDU/CSU in Government and Opposition 1945–1976*, London 1977.

27. Charles Eade (ed.), *The War Speeches of the Rt. Hon. Winston S. Churchill*, vol. 3, London 1952, p. 18. See also Lothar Kettenacker, 'Preußen-

Deutschland als britisches Feindbild im Zweiten Weltkrieg', in Bernd Wendt (ed.), *Das britische Deutschlandbild im Wandel des 19. und 20. Jahrhunderts*, Bochum 1983, pp. 145–68.

28. Lutz Niethammer, 'Die amerikanische Besatzungsmacht zwischen Verwaltungstradition und politischen Parteien in Bayern 1945', in *Vierteljahrshefte für Zeitgeschichte* 15, 1967, pp. 153–210; Christoph Henzler, *Fritz Schäffer 1945–1967. Eine biographische Studie zum ersten bayerischen Nachkriegs-Ministerpräsidenten und ersten Finanzminister der Bundesrepublik Deutschland*, Munich 1994; Konrad Maria Färber, 'Bayern wieder ein Königreich? Die monarchistische Bewegung in Bayern nach dem Zweiten Weltkrieg', in Wolfgang Benz (ed.), *Neuanfang in Bayern 1945–1949. Politik und Gesellschaft in der Nachkriegszeit*, Munich 1988, pp. 163–82.

29. Adolf M. Birke, 'Großbritannien und der Parlamentarische Rat', in *Vierteljahrshefte für Zeitgeschichte* 42, 1994, pp. 313–59; Gerd Wehner, *Die Westalliierten und das Grundgesetz, 1948–1949. Die Londoner Sechsmächtekonferenz*, Freiburg 1994; Karlheinz Nicklauß, *Demokratiegründung in Westdeutschland. Die Entstehung der Bundesrepublik 1945–1949*, Munich 1974; Volker Otto, *Das Staatsverständnis des Parlamentarischen Rates. Ein Beitrag zur Entstehung des Grundgesetzes für die Bundesrepublik Deutschland*, Düsseldorf 1971.

30. Cf. most recently Cornelia Rauh-Kühne, 'Die Entnazifizierung und die deutsche Gesellschaft', in *Archiv für Sozialgeschichte* 35, 1995, pp. 35–70; see also Clemens Vollnhals and Thomas Schlemmer (eds), *Entnazifizierung. Politische Säuberung und Rehabilitierung in den vier Besatzungszonen 1945–1949*, Munich 1991; Klaus-Dietmar Henke and Hans Woller (eds), *Politische Säuberung in Europa. Die Abrechnung mit Faschismus und Kollaboration nach dem Zweiten Weltkrieg*, Munich 1991; as well as the classic regional study by Lutz Niethammer, *Entnazifizierung in Bayern. Säuberung und Rehabilitierung unter amerikanischer Besatzung*, Frankfurt am Main 1972.

31. Ruth-Kristin Rößler (ed.), *Entnazifizierungspolitik der KPD/SED 1945–1948*, Goldbach 1994; Manfred Wille, *Entnazifizierung in der Sowjetischen Besatzungszone Deutschlands 1945–48*, Magdeburg 1993; Helga Welsh, *Revolutionärer Wandel auf Befehl? Entnazifizierungs- und Personalpolitik in Thüringen und Sachsen (1945–1948)*, Munich 1989.

32. Figures from C. Vollnhals and T. Schlemmer (eds), *Entnazifizierung*, p. 333.

33. Curt Garner, 'Public Service Personnel in West Germany in the 1950s. Controversial Policy Decisions and their Effects on Social Composition, Gender Structure, and the Role of former Nazis', in *Journal of Social History*, Fall 1995, pp. 25–80; Ulrich Herbert, *Best. Biographische Studien über Radikalismus, Weltanschauung und Vernunft 1903–1989*, Bonn 1996, especially pp. 467–9.

34. See the works cited in footnote 33 as well as H. Oberreuter and J. Weber (eds), *Freundliche Feinde*.

35. Marlis G. Steinert, *Hitlers Krieg und die Deutschen. Stimmung und Haltung der deutschen Bevölkerung im Zweiten Weltkrieg*, Düsseldorf 1970; Klaus-

Dietmar Henke, *Die amerikanische Besetzung Deutschlands 1944–45*, Munich 1995; Rolf Schörken, *Jugend 1945. Politisches Denken und Lebensgeschichte*, Frankfurt am Main 1994.

36. Policy Directive for the United States High Commissioner for Germany, in *Foreign Relations of the United States. 1949*, vol. III: *Council of Foreign Ministers; Germany and Austria*, Washington 1974, pp. 319–40, here p. 338.

37. Hermann-Josef Rupieper, *Die Wurzeln der westdeutschen Nachkriegsdemokratie. Der amerikanische Beitrag 1945–1952*, Opladen 1993; Nicholas Pronay and Keith M. Wilson (eds), *The Political Re-education of Germany and her Allies after World War II*, London 1985; Manfred Heinemann (ed.), *Umerziehung und Wiederaufbau*, Stuttgart 1981.

38. Hans Mommsen, 'Von Weimar nach Bonn: Zum Demokratieverständnis der Deutschen', in Axel Schildt and Arnold Sywottek (eds), *Modernisierung im Wiederaufbau: Die westdeutsche Gesellschaft der 50er Jahre*, Bonn 1993.

39. Werner Conze, *Jakob Kaiser. Politiker zwischen Ost und West 1945–1949*, Stuttgart 1969; Hans-Peter Schwarz, *Vom Reich zur Bundesrepublik. Deutschland im Widerstreit der außenpolitischen Konzeptionen in den Jahren der Besatzungsherrschaft 1945–1949*, 2nd edn, Stuttgart 1980; Rainer Dohse, *Der Dritte Weg. Neutralitätsbestrebungen in Westdeutschland zwischen 1945 und 1955*, Hamburg 1974; Arthur Schlegelmilch, *Hauptstadt im Zonendeutschland. Die Entstehung der Berliner Nachkriegsdemokratie 1945–1949*, Berlin 1991.

40. Richard Löwenthal, 'Prolog: Dauer und Verwandlung', in Richard Löwenthal and Hans-Peter Schwarz (eds), *Die zweite Republik. 25 Jahre Bundesrepublik Deutschland – eine Bilanz*, Stuttgart 1974, pp. 9–24, here p. 10.

41. Bernd Faulenbach, *Die Ideologie des deutschen Weges. Die deutsche Geschichte in der Historiographie zwischen Kaiserreich und Nationalsozialismus*, Munich 1980; *Deutscher Sonderweg – Mythos oder Realität. Kolloquium des Instituts für Zeitgeschichte*, Munich 1982. The later effects of specific German traditions of thought in the early postwar period is explored in an important example: Dirk van Laak, *Gespräche in der Sicherheit des Schweigens. Carl Schmitt in der politischen Geistesgeschichte der frühen Bundesrepublik*, Berlin 1993.

42. Anna J. Merritt and Richard L. Merritt (eds), *Public Opinion in Occupied Germany. The OMGUS-Surveys 1945–1949*, Urbana, Illinois 1970; Elisabeth Noelle and Erich Peter Neumann, *Jahrbuch der öffentlichen Meinung 1947–1955*, 2nd edn, Allensbach 1956; Elisabeth Noelle-Neumann and Edgar Piel (eds), *Eine Generation später. Bundesrepublik Deutschland 1953–1979*, Munich 1983; Gabriel A. Almond and Sidney Verba, *The Civic Culture. Attitudes and Democracy in Five Nations*, Princeton 1963; Klaus R. Allerbeck, *Demokratisierung und sozialer Wandel in der Bundesrepublik Deutschland. Sekundäranalyse von Umfragedaten 1953–1974*, Opladen 1976; Erwin K. Scheuch and Ute Scheuch, *Wie deutsch sind die Deutschen? Eine Nation*

wandelt ihr Gesicht, Bergisch-Gladbach 1991; Martin and Sylvia Greiffenhagen, *Ein schwieriges Vaterland. Zur politischen Kultur Deutschlands*, Munich
1979; Dirk Berg-Schlosser and Jakob Schissler (eds), *Politische Kultur in
Deutschland. Bilanz und Perspektiven der Forschung*, Opladen 1987.

43.   Hans Günther Hockerts, *Sozialpolitische Entscheidungen im Nachkriegsdeutschland. Alliierte und deutsche Sozialversicherungspolitik 1945–1957*,
Stuttgart 1980; Jens Alber, *Der Sozialstaat in der Bundesrepublik 1950–1983*,
Frankfurt am Main 1989; Gerhard A. Ritter, *Der Sozialstaat. Entstehung
und Entwicklung im internatiolen Vergleich*, 2nd edn, Munich 1991.

44.   Knut Borchardt, 'Die Bundesrepublik in den säkularen Trends der
wirtschaftlichen Entwicklung', in W. Conze and M.R. Lepsius (eds),
Sozialgeschichte, pp. 20–45, as well as the other essays in the book; Werner
Abelshauser, *Wirtschaftsgeschichte der Bundesrepublik Deutschland 1945–1980*,
Frankfurt am Main 1983; Werner Glastetter, Rüdiger Paulert and Ulrich
Spöl (eds), *Die volkswirtschaftliche Entwicklung in der Bundesrepublik
Deutschland 1950–1980*, Frankfurt am Main 1983; Wolfgang Zapf (ed.),
*Lebensbedingungen in der Bundesrepublik. Sozialer Wandel und Wohlfahrtsent-
wicklung*, 2nd edn, Frankfurt am Main 1979; Hartmut Kaelble (ed.),
*Der Boom 1948–1973. Gesellschaftliche und wirtschaftliche Folgen in der Bundes-
republik Deutschland und in Europa*, Opladen 1992; A. Schildt and A.
Sywottek (eds), *Modernisierung im Wiederaufbau*; Josef Mooser, *Arbeiterleben
in Deutschland 1900–1970. Klassenlagen, Kultur und Politik*, Frankfurt am
Main 1984. The social historical thesis, first put forward systematically
by Hans-Peter Schwarz (for example in his essay: 'Die Fünfziger Jahre
als Epochenzäsur', in Jürgen Heideking, Gerhard Hufnagel and Franz
Knipping (eds), *Wege in die Zeitgeschichte. Festschrift zum 65. Geburtstag von
Gerhard Schulz*, Berlin 1989, pp. 473–96) and developed and extended
by Schildt and Sywottek, of a break between epochs in the 1950s is
plausible in many respects. It cannot, however, call into question the
severity of the break in 1945, but only indicate that the period of
transition between the crisis-filled and convulsive epoch of the three
decades after 1914 and the new order of social, intrastate and interstate
relations that existed up to 1989/90 is to be assessed as longer than
the first three or four postwar years.

45.   John H. Backer, *The Decision to Divide Germany. American Foreign Policy in
Transition*, Durham 1978; Wolfgang Krieger, *General Lucius D. Clay und
die amerikanische Deutschlandpolitik, 1945–1949*, 2nd edn, Stuttgart 1988;
Josef Foschepoth and Rolf Steininger (eds), *Britische Deutschland- und
Besatzungspolitik*, Paderborn 1985; Ian D. Turner (ed.), *Reconstruction in
Post War Germany: British Occupation Policy and the Western Zones, 1945–55*,
Oxford 1989; Claus Scharf and Hans-Jürgen Schröder (eds), *Die Deutsch-
landpolitik Großbritanniens und die Britische Zone 1945–1949*, Wiesbaden
1979; Claus Scharf and Hans-Jürgen Schröder (eds), *Die Deutsch-
landpolitik Frankreichs und die Französische Zone 1945–1949*, Wiesbaden 1983;
Henri Ménudier (ed.), *L'Allemagne occupée 1945–1949*, Brussels 1990;

Werner Abelshauser, *Wirtschaft in Westdeutschland 1945–1948. Rekonstruktion in der amerikanischen und britischen Zone*, Stuttgart 1975; Nicholas Balabkins, *Germany under Direct Controls*, New Brunswick 1964; Helga Grebing, Peter Pozorski and Rainer Schulze, *Die Nachkriegsentwicklung in Westdeutschland 1945–1949*, 2 vols., Stuttgart 1980.

46. Gerhard L. Weinberg, *A World at Arms. A Global History of World War II*, Cambridge 1994; Lloyd C. Gardner, *Spheres of Influence. The Partition of Europe from Munich to Yalta*, London 1993; John Lewis Gaddis, *The United States and the Origins of the Cold War 1941–1947*, New York 1972; J. H. Backer, *The Decision;* W. Krieger, *General Lucius D. Clay*; Gabriel Kolko, *The Politics of War. The World and United States Policy 1943–1945*, New York 1968; Gabriel Kolko and Joyce Kolko, *The Limits of Power. The World and United States Foreign Policy, 1945–1954*, New York 1972; Josef Foschepoth (ed.), *Kalter Krieg und Deutsche Frage. Deutschland im Widerstreit der Mächte 1945–1952*, Göttingen 1985; Manfred Knapp (ed.), *Von der Bizonengründung zur ökonomisch-politischen Westintegration. Studien zum Verhältnis zwischen Außenpolitik und Außenwirtschaftsbeziehungen in der Entstehungsphase der Bundesrepublik Deutschland (1947–1952)*, Frankfurt am Main 1984; Ludolf Herbst, Werner Bührer and Hannes Sowade (eds), *Vom Marshallplan zur EWG. Die Eingliederung der Bundesrepublik in die westliche Welt*, Munich 1990; Christoph Buchheim, *Die Wiedereingliederung Westdeutschlands in die Weltwirtschaft 1945–1958*, Munich 1990; Gerold Ambrosius, *Die Durchsetzung der sozialen Marktwirtschaft in Westdeutschland, 1945–1949*, Stuttgart 1977; Charles S. Maier and Günter Bischof (eds), *The Marshall Plan and Germany. West German Development within the Framework of the European Recovery Program*, New York 1991. The controversies about the economic effect of the Marshall Plan and about the relation of Atlantic and West European integration are not of decisive importance in the context of my argument, especially as the political leadership of West Germany was not fixed on one certain form of Western ties.

47. Ludolf Herbst, *Der Totale Krieg und die Ordnung der Wirtschaft. Die Kriegswirtschaft im Spannungsfeld von Politik, Ideologie und Propaganda 1939–1945*, Stuttgart 1982.

48. K. Klotzbach, *Der Weg zur Staatspartei;* Kurt Thomas Schmitz, *Deutsche Einheit und Europäische Integration. Der sozialdemokratische Beitrag zur Außenpolitik der Bundesrepublik Deutschland unter besonderer Berücksichtigung des programmatischen Wandels einer Oppositionspartei*, Bonn 1978; Dieter Groh and Peter Brandt, *'Vaterlandslose Gesellen'. Sozialdemokratie und Nation 1860–1990*, Munich 1992, pp. 233 ff.

49. For a summary see H. Oberreuter and J. Weber (eds), *Freundliche Feinde;* Wolfgang Benz, 'Erzwungenes Ideal oder zweitbeste Lösung? Intentionen und Wirkungen der Gründung des deutschen Weststaats', in L. Herbst (ed.), *Westdeutschland 1945–1955*, pp. 135–46; for a regional study see Hans Woller, *Gesellschaft und Politik in der amerikanischen Besatzungszone. Die Region Ansbach und Fürth*, Munich 1986. On the reform

of the civil service Udo Wengst, *Beamtentum zwischen Reform und Tradition. Beamtengesetzgebung in der Gründungsphase der Bundesrepublik Deutschland 1948–1953,* Düsseldorf 1988; Ulrich Reusch, *Deutsches Berufsbeamtentum und britische Besatzung. Planung und Politik 1943–1947,* Stuttgart 1985; Curt Garner, '"Zerschlagung des Berufsbeamtentums"? Der deutsche Konflikt um die Neuordnung des öffentlichen Dienstes 1944–48 am Beispiel Nordrhein Westfalens', in *Vierteljahrshefte für Zeitgeschichte* 39, 1991, pp. 55–101; Curt Garner, 'Schlußfolgerungen aus der Vergangenheit? Die Auseinandersetzungen um die Zukunft des deutschen Berufsbeamtentums nach dem Ende des Zweiten Weltkrieges', in H.-E. Volkmann (ed.), *Ende des Zweiten Weltkriegs,* pp. 607–74; C. Garner, *Public Service Personnel.*

50. On the term see above all Reinhart Koselleck, 'Revolution', in *Geschichtliche Grundbegriffe,* vol. 5, Stuttgart 1984, pp. 653–788.

51. Ralf Dahrendorf, *Society and Democracy in Germany,* London 1968; David Schoenbaum, *Hitler's Social Revolution. Class and Status in Nazi Germany 1933–1939,* New York 1966. Taking up from this, for example, Michael Prinz and Rainer Zitelmann (eds), *Nationalsozialismus und Modernisierung,* Darmstadt 1991.

52. Bernhard R. Kroener, 'Auf dem Weg zu einer "nationalsozialistischen Volksarmee". Die soziale Öffnung des Heeresoffizierkorps im Zweiten Weltkrieg', in M. Broszat, K.-D. Henke and H. Woller (eds) *Von Stalingrad,* pp. 651–82; Militärgeschichtliches Forschungsamt (ed.), *Anfänge westdeutscher Sicherheitspolitik, 1945–1950,* 2 vols, Munich 1982, 1990; Detlef Bald, *Militär und Gesellschaft in Deutschland 1945–1990,* Baden-Baden 1993.

53. Horst Matzerath and Heinrich Volkmann, 'Modernisierungstheorie und Nationalsozialismus', in Jürgen Kocka (ed.), *Theorien in der Praxis des Historikers,* Göttingen 1977, pp. 86–116. See also Norbert Frei, 'Wie modern war der Nationalsozialismus?', in *Geschichte und Gesellschaft* 19, 1993, pp. 367–87; Hans Mommsen, *Der Nationalsozialismus und die deutsche Gesellschaft,* Reinbek 1991. See in general the collection of essays by Karl Dietrich Bracher, Manfred Funke and Hans-Adolf Jacobsen (eds), *Nationalsozialistische Diktatur 1933–1945. Eine Bilanz,* Bonn 1983.

54. More plausible than the thesis of a 'social revolution' of national socialism seems to me the reading of the 'seizure of power' in 1933–34 as a revolutionary change of the political system, in form and content, as proposed especially by Karl Dietrich Bracher. It is, in any case, compatible with my attempt at a definition.

JÜRGEN KOCKA

Reform and Revolution: Germany 1989–90

The classical revolutions remained extremely controversial long after they had been won or lost. As memories and symbolic actions, and in disparate interpretations, some of the battles of the French revolution were still being fought two hundred years later. Was François Furet right when he proclaimed, on the occasion of the bicentennial, that the French revolution was finally over and would eventually no longer be the object of controversy? The Russian revolution remained highly controversial, reflecting the different traditions associated with the victors and the victims. After the fall of communism, such controversies have calmed down internationally, but now, for the first time, they can be and are voiced inside Russia. And remember the German Revolution of 1918/1919, which in Weimar Germany became the object of bitter controversies, hatred and defamation. Those on the right alleged that the *Novemberverbrecher* (November criminals) had betrayed the nation; and on the left, Kurt Tucholsky ridiculed the event: 'Die deutsche Revolution hat 1918 im Saale stattgefunden' – 'The German revolution of 1918 took place in the assembly hall.'[1]

Nothing of that kind can be detected a few years after the East German revolution of 1989–90. There have been, and still are, varying interpretations of that deep turnaround, related to ideological and political arguments of the day (see below). But the main thing to be stressed is the relatively high degree of consensus, the lack of ideological battles, and even some indifference about the meaning of this remarkable discontinuity in recent German history, which in everyday language is nowadays mostly referred to as the *Wende* (turn, turning point). There are highly controversial, historical, public debates with strong political overtones in present-day Germany, but they deal much more with the character of the GDR, its more or less totalitarian nature, the injustices it produced and the arrangements it permitted, with collaboration and opposition, perpetrators and victims – and how they have subsequently been treated.[2] These debates are much less concerned with the way the GDR was brought to an end. Measured by the degree of controversy it has led to *post festum,* the turn of 1990 appears to have been no revolution at all.

Was it a revolution? In what sense, and in what sense not? What can we say about the internal and external causes? What was specific about the German case, compared with the breakdown of communism in the other countries under Soviet hegemony? How can we locate the place of 1990 in German history?

One can distinguish three phases of the 1990 transformation. The first phase extended from the beginning of the massive demonstrations in late September or early October to the opening of the Berlin Wall on 9 November 1989. The second phase began with the opening of the Wall and ended with the first and last free elections of the East German parliament (*Volkskammer*) on 18 March 1990. The third phase extended from those elections to 3 October 1990, when the GDR – by accession to the Federal Republic – formally ceased to exist.[3]

I.

Central to the first phase was a specific interplay of 'exit and voice', of mass exodus and mass demonstrations.[4] Gorbachev's *perestroika* had visibly demonstrated that change was possible even within the framework of 'real socialism'. Gorbachev was popular in the GDR; the uprising of the following months had virtually no anti-Soviet thrust. The scope of options and possibilities perceived by GDR citizens must have broadened, in view of the far-reaching changes in Hungary and Poland throughout the year – changes that were widely publicized in the GDR. When controls at the Hungarian and later Polish borders gradually loosened, with a breakthrough on 11 September, the lasting dissatisfaction of many East Germans showed itself in a quickly growing wave of migration into West Germany, at a rate of several thousand per day. This widely publicized mass exodus continued throughout the fall and the beginning of the winter. It remained a major concern for the GDR leadership and a major issue of controversy within East Germany. The exodus demonstrated the apparent weakness, even helplessness and certainly unattractiveness of the East German regime, whose attempts to stop it were futile. The exodus helped to further delegitimize the system. It triggered demands for reform as well as impressive street demonstrations by those who did not want to leave but who wanted to change the country.

Certainly, in the increasingly agitated months of September and October, small opposition groups, composed primarily of church people, intellectuals, artists, and academics, were formed and registered. The *Neue Forum* (Jens Reich), *Demokratie Jetzt* (Wolfgang Ullmann), *Demokratischer Aufbruch* (Rainer Eppelmann, Friedrich Schorlemmer) and the East German Social Democratic Party were founded. Partly under the protection of the Protestant Church, these groups emerged from numerous, previously illegal, semi-legal, or at least informal circles of dissent and opposition, which had crystallized during the previous years and particularly the previous months around anti-nuclear and peace protests and ecological issues, as well as in protest against election forgery and police (or Stasi) repression.

These small and fluid groups played a role in the process of popular mobilization, in discussion groups, church prayers, candlelight demonstrations, and increasingly in the streets. But these groups and activists neither engineered nor controlled the peaceful demonstrations, which were very spontaneous. They began in Leipzig in late September, usually on Monday evenings after service and prayer in the Nicolai church, with 25,000 people on 2 October, 80,000 on 9 October and 300,000 at the end of October. There were demonstrations, prayers and limited clashes with the police in other cities extending to the north as well, in Dresden, Karl-Marx-Stadt (Chemnitz), and so forth. They soon reached Berlin, where police arrested more than 1,000 demonstrators on 7 and 8 October when Gorbachev visited on the occasion of the fortieth anniversary of the GDR.

Monday 9 October appears to have been the decisive climax. It occurred in Leipzig, when demonstrators broke through police barriers to a greater extent than before, symbolically conquering space that they had not claimed before when police and even military reactions were expected and partly prepared. This was a situation full of tension and anxiety, but also of excitement and emancipation. Bloody Bejing-style suppression seemed possible, and indeed was evidently considered, but not carried out. Why not? The Soviets discouraged repressive reactions and made it clear that their troops would stay in the barracks. The ruling group around Honecker appears to have been well informed but wavering, not unanimous, already weakened by preceding challenges and the lack of Soviet support, partly paralysed. Local leaders were left to their own devices, and they responded to the dramatic appeal for non-violence from local notables, conductor Kurt Masur and local Party functionaries among them.

'Wir bleiben hier', 'Reisefreiheit statt Massenflucht', 'Wir sind das Volk', 'Versammlungsfreiheit', 'Stasi in die Volkswirtschaft' ('We're staying here', 'Freedom to travel instead of mass exodus', 'We are the people', 'Freedom of assembly', 'Put the Stasi to productive work') – these were some of the slogans of the October and early November demonstrations, which had no clearly formulated platform but called for civil liberties, democratic reforms, better living conditions, and improved relationships between the people and the government, in the spirit of dialogue, understanding, and cooperation. It was felt and said that the regime had lost touch with society. Mistakes had been made. Government had become unresponsive to the social needs of the citizens. Freedom to travel was a major aim. Without using the term, the rights of civil society were claimed. The language of non-violence, of community, of simplicity and of self-organization abounded, partly with Biblical allusions. Music – church chorales and rock bands – played a role. The conquest of space by peaceful means had a snowball effect.[5]

The mass demonstrations of October and early November did not aim at unification with the Federal Republic; they were not directed against the autonomous existence of the GDR. They did not challenge the basis of socialism nor did they advocate the dissolution of the Warsaw Pact. They did not even demand a new constitution. With minor exceptions, they didn't even violate the law. When the New Forum applied for registration, it formally claimed the rights guaranteed in article 129 of the constitution of the GDR.

But in regard to the constitutional reality of the GDR, the demonstrators did behave in an antisystemic way and pursued protests of an antisystemic nature. This was a system in which, although several parties existed on paper, one party, and ultimately its leadership, claimed and largely had a monopoly of authority; it was a system that did not forbid demonstrations but largely managed to control them closely; a system that did not abandon elections but manipulated them so that, in effect, free elections were impossible; a regime that denied its citizens basic human rights and civil liberties while claiming to provide them. It was an authoritarian regime that suppressed pluralism, basic criticism, and the autonomous self-organization of social groups as well as spontaneous movements; a dictatorship with paternalistic tutelage and pervasive suppression – whatever the written constitution said. If one sees this as the basic structure of the existing system, the practice of the spontaneous mass movements and the liberal-democratic aims pursued were indeed antisystemic. Given the authoritarian reality of the regime, these practices had a revolutionary thrust.[6]

The mood of protest and the spirit of change quickly spread, developing dynamic energy even within the SED membership, irritating the cadres and challenging the leaders who, without the accustomed support of their Soviet ally, reacted with uncertainty. In the meantime we know a lot about the internal debates, conflicts, and tendencies towards dissolution within the Party and even within the army. On 18 October, the *Politbüro* itself forced Honecker to step down. Egon Krenz, his successor, tried to stabilize the situation without success. The economic situation deteriorated, the mass exodus continued, and so did the mass demonstrations. They became even larger, despite mediation attempts between the authorities and speakers for the citizens' initiatives. On 4 November, about one million people participated in a very heterogeneous mass demonstration on Berlin Alexanderplatz. On 8 November, the old guard lost power and seats in the *Politbüro* as the Party tried to adjust to the new situation. In a situation of pressure and confusion, challenged by mass emigration and mass demonstrations, the Wall was opened on 9 November. This meant unlimited opportunities to travel to the West and the beginning of the end of the GDR, which, after all, had needed the Wall since 1961. All these dramatic events were direct consequences of the mass movement and the moving moments in the life of the nation that could be widely observed on TV.[7]

II.

On 10 November it was clear that the future of the GDR would not be a mere continuation of the past. But most, if not all, the actors and observers could not have said what future developments might be, which options would exist, and what choices would be made. The smoke cleared in the second phase, between 9 November and the elections for the GDR parliament (*Volkskammer*) on 18 March.

The mass demonstrations became more radical though less numerous. Hatred against the system and its representatives became more manifest. Popular anger and passion turned against the privileges of the leading functionaries. Their isolated housing in Wandlitz, a Berlin suburb of rather modest luxury, became the symbol of unacceptable inequality in a system whose claims of superiority were based on the rhetoric of equality. The Stasi – state security – became the major object of popular scorn and attack. Its headquarters were stormed and searched, occupied and sealed on 4 December in Leipzig, and on 15 January in Berlin. The Stasi was not only a symbol, but also a focus of power.

By attacking and taking Stasi headquarters and confiscating its seemingly unending stock of files, the oppositional movement posed the question of power more sharply than ever before or after. Although the mass movement was extremely successful in challenging the old system and bringing down the old leadership, it never produced a counter-elite of its own that would have competed or struggled for power. The ministers, scientists, artists, and intellectuals who served as representatives of the different opposition groups did not have a programme, or the will, or the background to lead them to a real fight for power. They were satisfied – or had to be satisfied – with small shares of power, with seats at the so-called Round Tables, newly emerging institutions of dialogue, negotiations, and conciliation that, between November and March and under the guidance of the Church, brought together representatives of the government, of the old and the new parties, of different opposition groups, and of other social formations. Like the Council Movement of 1917 to 1919, the Round Tables filled an institutional gap between the decline of the *ancien régime* and the rise of an effective parliamentary system. In contrast to the Russian Soviets and the German *Räte* of 1917 and 1918, they were not revolutionary forces' platforms for the quest for power, but reflections of an uneasy compromise or stalemate between the still-strong old elites and the *homines novi* who did not know or did not wish to translate the energy of a mass movement into the quest for power in the country. The East German revolution of 1989–90 had no Danton or Robespierre, nor a Lenin or Trotsky, not even a Lech Walesa or Vaclav Havel.

Why? On the one hand, until 1989, the SED had been strong, encompassing, and repressive enough to prevent the emergence of a substantial counter-elite outside its sphere of influence, with the partial exception of the Church. On the other hand the leaders of the opposition lost part of their popular base after the Wall had come down. Between mid-November and mid-January, the mass demonstrations not only shrank, but fundamentally changed.

Until 10 November, nationalistic slogans played no role in the East German uprising. The opposition had pursued aims of basic reform within the framework of the GDR. Now these demands were partly continued, but increasingly supplemented, overlapped, and pushed aside by national ones. The slogan 'Wir sind ein Volk' ('We are one people') frequently replaced 'Wir sind das Volk' ('We are the people'). Posters and flags, platforms and publications, and later party programmes and opinion polls showed that the quest for unification with West Germany was quickly gaining ground and was soon supported by a large majority of the East German population. The movement for anti-dictatorial and democratic change merged into a movement for national unification. In the course of this shift, the composition of the demonstrations changed. Those who went to the streets shortly before Christmas were not the same demonstrators as those who had been there in October and early November. The activists of the first phase frequently felt estranged from the national aims that became dominant in the second phase. This is why they lost power and often reduced their commitment.[8]

This leads me to a second stage, which became increasingly important: Bonn. It should be stressed that West Germany had not engineered the nationalistic aspect of the East German revolution. This nationalistic turn was the result of priorities set by the majority of East Germans who gave up their state long before it disappeared. Many East Germans did not believe in the future of their system, compared with the Western one. By pressing for quick national unification under West German conditions, they hoped to improve their economic, social, and political situation more quickly and thoroughly than they could have hoped for through internal, autonomous reforms. I still think they were right.

On the other hand, one cannot overlook the fact that West Germany had played an important, although indirect, role in the East German upheaval from its beginning. Earlier I tried to argue that the mass exodus of East Germans to the West was a triggering factor for the mass movement in the GDR and a major factor in the erosion of the East German power structure. This mass exodus would have been impossible or unlikely without the impact of the West German media, especially TV, within the GDR. Such a mass migration to the West would also have been much more difficult without West Germany's citizenship policy, which worked as a standing invitation to all ethnic Germans who could manage and were willing to come, GDR Germans included. Bonn probably helped to convince Budapest to relax its border controls in September, and the East German revolution would not have taken its nationalistic turn had it not been known that the Federal Republic stood for unification, in principle.

The West German government was surprised by the acceleration of change within the GDR. Even at the end of November, Kohl's 'Ten Points programme' saw a unified German national state as a goal for the distant future. Since the beginning of December, however, Kohl and his circle started to understand that unification might quickly become a real possibility, and from then on the Bonn government helped to bring it about with flexibility, skilful diplomacy, and firm determination. Kohl and his government thought and acted slightly ahead of German public opinion but the government's commitment to unification corresponded to the binding mandate of the Federal Republic's provisional constitution, the Basic Law, and to the long-term official commitments of all West German administrations throughout the preceding decades. Soon, it was also supported by a large majority of the West German 'political class' across party lines and by comfortable majorities at the polls. The West German dispute during the following months concerned questions of the modalities and speed of unification, rather than whether unification was desirable at all. There was enough national cohesion and conviction left among West Germans to make unification the 'natural' thing to do, once the external obstacles preventing it were eroding and if the East Germans wanted it. The West German government did not specify the costs of unification, nor the price the West Germans might have to pay, nor the sacrifices East Germans would have to make. Had there been a clearer public notion of the eventual costs and sacrifices, the national consensus in favour of fast unification would have been less overwhelming.

Be that as it may, starting in December, West Germany increasingly influenced East German developments rather directly: through negotiations with the East German government, by granting, refusing, and promising badly needed economic aid to the GDR, through the media and political opinion makers, visiting politicians and campaigns, party and interest group activities, a lot of grassroot contact between West and East Germans, and through skilful diplomacy in the international arena.[9]

Ultimately the fate of the GDR and of the German unification was decided in the arena of international relations. The formation of a strong nation state in the middle of Europe had always been a problem of international politics and the balance of power in Europe; and so it was again in 1990. The division of Germany and the creation of two German states had been the result of the unfolding Cold War in the 1940s. Correspondingly, unification had now to be part of the complicated process of international diplomacy bringing the Cold War to an end.

There is no need to reconstruct the fascinating interchange between the major actors in Moscow and Washington, Bonn and Berlin, Paris and London – from the Malta meeting between Presidents Bush and Gorbachev in early December through the Ottawa conference in February and the ensuing 'Two-Plus-Four' process up to the Gorbachev–Kohl Caucasus meeting in July. Reading the available accounts and analyses, most recently that by Zelikow and Rice, one is impressed to see what a process of unexpected acceleration this was, following rules of its own, but again and again pushed forward by developments inside Germany: by the mass movement in the GDR, the fall of the Wall, the collapse of the old GDR leadership, the economic crisis and the threatened breakdown of the GDR, and finally the skilful pressure exerted by Bonn. As the late François Mitterrand put it when he looked back in 1995:

> The question was whether reunification was unavoidable or whether one could have prevented it. Certainly for us Frenchmen a Germany of 60 million would have been less dangerous than a nation with 80 million. We would have preferred to keep Germany divided. But nobody could carry this through. Not the superpowers. Not the East German military (. . .). The Wall just came down. It was a people's revolution in which common people forced their opinion upon the whole world. While Margaret [Thatcher] and I had the same historical anxiety regarding a unified Germany, we still differed in the following respect: I considered it an unshakeable fact that could no longer be changed by anyone. In July 1989, I already said that if Germany wanted to reunite democratically, after a general election, and peacefully, nothing could prevent it. And that's exactly what happened. In the last analysis there was a pressure in favour of reunification that overwhelmed all treaties.[10]

This may be exaggerated, and there were moments when Mitterrand saw things differently.[11] But the quotation reflects a basic belief that Mitterrand shared with Gorbachev, Bush, and other decision-makers – a deep belief in the historical legitimacy and unavoidability of the nation state whose tremendous vitality would be difficult and somehow wrong to stop. The quote also correctly makes clear that the major actors were indeed confronted and surprised by a powerful movement inside Germany, one they had not engineered and could not control, except at a price they were not prepared to pay. Only Prime Minister Thatcher was willing to stem the tide of change and try to prevent the reconstruction of a German nation state that she feared would dominate Europe. She did not prevail.[12] Other diplomatic constellations were conceivable. They could have emerged, they were indeed sought, they might have slowed down unification immensely, and a difference in timing would probably have resulted in different results.

But, since February 1990, it became increasingly clear that some arrangements would be reached, and that Gorbachev's reorientation towards internal reform, towards Europe and the West, away from the old Brezhnev doctrine, would probably prevail within Moscow, which would in turn severely limit Soviet options *vis-à-vis* the dynamics of unification. Economic considerations played an increasing role. Gorbachev was keenly aware of the Soviet Union's deep economic problems. He discovered the GDR's tremendous international debt with surprise and alarm. He feared that this would add to the burdens that the Soviet economy was facing anyway, and he expected substantial economic help from the West and particularly from the Federal Republic of Germany, whose economic and political strength he highly respected. Still, even then, it was difficult and painful for the Soviets to give up a sphere of influence they regarded as well-deserved compensation for their tremendous sacrifices during the Second World War. It was only in July that the deal was finally struck, as part of a broader international agreement to be reached in November 1990.[13]

The situation of the GDR government, now under Hans Modrow (a pragmatic, slightly reform-oriented Party secretary), was increasingly difficult. There were still demonstrations, increasingly in favour of unification. There were growing economic difficulties, indebtedness, threatening bankruptcy, and the loss of productivity. The exodus of qualified people continued. Pressure from Bonn mounted, and the Soviet ally was unwilling to unequivocally guarantee the continuous existence of the GDR as an autonomous state – on the contrary. Modrow's government had to share power with the Round Table. Constitutional and legal reforms were cautiously enacted, first steps were taken towards partial privatization, and the date for free elections was set. The SED adopted a new programme, a new name, a new leadership – and lost more than half of its membership. The other parties, until then dependent satellites of the SED, regained independence, but quickly lost it again by affiliating with the corresponding West German parties, which extended their scope of action into the GDR. West German parties and politicians dominated the election campaign, whose central issue became unification.

Ninety-three per cent of East Germany's electorate voted in the *Volkskammer* elections of 18 March. The parties that had advocated quick unification on West German terms gained a comfortable majority. The communists lost, along with the civil rights activists, dissidents, and reformers who had led the revolution during its first phase and had long hoped for a 'third way' between the capitalist Federal Republic and the dictatorial state socialism that they had helped bring down. A large majority of the voters decided against the continuation of an autonomous GDR.[14]

III.

Some authors see 18 March as the point at which the East German revolution ended.[15] Major issues had been decided, in favour of unification on West German terms. Popular demonstrations died down, the Round Tables disappeared, the demobilization of the masses accelerated, the centre of action and energy moved away from the streets into parliamentary and bureaucratic institutions. While the first phase had clearly been initiated and carried out by people, decisions, and actions within the GDR, the second phase saw the centre of gravity gradually moving from the East to the West, an unstable mix of East German and West German input. Now, in the third phase (between March and October 1990), Bonn became the centre of decision-making and West Germans took over. East German majorities had agreed to it, East German speakers cooperated and participated. Still, it cannot be denied: the East Germans once again became the objects of change, after pushing it forward as subjects for some months at a great historical moment. This is particularly true for the dissidents, the opposition, the activists of the first phase. It is understandable that some historians see the East German revolution as ending in March, at the latest.

On the other hand, one has to admit that rapid restructuring continued after 18 March, modifying but also continuing the basic decisions of the second phase. Between March and October, legal, social, and economic change even accelerated, under the influence from the West, but formally under the leadership of the freely elected *Volkskammer*. The restructuring of the economic, social, and political system accelerated, following the West German model. The replacement of the old elites gained new momentum, and West Germans moved in. What had started as a revolution from below was now continued as a revolution from above and, in a way, from outside (namely Bonn).

On 1 July, the West German currency and the West German economic and social system were extended to the East, against the warning of most economists, on the basis of a political decision welcomed by most East Germans. International acceptance of unification was definitely gained in July. The Treaty of Unification was negotiated between two unequal partners: Bonn and East Berlin, Kohl and de Maizière, Schäuble and Krause. It provided for unification in the form of the East's accession to the Federal Republic; the latter would continue to exist in an enlarged form. Minorities on the left had advocated the joint creation of a new constitution. It would replace both the West German and the East German constitution and mark a new departure for both the West and the East. These voices did not prevail. Unification was scheduled to be brought about by the extension of the West German system to the East. The basic decision of 1990 was not in favour of creating something new that might, as the defeated minority hoped, combine the strengths of both the West and the East, or that might, as the prevailing majority feared, embark on an uncertain journey into unknown waters, with great foreign and domestic policy risks. On 3 October 1990, the Treaty of Unification went into effect and the GDR ceased to exist.[16]

IV.

The deep ruptures that occurred in the GDR and consequently in West Germany during 1989–90 lacked some of the basic elements usually associated with the concept of a modern revolution. They were not based on, nor did they produce, a new set of ideas. They were non-violent. Mostly, they even avoided breaking the law. There was no showdown or clear-cut power struggle between the old ruling elite and a rising new counter-elite. There was no stiff resistance from those in power, and there was no real attempt at counter-revolution. It is understandable that many observers and some historians avoid the term 'revolution', preferring less ambitious expressions like 'transition', 'fundamental change', *Wende* or *Umwälzung*.[17]

Yet the ruptures of 1989–90 contained at least strong revolutionary elements. First, endogenous mass movements were central. They were powerful and decisive during phase one and important during phase two. Second, the demonstrations may not have been antisystemic with respect to the formal constitution of the GDR, which, after all, preserved certain principles of a civil society as a reservoir of unfulfilled claims, but they were indubitably antisystemic in terms of practice, thrust, and effect if measured against the constitutional reality of this communist dictatorship. Third, change was fundamental and comprehensive. It concerned the whole system, not just one or two subsystems. There was basic institutional change; both the principles and the leaders of the previous economic, social and political order were replaced. So were the bases of legitimation. Change turned out to be more fundamental and radical in the GDR than in any other of the East European countries abandoning communism. Fourth, these changes occurred in a relatively short period of time. In this respect, the GDR experience differed from the Polish and the Hungarian pattern of change, which extended over a longer period of time. In this respect, the developments within the GDR were more revolutionary than in most neighbouring countries.

Whether one chooses the term 'revolution' or not is partly a semantic, partly a political question. It should not become a scholastic one. German history is not rich in revolutions, particularly not rich in successful ones. Seen against this background, the East German turn was quite revolutionary even if it contained many reformist traits.

Certainly, there were many exogenous factors that triggered this revolution. No one can overlook the role played by the changes within the Soviet Union and particularly by Gorbachev, the example provided by Poland and Hungary, or the opening of the Hungarian border. What happened in the GDR was part of a cycle of basic changes occurring all over East Central and Eastern Europe. The success of the East German revolution was largely influenced by international developments. [18]

There were also strong internal factors. The uprising needed external stimuli to unfold, but it was based on anger, dissatisfaction, and protest responding to a home-grown crisis: to the deepening difficulties of the GDR economy, to the increasing rigidity of the social order and the increasingly blocked opportunities for upward mobility, and to ideological disintegration, particularly among the young.[19] Although the results were strongly influenced by external factors, by diplomatic decisions, and by international movements, these diplomatic decisions and international movements were largely reacting to what came from inside (East) Germany, as Mitterrand observed.

Compared with the neighbouring countries in the East and their movement away from communism, the East German case had its own particular structure and flavour, due to the fact that the GDR was confronted with another, much stronger state of the same nationality, which had never fully accepted the nation's division. The relation between nation and revolution was different for the GDR than in any other place.[20] The specific national situation influenced the East German uprising from the start. The East German revolution took a national turn at the end of which the GDR disappeared.

The interpretation of this national turn remains controversial. There are those who hold that it basically betrayed the revolution and brought it to an untimely end. According to this view, the original aims were suppressed, activists of the early phase were pushed to the margin, the direction was changed, and West German politicians took over. What had started as an endogenous uprising became a process of change engineered from above and from the West. According to this view, the East German revolution led to colonization by West Germany.[21]

But this argument rests on doubtful presuppositions and neglects important aspects of historical reality. First of all, it needs to be stressed that the national turn of the East German revolution came from inside the GDR, was legitimized by democratic procedures, and was supported by a large majority of the East German population.

And what were the aims pursued by the revolutionaries and reformers of the first phase and allegedly suppressed by the national turn of the second phase? There were indeed elements of radical, participatory, and consensus-oriented democracy in the mass demonstrations and Round Tables. These elements were different from and alien to the West German constitutional system that would later be extended to the East. But how strong were they really, and would they have had any chance to be routinized and endure? There were some weak attempts among reform-minded intellectuals within the SED to formulate the socioeconomic program of a 'third way' between the bankrupt state-socialist dictatorial model of the East and the relatively successful liberal-democratic, pluralist, mixed-economy model of the West. But nothing came of them. By and large, it is not at all clear whether and how the internal structures of a thoroughly reformed, post-communist but independent GDR might have differed from the internal structures of the FRG. But then, what would have been saved, preserved, or made possible had the revolution not taken its national turn?

Finally one may wonder whether the East Germans, left to themselves, would have been strong enough to achieve the basic democratic reform of their system. The forces of the *ancien régime* were still powerful at the end of 1989 and the beginning of 1990. They tried to adjust to the new situation and reconsolidate themselves. The mass demonstrations could not have been kept alive forever. Measured by political skill, instinct for power, and real influence in everyday politics, the endogenous forces of reform were weak. After nearly sixty years of dictatorial rule and with a deeply damaged economy, East German society was probably ill-prepared to master an autonomous transition to democracy without disappointment and backlash. Seen from this perspective, the turn towards unification was not a betrayal of the revolution, but a way to realize its basic liberal-democratic aims that would have been hard to secure otherwise.

Certainly, the ruptures of 1989–90 marked a major caesura in recent German history. Sometimes 1989–90 is seen as a revision of what the shift of 1945–49 had brought. According to this view, the changes of 1945–49 led primarily to the loss of the German nation state and began more than forty years of a new German anomaly, the life of a nation in two states. The changes of 1989–90 restored the German nation state, though not in its old borders. It ended the German and European division. The shift of 1989–90 thus corrected the decision of 1945–49. This is how the relation between the two last German turning points can appear if interpreted from the perspective of the history of the nation state.[22]

But the caesura of 1945–49 can be seen in a different way. It can be seen as the beginning of the end of the 'German divergence from the West', which had started in the nineteenth century and had reached its extreme in the Nazi period. In the years after 1945, a historical development began that made the bulk of Germany an integrated part of the Western world, with respect to its constitutional order and its economic system, its open society and its pluralist culture, with respect to values, lifestyle, communication, and alliances. The basic principles of civil society were successfully anchored in the reality of the Federal Republic, more than in any previous period of German history. In the Federal Republic, the German *Sonderweg* between West and East came to an end.[23]

Seen from this point of view, the break of 1989–90 – the revolution in the GDR, its transformation into a movement for unification with the FRG, and the accession of the GDR to the FRG – appear to be the completion, not the correction, of 1945–49. It extended the system of the West to the Germans in the East, who had opted for it by a large majority. It provided the opportunity to include the East Germans in a relatively successful development toward civil society, from which they had been excluded. Whether and how this will work remains to be seen.

Notes

1. Cf. Werner Bramke, 'Ungleiches im Vergleich. Revolution und Gegen-
    revolution in den deutschen Revolutionen von 1918/19 und 1989', in
    Matthias Middell (ed.), *Widerstände gegen Revolutionen 1789–1989*, Leipzig
    1994, pp. 263–79.

2. The hearings, expertise and reports of a parliamentary committee
    (1992–94) give a good summary of the controversial assessment of the
    legacy of the GDR and the *Wende* in recent years. See Deutscher
    Bundestag (ed.,) *Materialien der Enquête-Kommission Aufarbeitung von Geschichte
    und Folgen der SED-Diktatur in Deutschland (12. Wahlperiode des Deutschen
    Bundestages)*, 18 vols, Frankfurt am Main 1995. See also Klaus Sühl (ed.),
    1945–1989. Ein unmöglicher Vergleich?, Berlin 1994; the volume documents
    an interesting discussion in Potsdam 1992.

3. Good introductory overviews are available, with bibliographical informa-
    tion for further reading: Charles S. Maier, *The End of East Germany*,
    Cambridge, Mass. 1996; Konrad Jarausch, *The Rush to German Unity*, New
    York 1994 (German edition: *Die unverhoffte Einheit 1989/1990*, Frankfurt
    am Main 1995); Mary Fulbrook, *Anatomy of a Dictatorship. Inside the GDR
    1949–1989*, Oxford 1995. On the international dimensions: Philip Zelikow
    and Condoleezza Rice, *Germany Unified and Europe Transformed. A Study in
    Statecraft*, Cambridge, Mass. 1995.

4. Albert O. Hirschman, 'Exit, Voice and the Fate of the German Demo-
    cratic Republic', in A. O. Hirschman, *A Propensity to Self-Subversion*,
    Cambridge, Mass. 1995, pp. 9–44.

5. The best accounts are by the historian and participant observer Hartmut
    Zwahr. See his *Ende einer Selbstzerstörung. Leipzig und die Revolution in der
    DDR*, Göttingen 1993; Hartmut Zwahr, 'Die Revolution in der DDR
    1989/1990 – Eine Zwischenbilanz', in Alexander Fischer and Günther
    Heydemann (eds.), *Die politische Wende 1989–90 in Sachsen. Rückblick und
    Zwischenbilanz*, Weimar 1995, pp. 205–52. Good documentation is provided
    in Charles Schüddekopf (ed.), *Wir sind das Volk! Flugschriften, Aufrufe und
    Texte einer deutschen Revolution*, Reinbek 1990.

6. One of the best analytical pieces: Ralph Jessen, 'Die Gesellschaft im
    Staatssozialismus. Probleme einer Sozialgeschichte der DDR', in *Geschichte
    und Gesellschaft* 21, 1995, pp. 96–110. Jessen responds to Sigrid Meuschel,
    'Überlegungen zu einer Herrschafts- und Gesellschaftsgeschichte der
    DDR', in *Geschichte und Gesellschaft* 19, 1993, pp. 5–14.

7. See the lively eye-witness account by Robert Darnton, *Berlin Journal 1989-
    1990*, New York 1991. Interesting evidence from the point of view of the
    Soviet ambassador as well as a good analysis may be found in Igor F.
    Maximytschew and Hans-Hermann Hertle, 'Die Maueröffnung. Eine
    russisch-deutsche Trilogie', in *Deutschland Archiv* 27, 1994, pp. 1137–58,
    1241–51. From the perspective of Erich Honecker's successor: Egon
    Krenz, *Wenn Mauern fallen. Die Friedliche Revolution: Vorgeschichte, Ablauf*

Auswirkungen, Wien 1990. The account of an active member of the Politbüro: Günter Schabowski, *Der Absturz*, Berlin 1991.

8. See the good account in C.S.Maier, *The End of East Germany*, Chapter 4. The most important documents in Volker Gransow and Konrad H. Jarausch (eds), *Die deutsche Vereinigung. Dokumente zu Bürgerbewegung, Annäherung und Beitritt*, Cologne 1991, Chapters III and IV. The changing situation is reflected in the writings of one of the most important representatives of the opposition movement: Jens Reich, *Rückkehr nach Europa. Bericht zur neuen Lage der deutschen Nation*, Munich 1991, pp. 184–274.

9. Cf. Horst Teltschik, *329 Tage. Innenansichten der Einigung*, Berlin 1991 (Teltschik was the most important foreign policy advisor to chancellor Kohl during this period); Elizabeth Pond, *Beyond the Wall: Germany's Road to Unification*, New York 1993; M. Donald Hancock and Helga A. Welsh (eds), *German Unification. Process and Outcomes*, Boulder 1994.

10. Quoted (and translated) from the German transcript of a discussion between George Bush, Mikhail Gorbachev, François Mitterrand and Margaret Thatcher in the fall of 1995, as quoted in *Die Zeit*, no. 11, 8 March 1996, pp. 9–11, especially p. 10.

11. See the account by Jacques Attali, *Verbatim III*, Paris 1995, pp. 340–54, 366–92, 416, 495, 541. See also François Mitterrand, *De l'Allemagne, de la France*, Paris 1996.

12. Margaret Thatcher, *The Downing Street Years*, London 1993, pp. 768–96.

13. See P. Zelikow and C. Rice, *Germany Unified*; Michael R. Beschloss and Strobe Talbott, *At the Highest Levels. The Inside Story of the End of the Cold War*, Boston 1993; Karl Kaiser, *Deutschlands Vereinigung. Die Internationalen Aspekte. Mit den wichtigen Dokumenten*, Bergisch-Gladbach 1991; Mikhail Gorbachev, *Erinnerungen*, Berlin 1995; Juliy A. Kwizinskij, *Vor dem Sturm. Erinnerungen eines Diplomaten*, Berlin 1993; Wjatscheslaw Kotschemassow, *Meine letzte Mission. Fakten, Erinnerungen, Überlegungen*, Berlin 1994; Hans-Dietrich Genscher, *Erinnerungen*, Berlin 1995, Chapter 17.

14. See Hans Modrow, *Aufbruch und Ende*, Hamburg 1991; Russell J. Dalton (ed.), *The New Germany Votes: Unification and the Creation of the New German Party System*, Oxford 1993; Helmut Herles and Ewald Rose (eds), *Vom Runden Tisch zum Parlament*, Bonn 1990; Uwe Thaysen, *Der Runde Tisch. Oder: Wo blieb das Volk?*, Opladen 1990. Results of the elections of 18 March 1990 in: V. Gransow and K.H. Jarausch (eds), *Die deutsche Vereinigung*, p. 148.

15. This is the view in C.S. Maier, *The End of East Germany*, Chapter 4.

16. See K.H. Jarausch, *Rush to German Unity*, part 3; Wolfgang Schäuble, *Der Vertrag. Wie ich über die deutsche Einheit verhandelte*, Stuttgart 1991. The documents in V. Gransow and K.H. Jarausch (eds), *Die deutsche Vereinigung*, pp. 163–234. Several contributions in Eckhard Jesse and Armin Mitter (eds), *Die Gestaltung der deutschen Einheit. Geschichte – Politik – Gesellschaft*, Bonn 1992; Werner Weidenfeld and Karl-Rudolf Korte (eds), *Handwörterbuch zur deutschen Einheit*, Frankfurt am Main 1992.

17.   See C.S. Maier, *The End of East Germany*, Chapter 3. There is an excellent discussion of the changing and different meanings of revolution in Reinhart Koselleck, 'Revolution. Rebellion, Aufruhr, Bürgerkrieg', in *Geschichtliche Grundbegriffe. Historisches Lexikon zur politisch-sozialen Sprache in Deutschland*, vol. 5, Stuttgart 1984, pp. 653–6, 689–788. See also Crane Brinton, *Anatomy of Revolution*, New York 1938 (rev. eds 1952, 1965). See Michael Richter, *Die Revolution in Deutschland 1989–90. Anmerkungen zum Charakter der Wende*, Dresden 1995.

18.   See Timothy Garton Ash, *We The People. The Revolution of '89*, Cambridge 1990; Bernard Gwertzman and Michael T. Kaufman (eds), *The Collapse of Communism. By the Correspondents of The New York Times*, New York 1990; Olivier J. Blanchard, Kenneth A. Froot and Jeffrey D. Sachs (eds), *The Transition in Eastern Europe*, vol. 1, Chicago 1994. As to the role of the Soviet Union: Klaus Segbers, *Der sowjetische Systemwandel*, Frankfurt am Main 1989; 'Schön, ich gab die DDR weg. Michail Gorbatschow über seine Rolle bei der deutschen Vereinigung. Spiegel-Gespräch', in *Der Spiegel* 40, October 1995, pp. 66–81.

19.   A survey of the internal causes of the East German revolution in C.S. Maier, *The End of East Germany*, Chapters 1 and 2. With respect to the economic dimensions see the revealing interviews and analyses in Theo Pirker, M. Rainer Lepsius, Rainer Weinert and Hans-Hermann Herth (eds), *Der Plan als Befehl und Fiktion. Wirtschaftsführung in der DDR*, Opladen 1995. Blocked opportunities for social mobility in the 1980s and 1990s (compared with the 1970s and 1960s) are well documented in Heike Solga, *Auf dem Weg in eine klassenlose Gesellschaft? Klassenlagen und Mobilität zwischen Generationen in der DDR*, Berlin 1995. Traditions of dissent within the GDR are documented in Markus Meckel and Martin Gutzeit, *Opposition in der DDR. Zehn Jahre kirchliche Friedensarbeit – kommentierte Quellentexte*, Cologne 1994; Ulrike Poppe, Rainer Eckert and Ilko Sascha Kowalczuk (eds), *Zwischen Selbstbehauptung und Anpassung. Formen des Widerstandes und der Opposition in der DDR*, Berlin 1995.

20.   See Jürgen Kocka, 'Revolution und Nation 1989. Zur historischen Einordnung der gegenwärtigen Ereignisse', in Jürgen Kocka, *Vereinigungskrise. Zur Geschichte der Gegenwart*, Göttingen 1995, pp. 9–32; revised English version Jürgen Kocka, 'Revolution and Nation. 1989–90 in Historical Perspective', in *European Studies Journal* 10, 1993, pp. 45–56.

21.   See Michael Schneider, *Die abgetriebene Revolution. Von der Staatsfirma in die DM-Kolonie*, Berlin 1990; Wolfgang Dümcke and Fritz Wilmar (eds), *Kolonialisierung der DDR. Kritische Analysen und Alternativen des Einigungsprozesses*, Munich 1995.

22.   See Horst Möller, 'Die Relativität historischer Epochen: Das Jahr 1995 in der Perspektive des Jahres 1989', in *Aus Politik und Zeitgeschichte* 1995, B 18/19, pp. 3–9. Arnulf Baring (ed.), *Germany's New Position in Europe. Problems and Perspectives*, Oxford 1994.

23. See Jürgen Kocka, 'German History Before Hitler: The Debate about the German "Sonderweg"' , in *Journal of Contemporary History* 23, 1988, pp. 3–16; Jürgen Kocka, 'Ende des deutschen Sonderwegs?', in Wolfgang Ruppert (ed.), *Deutschland, bleiche Mutter oder eine neue Lust an der nationalen Identität?*, Berlin 1992, pp. 9–31; Jürgen Kocka, 'The Difficult Rise of a Civil Society. Societal History of Modern Germany', in Mary Fulbrook (ed.), *German History since 1000*, London (in press).

REINHARD RÜRUP

Problems of Revolution in Germany, 1525–1989

Karl Marx, who was famous for his love of pointed turns of phrase, complained as early as 1843 in his 'Critique of Hegel's Philosophy of Law' of a dearth of revolutions and of a glut of counter-revolutionary 'restorations' in Germany. He wrote:

> We have, namely, shared the restorations of modern peoples, without sharing their revolutions. The old order was restored to us, firstly, because other peoples dared to countenance revolution, and secondly, because other peoples suffered a counter-revolution, in the first instance, because our princes were afraid, in the second instance, because our princes were not afraid. We, with our shepherds in the lead, found ourselves in the society of freedom on just one occasion, on the *day of its burial.*[1]

Certainly, this was contemporary political polemic rather than detached historical analysis, but it set the tone for left-wing intellectual discourse inside and outside Germany right up until the present day. A belief in the necessity of revolution established itself in the Marxist-influenced workers' movement, but for left-wing intellectuals the theme of 'Germany and the revolution' developed, above all in the twentieth century, to the point of satire. Significantly, Lenin's remark that German revolutionaries would first buy tickets before they would storm the railway station became a standard quotation. Germans are, so ran the verdict in many variations, incapable of the revolutionary act.

This corresponded to the historical and political self-conception of the German middle classes, which had become dominant by the middle of the nineteenth century at the latest. Here, the thesis that Germany was 'the land without revolution' was understood in a positive sense. Luther's Reformation was interpreted as the real German revolution, and the absence of revolutions was believed to be proof of the receptivity of German politics towards reform. The 'Prussian reforms', which started in 1807, were systematically opposed to the French revolution of 1789 as a specifically German path of moderate progress. The historian Rudolf Stadelmann summarized this understanding of German history as late as 1948 in the following words: 'The heydays of our national past are not victories over the monarchy, but rather victories of the monarchy, military feats of glory and the achievements of statesmen, Frederick the Great and Bismarck.'[2] In this conception of history, there was no room for revolutions. When their existence could not be overlooked, as in 1848 or 1918, they were dismissed as mere disturbances, as turmoils without historical legitimization. According to this view of history revolutions were, by their very nature, 'un-German'.

Of course, by 1948, after two world wars and the experience of the Nazi system of terror, the exponents of such opinions found themselves unmistakably on the defensive. The German people, Stadelmann maintained,

> is, as far as its political aspirations are concerned, pushed almost unseen by the other nations into a reactionary pigeon-hole and a label is affixed to it with the inscription: the people without revolution. Our history has been marked out as that of a pariah for three generations because it lacks experience of, and education characterised by, a radical rejection of the absolutist past of recent centuries. The ostracizing of Germany's name has its first and probably most important root in the absence of a normal, revolutionary crisis of puberty in German development.[3]

The 'ostracizing of Germany's name' that is complained of here, had, without doubt, other causes, in view of the Nazi crimes. Nevertheless, the new, critical view of German history is accurately summarized in these sentences, although with a negative accent. It was liberal and democratic historians, above all in Anglo-Saxon countries, who no longer sought the causes of National Socialism in the treaty of Versailles or the Great Depression, but in long-term, abortive developments in German history.

Since the 1960s, these problems have also been addressed by a new generation of historians in the Federal Republic. Attention was focused above all on the absence of a successful revolution, on the weaknesses of the liberal and democratic middle classes or *Bürgertum*, on the founding of the German nation state by means of a 'revolution from above', and on the authoritarian structures of imperial Germany. Within the framework of new theories of modernization, it soon became common to talk of a typically German form of 'partial modernization', of a dichotomy between a very successful economic modernization and an interrupted political and social modernization. In comparison with the democratically developed societies of the 'West', historians began to refer to a specifically German path – or *Sonderweg* – to modernity, which was depicted in negative terms. The 'ideology of a German way', which had been developed during the nineteenth century, was turned on its head, as it were: because Germany was a country that had not experienced a successful liberal, bourgeois revolution, it followed a special path, which ended ultimately in the catastrophe of the Nazi system. Although this view never went unchallenged, it began to dominate West German historiography from the early 1970s onwards. Its appeal lay in the fruitful connection that it made between democratic commitment and a change of method within the historical discipline – from classical historicism to a historical social science. A great number of critical historical studies of the German Empire have been carried out on this basis.[4]

There are at least three reasons why it seems sensible to discuss anew the question of the significance of revolution in German history. Firstly, there have in recent decades been a great number of historical studies of revolutions, whose manifold findings have not, hitherto, been assessed collectively. It remains to be seen whether a changed picture of the whole will emerge from the abundance of separate findings. Secondly, the *Sonderweg* thesis has already been subject to criticism for more than a decade – not least as a result of a frontal attack by the British historians David Blackbourn and Geoff Eley – and it is represented by its defenders today in an obviously and reductively modified form. Even Hans-Ulrich Wehler, one of the most influential representatives of the *Sonderweg* thesis, made substantial modifications in the third volume of his *Deutsche Gesellschaftsgeschichte*, which came out in 1995: the revolution of 1848 is no longer portrayed exclusively as a defeat of the liberal middle classes, the 'revolution from above' at the time of national unification is assessed more positively, and the political 'backwardness' of the German Empire is limited to a relatively narrow political sphere.[5] Thirdly, in the autumn of 1989 we experienced a mass movement in the German Democratic Republic, which, to its own amazement, released revolutionary forces and eventually brought down not only the political regime, but also, contrary to its own aspirations, the state. In view of this 'autumn revolution', it might prove difficult in the future to claim categorically that the German people are incapable of successful revolutionary action. The fact that the category of 'revolution' has itself been brought into question by the structural changes in the Communist states of central and eastern Europe will be discussed in the final part of this chapter.[6]

I.

The notion of an 'early bourgeois revolution', which historians of the GDR developed for the great upheavals of the early sixteenth century, has been proven to be unsustainable. Still, it is undisputed that this juncture constitutes the beginning of what we call the 'early modern' period, or *Neuzeit*, and that the Reformation played a major, perhaps decisive, role in Germany's transition from the late Middle Ages to the early modern era. I do not want to return to older conceptions of the Reformation as the German revolution – a revolution of the mind. It is perhaps worth recalling, however, that both the European Enlightenment and the French revolution referred to Luther and the Reformation as the first step towards freedom of thought and individual self-determination in Europe. For our purposes, it is more important that recent research has emphasized the revolutionary nature of the German peasants' war of 1525. What Friedrich Engels, full of admiring partisanship, had described as 'the most radical fact in German history' – the armed struggle of rebellious peasants in large parts of the German Reich – is now also recognized by researchers as the 'revolution of 1525', to cite the title of an important book by Peter Blickle. True, the authorities' victory over the peasants was not only clear-cut – it was also bloody and cruel. Yet it remains a fact of fundamental significance that there was a mass uprising, with a far-reaching revolutionary programme, at the beginning of the early modern period in Germany – in contrast to other European states.[7]

At the start of modern German history, there was, as has become clear from the research of the 1960s onwards, not only the Reformation, but also a revolution, if, admittedly, a failed one. Furthermore, the classic argument that the peasantry did not make a political appearance in the centuries following its crushing defeat in the peasants' war, but rather disappeared for a long time from the German historical stage, is no longer tenable. From the sixteenth to the eighteenth century, there was, as both Blickle and Winfried Schulze have demonstrated, 'an unbroken chain of resistance movements' within the peasant population in many areas of the Holy Roman Empire. In the eighteenth century alone, the existence of more than fifty peasant revolts has already been proven. And a considerable number of peasants' complaints against unjust exactions came before the high courts of the Reich. The much-maligned deference of peasants was, at the very least, not so uniform as has been believed.[8]

This was also true of Germany during the era of the French revolution. The Enlightenment movement was considerably more political and more sophisticated in its organization than had been thought until relatively recently. There was a political public sphere, which oriented itself towards human and civil rights, and which strove to overcome the old feudal order in the interests of the freedom of the individual and of property. In this respect, before the French reform movement transformed itself into the revolution, the difference between France and Germany was not nearly as great as it appeared to be in the older historical literature. As there were at least the beginnings of reform politics in Germany, in alliance with absolutist princes against the privileged estates of the old order, a violent coup did not seem necessary, in contrast to France. Thus, on the one hand, the French revolution was at first greeted enthusiastically by German public opinion as a victory for theory and a triumph for enlightened philosophy; on the other hand, it was condemned decisively after it suddenly inaugurated the period of the Terror (and of 'anarchy', as it was frequently argued). The French revolution was usually seen as proof that the dangers of revolution were so great that it should not be entered into unnecessarily.[9]

It was not as quiet in Germany, though, as it was said to be in the older literature. Regional and local histories have, in the meantime, established the existence of rural and urban unrest and rebellion in many parts of the empire, from local apprentices' revolts to more significant rural uprisings (with up to 10,000 participants in Saxony in 1790). Admittedly, these results should also not be overestimated, given that all such rebellions remained isolated and, as a rule, could be put down without great difficulty.[10] Part of the new findings is the discovery that there were groups of supporters of the French revolution, not only in the Rhineland, but also in north and south Germany, and even in Vienna, who hoped to precipitate the revolutionary process in Germany as well. So-called 'Jacobin research' has succeeded in tracing democratic traditions in German history back to the era of the French revolution. Meanwhile, it has also become clear that the name 'Jacobin' is rather misleading, because these German revolutionaries did not orient themselves towards the rule of the Jacobins, but towards the first phase of the revolution and towards the constitution of 1791. They were, as has recently been formulated, Girondins rather than Jacobins.[11]

Still more important than the changes, which I have already outlined, in our understanding of German history during the period of the French revolution is the fundamental reassessment of reform politics in German states. As Lothar Gall put it: 'The first fifteen years of the nineteenth century can in many respects be seen as the truly revolutionary years in German history. It is then, and this is even more the case in the South than in the North, that the foundations were laid for subsequent developments in its entirety, and no caesura until 1945 has proved more decisive than this one.'[12] In the German states, the real breakthrough onto the path towards a modern society occurred during the era of Napoleon, who appeared in Germany not only as a conqueror, but also as the heir and executor of the French revolution. This happened in an incomplete way and with different emphases, but the direction was clear: a civil and liberal society was to take the place of the old feudal order. Enlightened, liberal ideas might well have been fragmented, but they determined the main themes of German politics.

The concept of a 'revolution from above' is taken much more seriously in more recent research than was the case previously, as it has been recognized in the meantime that it in fact involved revolutionary interventions in the existing order. Although reforms in the south German states were formerly labelled the products of 'foreign rule' and the 'import of abstract ideas', it has since become uncontentious that Montgelas in Bavaria, Reitzenstein in Baden and also, King Frederick in Württemberg pursued relatively independent policies, which were shaped by the traditions of the German Enlightenment as well as by the ideas of the French revolution. The emphasis lay on political reforms, which included the introduction of a representative constitution and made the south and south-west into the centre of German liberalism in the period until 1848.

As far as the Prussian reforms are concerned, it is no longer, as in conservative historiography, Freiherr vom Stein who is of primary interest, but rather Hardenberg, since the latter was committed in far greater measure to the political and, above all, to the economic ideas of early liberalism. As Reinhart Koselleck has formulated it, an attempt was made to overcome Napoleon with the help of Adam

Smith. Economic and societal reforms were carried out in Germany with considerable determination, whereas constitutional promises remained unfulfilled until 1848. Prussia did not become a constitutional state, but it was so receptive to modern economic developments that it became the leading economic and industrial power in Germany within a few decades. Of course, the reformers suffered defeats, as well as having to compromise with the aristocracy, which remained strong. Nonetheless, there can be no doubt that the foundations were laid during this period for modern political and societal development. There was not only a 'defensive' reaction to the challenge of Napoleon and the French revolution, but also an attempt to use the ideas of the Enlightenment and the French revolution in order to shape the future. A 'revolution from above', as was practised in both the South German states and in Prussia, was revolutionary in its content, if not in its methods. It is said, with good reason, that Germany and France probably had fewer differences after 1815 than they had had before 1789. The 'era of the revolution' left behind deep imprints in Germany, too.[13]

Before we turn to the revolution of 1848, it is important to remember that there were, in the wake of the French July revolution of 1830, mass movements, popular unrest and revolutionary tremors, the extent and significance of which are still, as a rule, underestimated. Numerous cities were hit by workers' disturbances and more than half of the German universities were affected by student unrest of various sorts. In Braunschweig the Grand Duke's castle was burned down; in Dresden the town hall was stormed and the police building razed to the ground; in many places there were clashes with the military and in Oberhessen revolutionary peasants' columns were formed with many thousands of participants. Certainly, the respective arenas remained isolated and the troubles did not escalate uncontrollably, but individual rulers did abdicate their thrones, governments were reconstituted, modern constitutions were introduced, and social reforms were enacted. The *Frankfurter Wachensturm* (the attack on the Frankfurt guardhouse) of the revolutionary students, Georg Büchner and the *Hessische Landbote*, also belong in this context. All in all, it seems thoroughly justified to speak, like Heinrich Volkmann, of a 'forgotten revolution' for the period around 1830.[14]

The revolution of 1848–49 alone would justify a separate chapter and I intend here to limit myself to a few observations and judgements. In a certain sense, the revolution of 1848 has been rediscovered by recent research, at least insofar as its genuinely revolutionary nature is concerned. Historians have overcome their fixation with the so-called 'parliament of the professors' in Frankfurt's church of St Paul just as they have overcome their one-sided emphasis on the national question. Instead, the role of the popular masses, the armed struggles and the national and international dynamics of revolutionary – and also of counter-revolutionary – developments have been investigated more closely. The quick victory in March/April – the so-called 'achievements of March' –, the postponement of revolutionary decisions in the following weeks and months, and, not least, the recovery of the old powers by the start of the summer of 1848, are now easier to recognize than was previously the case, as are the conflicts of interest between the lower orders and the liberal bourgeoisie, which, quite rightly, saw its position threatened from below. There were not fewer violent struggles on the territory of the German Confederation than in other European states, not to mention France and Paris – if the counter-revolutionary massacre in the French capital of June 1848 is exempted.[15]

In a comparative European history of the revolution of 1848–49, the *Sonderweg* thesis loses its explanatory power. The fact that the German revolutionaries tried to steer a moderate course does not distinguish them from the men of 1789, and the fact that they failed to attain many of their goals makes their fate no different from that of all the other revolutionaries in Europe during those years, including the French, who more or less immediately saw the Republic replaced by the Empire of Napoleon III. And finally, doubts have increasingly been raised in the more recent scholarly literature about the simplistic formula of revolutionary failure – *'die allzu glatte Formel'*, in Hans-Ulrich Wehler's words. The revolution did not achieve its ultimate ends and it was, above all, dominated by the national question. Yet it was not only about the nation state, but also about constitutional questions, and about liberal economic and societal change, and in this respect the revolution was certainly successful. Without the revolution, Prussia and Austria would not have become constitutional states, the agricultural reforms would still not have reached their conclusion, other feudal rights would have remained in place, and the industrial revolution would have encountered considerably larger obstacles in the German states. Beside the defeats of the revolution stood enduring successes; and the fact that revolutionaries fought to establish a liberal-democratic nation state was of importance for the future. One can agree with Hans-Ulrich Wehler, when, in the second volume of his *Deutsche Gesellschaftsgeschichte*, he ends his discussion of the 1848 revolution with the sentence: 'The standards which it set for the constitution of state and society, for rights to freedom and equality, retained thereafter the luminosity of an ideal that, for many people, remained binding, in spite of all the setbacks after 1848 – and that is why, as a basic fact, it could not be circumvented over the longer term.' The revolution failed, but it had important positive ramifications for the course of German history. [16]

If the nineteenth century is often described as the 'century of revolutions' in European history, then this only applies, on closer inspection, to the first half of the century. The second half merely witnessed the failed revolt of the Paris Commune in 1871, before the new century was inaugurated by the Russian revolution of 1905, which also ended in failure. Revolutionary upheavals proper only reappeared, in considerable style, towards the end of the First World War, as the Russian revolution of 1917 – in both its democratic and its socialist guise – seemed to presage a new age. The German revolution of 1918–19 is of particular significance in this respect: it was the largest revolutionary mass movement outside Russia, and one that was successful in its early stages. It was also the event in which Lenin invested his greatest hopes for a communist world revolution. In German historiography, as in German political consciousness, this revolution was suppressed for decades before a process of reappropriation of its history began in the 1960s. I should add, however, that this revolution, termed the 'November revolution', had always been central to the communist tradition and thereby also to the historiography of the GDR, because it engendered the German Communist party and, so it was said, finally exposed the counter-revolutionary nature of social democracy. The Communist position, which was laid down in detail by the resolutions of the central committee of the Socialist Unity Party, has not, in terms of scholarship, proved very fruitful. The decisive advances of the research into the revolution were made, for the most part, in the Federal Republic. [17]

One of the most important results of this research was the recognition that it was not merely a question of an upheaval (*Umsturz*) or of a 'period of transition' (*Übergangszeit*) between the *Kaiserreich* and the Weimar Republic, but rather a revolution. Both in its programme and in its action this revolution was, admittedly, conspicuously 'moderate'. It was a social democratic revolution, and not only to the extent that the new governments in the Reich and in the federal states were led by Social Democrats, but also because the revolutionary masses, who organized themselves into soldiers' and workers' councils, had a social democratic programme – a National Assembly, parliamentary democracy, combating militarism, societal democratization, and prudent socialization. In the first stages, far greater successes were achieved than in 1848: for some days, and even weeks power did actually lie in the hands of workers and soldiers, but it was only used hesitantly in the direction of a new democratic order, with governments as well as workers' and soldiers' councils devoting most of their energy to the resolution of actual crises, from demobilization and provisioning to reviving industry. The restructuring of society in the direction of social democracy remained in abeyance, with important structural decisions being left to the National Assembly, which was to be elected in mid-January 1919, but which, as a result of its composition, was hardly in a position to make such decisions. Thus, a social democratic counter-example to the Bolshevik system in Russia did not materialize.

The revolution had some successes, however: the dissolution of the monarchy proved irreversible; the democratic electoral law, which included women, and the liberal-democratic constitution were perceived in many respects to be exemplary, and the fundamental achievements in social policy continued the expansion of a socially interventionist state. But antidemocratic forces had not really been cowed. After a relatively short period, they were already able to offer effective opposition to the republic and, in the end, they were so successful at destroying that republic from within that it was replaced by the National Socialist rule of terror less than a decade and a half after its inception. In the wake of the revolution of 1830 in France, Heinrich Heine had once argued that each revolution is a misfortune, but that a still greater misfortune is an unsuccessful revolution. This was particularly the case with the revolution of 1918–19, which aggravated and eventually poisoned domestic conflicts, precisely because there was no real clarification of power relations.

I intend to leave aside the question of whether it was right, in 1933, to speak of a 'national' or of a 'National Socialist revolution', nor do I intend to discuss whether, and in what way, the structural changes which resulted from defeat in 1945 can be compared to a revolution.[18] Similarly, I am prevented by the constraints of space from examining the very interesting question of whether the so-called 'student revolt' of 1968 can be interpreted as a successful 'cultural revolution' – and, for the same reason, I shall have to forego discussion of the revolutionary content of events around the 17 June 1953 in the GDR.[19] Instead, I am going to turn immediately to the events of autumn

1989, which have been described, with good reason, as a 'peaceful revolution'.

From a comparison of 1918 and 1989, some similarities stand out: The social and political system seemed unshakeable until shortly before its demise. The mobilization of malcontents and protesters, who became opponents of the system as a matter of principle in the course of events, occurred publicly in demonstrations, which took place in the streets and squares of towns and cities. There was no planning and no central organization, but there was a common mood of the masses, from which an unforeseen and irresistible momentum developed. True, this irresistibility resulted to a considerable degree from a loss of confidence on the part of the old regime and its representatives and from a failure to use – or to use consistently – the available instruments of power. In 1918 this breakdown was connected to the shock of military defeat, and in 1989 to precipitate developments in the Soviet Union and in some of the European states that were dependent on the USSR. The demands of the masses did not aim initially at an upheaval (*Umsturz*) but at changes within the existing framework. More radical demands, which destroyed the system, only followed the acknowledged incapability of the old regime to enact reforms, and it was only the unexpected breakdown of the old powers within the state that created the possibility of a revolutionary new beginning.[20]

Admittedly, the parallels end here. In 1918 the workers' and soldiers' councils, and the governments that they appointed, were in a position to take over power and to control military and civil institutions. They could fall back on the political schooling and organizational experience of the German workers' movement, and they could rely on the Social Democratic Party and the unions. All these conditions were absent in the GDR, where the opposition was not able to create viable organizations and where established parties and mass movements did not constitute reliable allies. The mass movement was not – and, indeed, could not be – prepared for the power vacuum that suddenly appeared, so that so-called 'reformers' in the Socialist Unity Party and, above all, the previous 'bloc parties', received an unanticipated and unearned opportunity to assume power. This was the end of the revolution proper, and there followed a transition phase, whose nature was soon determined by the prospect of a union with the Federal Republic. Into the places of those who wanted a reformed, democratic GDR stepped those who no longer wanted the GDR at all, but rather a united Germany. People suddenly realized that they did not have to reform the GDR, but that they could simply give it up, that the union with the Federal Republic could replace the disputes over internal reorganization. The truly revolutionary slogan 'We are the people!' changed into: 'We are one people!' There was no more talk of revolution. Nevertheless, those days in the autumn of 1989 remain not only high points of German political history, but also part of a history of revolution in our century. Jens Reich had already formulated this very impressively in January 1990:

> They [the autumn days] belong to those wonderful moments of German history, in which 'the people' has itself, as a single, acting unit, determined its own fate with imagination and resolve, after 45 years (and more) of foreign interference, faint-heartedness, cowardice, conformity and resignation.[21]

II.

Summing up the results of this speedy passage through German history from 1525 to 1989, it should be incontestable that the thesis that sees German history characterized by a conspicuous absence of revolutions is no longer tenable. One should not make the mistake of claiming the exact opposite, however, and calling Germany a land of successful revolutions. There were no epochal upheavals akin to 1789 and 1917. Such events are not the rule, but the exception in the historical process. Most revolutions in Germany failed or were, at most, only partly successful, but it is also true that the great majority of all revolutions in Europe have failed. Polish history, with its revolutionary image in the nineteenth century, includes no small number of revolutions, but none were successful. And even in France, the history of revolutions is anything but a pure success story: The Terror followed 1789, Napoleon followed the Directory, and finally there was a restoration of the Bourbons; the July revolution had very mixed results, and the 1848 republic was succeeded by another empire; the revolt of the Paris Commune failed, and the Third Republic passed through a long phase of domestic crises before it finally consolidated its position. The difference between Germany, on the one hand, and France and Poland, on the other, is, however, that revolutions in the latter had a tradition-building effect and became central points of a general historical understanding, whereas this was not the case in Germany.

I will try to illustrate this with two examples: the revolutions of 1848 and 1918–19. With regard to 1848, it is conspicuous that the attempt has been made again and again, and not only in the nineteenth century, to use the history of the revolution in order to convey to the German people a feeling of political dependence and to give the impression that Germany could not shape its own destiny responsibly. Thus, there was talk of a 'parliament of professors' (although it was actually a parliament of lawyers), of the alleged 'doctrinairism' of liberals and democrats, of 'inactive idealism', of the absence of a sense of power, or of the exclusively destructive effect of radicalism. All these were supposedly 'lessons' of the revolution, which served, in the first instance, to stifle any thought of a repetition and to prepare the German people for the continuance of the authoritarian state. The fact that the revolution also included successes and that its aims were worth the effort was not only forgotten, but rather fell victim to a conservative understanding of history and politics.

The suppression of any positive recollection of the revolution of 1918–19 appeared even more clearly, perhaps, than it had done after 1848. The self-understanding of the Weimar Republic was based, not on the revolution, but on overcoming the revolution. Not only middle-class democrats, but also Social Democrats distanced themselves very quickly from the revolution that they had themselves led. When Philipp Scheidemann proclaimed the republic from a balcony of the Reichstag on 9 November 1918, he began with the words: 'The German people have won all along the line.' With his speech, he attempted – successfully – to place social democracy at the head of the revolutionary movement. As he depicted the same event ten years later in his memoirs, he stylized it into a decision between 'democracy' and 'Bolshevism'. On the (false) assumption that his speech had not been recorded verbatim, he produced a completely new version, in which there was no more talk of a victory of the people, but rather of defeat in war and of those who were responsible for war and defeat. Thus, 'defence against Bolshevism' became the real justification for the founding of the republic. One had no longer made a revolution, but rather, as Friedrich Ebert already formulated it in late September 1918, one had, in a moment of crisis, 'to leap into the breach', in order to prevent worse things from happening. Thus, the revolution became a breakdown or *Zusammenbruch*, with which no one could identify positively.[22]

The international socialist movement has demonstrated impressively, with the example of the Paris Commune, that a failed revolution can become a source of strength for the losers. What this could have meant for the development of revolutionary traditions in Germany can be read from an article that Ernst Fraenkel, the great jurist and political scientist, published in the German-language, New York-based *Neue Volkszeitung* in 1943, in order to mark the twenty-fifth anniversary of the revolution of 1918. It ran: 'Whatever else one thinks of the 9th of November, this event will still make history. A people that has once, at a critical moment, taken its fate into its own hands, will in the long run never be deprived of the right of decision.' This was, at such a time, certainly a bold claim, and was wishful thinking rather than sober analysis, and Fraenkel himself suggested that, fourteen years later, Germany had suffered 'a complete defeat' because there had only been 'half a revolution' in 1918. But, nevertheless, the thesis does show what meaning could be given to a conception of history in which revolutionary traditions constitute a vital component.[23]

III.

Thirty years later, Richard Löwenthal, starting from a discussion of the missed opportunities of 1918, began to examine systematically the fundamental difficulties of democratic revolutions in developed industrial societies. He spoke of an 'anti-chaos-reflex' experienced by large parts of the population at times of crisis. Political actors, precisely when they wish to effect structural changes in the political and societal system, are under pressure, first of all, to secure the 'technical and organizational continuity of daily life'. Löwenthal illustrated this with the example of 1918–19:

> The provisioning of cities with food, the transport of demobilized soldiers back home, their reintegration back into economic life, the supply of fuel and raw materials to industry, the fight against infection - all this depends on the functioning of the public transport system and other areas of administration. The breakdown of support and administrative chaos appear to be the most pressing dangers, for the sake of which the continued existence of available instruments of power are 'temporarily' accepted. The desire for assured survival becomes a support for the existing institutions of order, even on the part of many of those who are critical of the regime whose institutions are in question.[24]

If one were to continue this line of thinking – and there are, in my opinion, good reasons for doing so – then revolutions that accord with the 'classic' paradigm of 1789, 1848 and 1917 are now, in fact, barely imaginable. Even those who want to effect a change of system must make compromises in order to avoid the dreaded 'chaos', which endangers the survival of all. An abrupt break with the past is replaced by a process of change over the longer term, which is unable to renounce democratic legitimization by means of general elections and independent parliaments instead of popular assemblies and revolutionary committees. In 1981, in a publication in honour of Francis Carsten, Löwenthal attempted to show from a series of examples – of the internal development of the Third Republic in France and, above all, the replacement of authoritarian regimes in Greece and Spain – that fundamental shifts of power and changes of system are still possible, even though the instruments of the 'classic' revolution are no longer effective. Neither the beginning nor the success of processes of democratization are dependent on revolutionary upheavals as they have traditionally been understood.[25]

Such reflections make clear that the traditional opposition of revolution and reform in developed societies is outdated, and the old debates over the question 'reform or revolution?' as they have been conducted, above all, in the Marxist tradition of the European workers' movement, obstruct rather than promote objective analysis of profound changes in political and societal life. If we look back at developments in the former Soviet bloc between 1989 and 1991, then it appears that there are no clear distinctions between revolution and reform for the ending of communist rule and the beginning of processes of democratization – not to mention the dissolution of the Soviet Union and the disappearance of the GDR. The results have – notwithstanding all the uncertainties concerning future developments – an evident revolutionary quality, because a powerful political and societal system has broken up, and communism has abdicated as an alternative in world politics to the liberal-capitalist order of the West. But the process of transformation itself was, of its nature, overwhelmingly reformist. There are obviously revolutions – one only has to think of 1830 and 1848 in France – which merely produce relatively short-term and superficial changes. And there are reforms that restructure society effectively and over the long term. Reforms can, as has been shown, not least, in communist states, unleash forces that destroy entire systems. Revolutionary changes are not necessarily linked to violence and the spilling of blood. In dictatorships and totalitarian systems, democracy can – despite what the theory of totalitarianism would have us believe – be realized by means of a gradual alteration of the system or a bloodless accession to power.

These reflections, which result from our contemporary political experiences, find their confirmation in recent historical research. In a joint work of German and French historians, which was published in 1989 under the title 'Germany and France in the Age of the French Revolution', an attempt was made to analyse and compare social change in both countries between 1770 and 1820. One of the most important results consisted in relativizing the traditional connotations of revolution and reform. The editors expanded this point in the introduction: 'Comparison [between France and Germany] no longer allows revolution and reform to appear as contrary paths to modernity. To formulate it exaggeratedly and paradoxically: The French revolution takes on reformist aspects and the era of reform in Germany takes on revolutionary ones.'[26] This finding corresponds to the results of other research projects on the era of the French revolution and Napoleon, although a systematic discussion of the subject has yet to appear.

I have already pointed out that the revolutionary character of the political and societal reforms in a number of German states has been emphasized in recent years much more than was previously the case. Revolutionaries and reformers were similar in that they wanted to change existing conditions according to 'fixed principles' – according to the theoretical insights of the Enlightenment. Man was stood on his head, as Hegel formulated it somewhat later – this was the case for the reformers no less than for the revolutionaries of 1789. Revolution and reform were viewed by contemporaries as different paths towards modernity, but as paths in the same direction. If one considers the advances that were actually achieved, then the differences between revolution and reform become less important, and it has already been mentioned in passing that the differences between Germany and France around 1815 were less significant than those that had existed around 1789.[27]

Revolutions may have the advantage that conflicts are formulated sharply, fronts are clarified and decisions are forced. On the other hand, they also carry considerable risks. Revolutions, as a rule, take a different course to that which was originally planned; they always run the risk of degenerating into terror or anarchy; they demand human lives and they threaten to split the nation over the long term. By contrast, reforms often cannot completely override resistance from the privileged and powerful of a society, they are weakened by compromises and often misrepresented with regard to their original intentions. According to this line of argument, it is a question of weighing up the costs and gains of the different paths to modernity for societies that are to be founded on the freedom of the individual and of property. There is, then, no clear hierarchy between revolution and reform, no advantage in principle for one or the other course of historical transformation.

As a rule, reform movements precede revolutions, and the revolutionary act is a last attempt to push through those reforms that are believed to be necessary against resistance, which could not be overcome in other ways. Somewhat crudely, one could say: revolutions are an extreme means of imposing reforms, at least in the age of so-called 'bourgeois revolutions'. On the other hand, there is much to be said for the view that the politics of profound reform only became possible with the French example of a successful revolution. Equally crudely, this means: no reform without revolution. Or to put it another way: experience of a successful and momentous revolution – not necessarily in one's own country – is a precondition of a structural change in politics and society by means of reform.

Johann Gottlieb Fichte, who belonged to those who had emphatically welcomed the French revolution, wrote in 1793: 'Violent revolutions are always a bold gamble for humanity; if they succeed, then the victory won is well worth the trouble they had to go through; if they do not succeed, then you push your way through from misery to still greater misery.' From this, he drew the conclusion: 'It is safer to make gradual advances to greater enlightenment and thereby to improve the constitution of the state. The steps forward which you make are less noticeable whilst they are happening; but look behind you, and you will see a great stretch of covered ground.'[28] This is a recognition of the opportunities that revolution offers – and also, in certain circumstances, of its necessity – but it is, at the same time, a plea for the course of reform.

In European history, both revolutions and reforms confront us. If I tried to show in the first part of this essay that revolutions have been of much greater significance in recent German history than is commonly conceded, then this was motivated by a desire to correct historical orthodoxies, but it had nothing to do with a backward-looking glorification of revolution. It was Heinrich Heine who once warned that a revolution looks nice as long as we read about it in the books, but that it would be dangerous to confuse images and the harsh reality. This warning should also apply to historians. We should neither glorify revolutions, nor play down their potential for violence. It is for this reason that in the later parts of this essay I have tried to show, on the one hand, that the notion of revolution in the twentieth century, at least in developed societies, is no longer really relevant, and, on the other, that in the nineteenth century, too, the concepts of revolution and reform were not only thought of as stark alternatives, but also as different paths in the same direction. The goal, to which both paths were intended to lead, was a society in the spirit of the Enlightenment, of human and civil rights, and of the free development of individuals. Historians, too, should therefore devote at least as much attention to the common goal of a humane society as to the different paths towards that society.

Notes

1. Karl Marx, 'Zur Kritik der Hegelschen Rechtsphilosophie', in *Die Frühschriften*, edited by Siegfried Landshut, Stuttgart 1953, p. 209.
2. Rudolf Stadelmann, 'Deutschland und die westeuropäischen Revolutionen', in R. Stadelmann, *Deutschland und Westeuropa*, Laupheim 1948, p. 17.
3. Ibid. p. 14.
4. See Bernd Faulenbach, *Ideologie des deutschen Weges. Die deutsche Geschichte in der Historiographie zwischen Kaiserreich und Nationalsozialismus*, Munich 1980; Dietrich Rüschemeyer, 'Partielle Modernisierung', in Wolfgang Zapf (ed.), *Theorien des sozialen Wandels*, 2nd edn, Cologne 1970, pp. 382–96; on the German *Sonderweg* see in particular Jürgen Kocka, 'Deutsche Geschichte vor Hitler. Zur Diskussion über den "deutschen Sonderweg"', in J. Kocka, *Geschichte und Aufklärung*, Göttingen 1989, pp. 101–13.
5. Hans-Ulrich Wehler, *Deutsche Gesellschaftsgeschichte*, vol. 3, Munich 1995, pp. 449–86; David Blackbourn and Geoff Eley, *The Peculiarities of German History. Bourgeois Society and Politics in Nineteenth-Century German History*, Oxford 1984.
6. Any attempt to summarize briefly what to my mind are the most important results of recent historical research into revolutionary events must necessarily be broad in its scope. I have been obliged, therefore, to ignore many of the nuances of the subject.
7. *Marx-Engels-Werke*, vol. 1, Berlin 1972, p. 386. Peter Blickle, *Die Revolution von 1525*, Wien 1975.
8. See Winfried Schulze, *Bäuerlicher Widerstand und feudale Herrschaft in der frühen Neuzeit*, Stuttgart 1980; Winfried Schulze (ed.), *Europäische Bauernrevolten in der frühen Neuzeit*, Frankfurt am Main 1982; Peter Blickle, *Aufruhr*

und Empörung? Widerstand im Alten Reich, Munich 1980; Peter Blickle (ed.), *Revolte und Revolutionen in Europa,* Munich 1976 (*Historische Zeitschrift, Beihefte, N. F.,* vol. 4).

9. See my essay on Germany and the French Revolution in this volume. See in particular Elisabeth Fehrenbach, *Vom Ancien Régime zum Wiener Kongreß,* Munich 1981; Helmut Berding and Hans-Peter Ullmann (eds), *Deutschland zwischen Revolution und Restauration,* Düsseldorf 1981; Helmut Berding, Etienne François and Hans-Peter Ullmann (eds), *Deutschland und Frankreich im Zeitalter der Französischen Revolution,* Frankfurt am Main 1989. On the intellectual reactions see Jacques Droz, *L'Allemagne et la Révolution Française,* Paris 1959; Rudolf Vierhaus, '"Sie und nicht wir". Deutsche Urteile über den Ausbruch der Französischen Revolution', in Jürgen Voss (ed.), *Deutschland und die Französische Revolution,* Munich 1983, pp. 1–15; Claus Träger (ed.), *Die Französische Revolution im Spiegel deutscher Literatur,* Leipzig 1979.

10. The best summary on the social unrest is Helmut Berding (ed.), *Soziale Unruhen in Deutschland während der Französischen Revolution,* Göttingen 1988.

11. See Helmut Reinalter, *Die Französische Revolution und Mitteleuropa. Erscheinungsformen und Wirkungen des Jakobinismus. Seine Gesellschaftstheorien und politischen Vorstellungen,* Frankfurt am Main 1988; Volker Reinhardt, 'Reformer oder Revolutionäre? Deutscher und italienischer Jakobinismus im Vergleich', in *Zeitschrift für Historische Forschung* 21, 1994, pp. 203–20.

12. Lothar Gall, *Der Liberalismus als regierende Partei. Das Großherzogtum Baden zwischen Restauration und Reichsgründung,* Wiesbaden 1968, p. 3.

13. On the reform era in Prussia see Reinhart Koselleck, *Preußen zwischen Reform und Revolution. Allgemeines Landrecht, Verwaltung und soziale Bewegung von 1791 bis 1848,* Stuttgart 1967; Barbara Vogel, *Allgemeine Gewerbefreiheit. Die Reformpolitik des preußischen Staatskanzlers Hardenberg (1810–1820),* Göttingen 1983; Barbara Vogel (ed.), *Preußische Reformen 1807-1820,* Königstein. 1980. On the comparison between France and Germany see H. Berding, E. François and H.-P. Ullmann (eds), *Deutschland und Frankreich im Zeitalter der Französischen Revolution,* p. 18.

14. Heinrich Volkmann, *Die Krise von 1830. Form, Ursache und Funktion des sozialen Protests im deutschen Vormärz,* Berlin 1975 (*Habil.* thesis, unpublished).

15. The state of research in Dieter Dowe, Heinz-Gerhard Haupt and Dieter Langewiesche (eds), *Europa 1848. Revolution und Reform,* Bonn 1948; Wolfgang Hardtwig (ed.), *Revolution in Deutschland und Europa 1848/49,* Göttingen 1998. See also Wolfram Siemann, *Die deutsche Revolution von 1848/49,* Frankfurt am Main 1985; Rüdiger Hachtmann, *Berlin 1848. Eine Politik- und Gesellschaftsgeschichte der Revolution,* Bonn 1997; Manfred Gailus, *Straße und Brot. Sozialer Protest in den deutschen Staaten unter besonderer Berücksichtigung Preußens, 1847–1849,* Göttingen 1990; for a summary discussion see Reinhard Rürup, 'Revolution und Volksbewegung. 1848/49 im Kontext der deutschen Geschichte', in Bernd Faulenbach and

Heinrich Potthoff (eds), *Die Revolution von 1848/49 und die Tradition der sozialen Demokratie in Deutschland,* Essen 1999, pp. 22–36. See also the essay by Rüdiger Hachtmann in this volume.

16. See Hans-Ulrich Wehler, *Deutsche Gesellschaftsgeschichte,* vol. 2: *Von der Reformära bis zur industriellen und politischen Deutschen Doppelrevolution, 1815– 1845/49,* Munich 1987, pp. 759–79 ('Die Gründe des Scheiterns und die Ergebnisse der Revolution: Niederlagen und Erfolge'); there is also a brief discussion of failure and success in Reinhard Rürup, *Deutschland im 19. Jahrhundert, 1815–1871,* 2nd edn., Göttingen 1992, pp. 195–7. See also Hans-Ulrich Wehler's essay on the 'German Double Revolution' in this volume.

17. See Gerald D. Feldman, Eberhard Kolb and Reinhard Rürup, 'Die Massenbewegungen der Arbeiterschaft in Deutschland am Ende des Ersten Weltkrieges (1917–1920)', in *Politische Vierteljahresschrift* 13, 1972, pp. 84–105; Eberhard Kolb (ed.), *Vom Kaiserreich zur Weimarer Republik,* Cologne 1971; Eberhard Kolb, *Die Weimarer Republik,* 4th edn, Munich 1998, pp. 1–22, 147–68; Heinrich August Winkler, *Weimar 1918–1933. Die Geschichte der ersten deutschen Demokratie,* Munich 1993, pp. 13–108; Reinhard Rürup, *Die Revolution von 1918/19 in der deutschen Geschichte,* Bonn 1993. See also the essay by Heinrich August Winkler in this volume.

18. See the essays by Hans Mommsen and Peter Brandt in this volume.

19. On the June 1953 upheaval in the GDR see Arnulf Baring, *Der 17. Juni 1953,* 2nd edn, Stuttgart 1993. On the 1968 movement see Ingrid Gilcher-Holtey (ed.), *1968. Vom Ereignis zum Gegenstand der Geschichtswissenschaft,* Göttingen 1998; Wolfgang Kraushaar, *1968 – das Jahr, das alles verändert hat,* Munich 1998; Peter Mosler and Wolfgang Kraushaar, *Was wir wollten, was wir wurden. Studentenrevolte – 10 Jahre danach,* Reinbek 1977.

20. See Charles S. Maier, *Dissolution. The Crisis of Communism and the End of East Germany,* Princeton 1997; Konrad H. Jarausch, *The Rush to German Unity,* Oxford 1994, enlarged German edition: *Die unverhoffte Einheit, 1989–1990,* Frankfurt am Main 1995; Hartmut Zwahr, *Ende einer Selbstzerstörung. Leipzig und die Revolution in der DDR,* Göttingen 1993. See also Jürgen Kocka's essay in this volume.

21. Jens Reich, *Rückkehr nach Europa. Bericht zur neuen Lage der deutschen Nation,* Munich 1991, p. 204.

22. See Manfred Jessen-Klingenberg, 'Die Ausrufung der Republik durch Philipp Scheidemann am 9. November 1918', in *Geschichte in Wissenschaft und Unterricht* 19, 1968, pp. 649–56; Philipp Scheidemann, *Memoiren eines Sozialdemokraten,* vol. 2, Dresden 1928, pp. 313 f.; Reinhard Rürup, 'Friedrich Ebert und das Problem der Handlungsspielräume in der deutschen Revolution 1918/19', in Rudolf König, Hartmut Soell and Hermann Weber (eds), *Friedrich Ebert und seine Zeit. Bilanz und Perspektiven der Forschung,* Munich 1990, p. 84.

23. Ernst Fraenkel, 'November-Gedanken', in *Neue Volkszeitung*, New York, 13 November 1943, p. 2.
24. Richard Löwenthal, 'Die deutsche Sozialdemokratie in Weimar und heute. Zur Problematik der "versäumten demokratischen Revolution"', in R. Löwenthal, *Sozialismus und aktive Demokratie. Essays zu ihren Voraussetzungen in Deutschland*, Frankfurt am Main 1974, pp. 97–115; Richard Löwenthal, 'Bonn und Weimar Zwei deutsche Demokratien', in Heinrich August Winkler (ed.), *Politische Weichenstellungen im Nachkriegsdeutschland 1945–1953*, Göttingen 1979, pp. 9–25.
25. Richard Löwenthal, 'The "Missing Revolution" in Industrial Society. Comparative Reflexions on a German Problem', in Volker R. Berghahn and Martin Kitchen (eds.), *Germany in the Age of Total War*, London 1981, pp. 240–57.
26. H. Berding, E. François and H.-P. Ullmann (eds), *Deutschland und Frankreich im Zeitalter der Französischen Revolution*, p. 18. The French edition (Paris 1989) was entitled: *La Révolution, la France et L'Allemagne. Deux modèles contraires d'évolution sociale?*
27. Ibid., pp. 17 f.
28. Johann Gottlieb Fichte, 'Zurückforderung der Denkfreiheit von den Fürsten Europas', in J. G. Fichte, *Schriften zur Revolution*, Frankfurt am Main 1967, p. 12.

Notes on Contributors

PETER BRANDT, Professor of Modern History, Fernuniversität Hagen. His publications include *Antifaschismus und Arbeiterbewegung. Aufbau – Ausprägung – Politik in Bremen 1945/46,* Hamburg (Christians) 1976; *Preußen. Zur Sozialgeschichte eines Staates (Preußen. Versuch einer Bilanz,* vol. 3), Reinbek (Rowohlt) 1981; *Karrieren eines Außenseiters. Leo Bauer zwischen Kommunismus und Sozialdemokratie 1912–1972,* Berlin (Dietz) 1983 (with J. Schumacher, G. Schwarzrock and K. Sühl); *'Vaterlandslose Gesellen'. Sozialdemokratie und Nation, 1860–1990,* Munich (C. H. Beck) 1992 (with Dieter Groh).

RÜDIGER HACHTMANN, *Privatdozent* and Research Fellow, Institut für Geschichtswissenschaft, Technische Universität Berlin, Visiting Professor of Modern History at the University of Freiburg. Among his publications are *Industriearbeit im 'Dritten Reich'. Untersuchungen zu den Lohn- und Arbeitsbedingungen in Deutschland 1933 bis 1945,* Göttingen (Vandenhoeck und Ruprecht) 1989; *Berlin 1848. Eine Politik- und Gesellschaftsgeschichte der Revolution,* Berlin (Dietz) 1997; (editor) *Geschichte und Emanzipation. Festschrift für Reinhard Rürup,* Frankfurt am Main (Campus) 1999 (with Michael Grüttner and Heinz-Gerhard Haupt).

JÜRGEN KOCKA, Professor of Modern History, Freie Universität Berlin; Permanent Fellow, Wissenschaftskolleg zu Berlin (Institute for Advanced Study, Berlin). Among his many publications are *Weder Stand noch Klasse. Grundlagen der Klassenbildung im 19. Jahrhundert,* Berlin (Dietz) 1990; (editor) *Bürgertum im 19. Jahrhundert. Deutschland im europäischen Vergleich,* 3 vols, Göttingen (Vandenhoeck und Ruprecht) 1988; (editor) *Historische DDR-Forschung. Aufsätze und Studien,* Berlin (Akademie Verlag) 1993; *Vereinigungskrise. Zur Geschichte der Gegenwart,* Göttingen (Vandenhoeck und Ruprecht) 1995.

WOLFGANG KRUSE, Senior Lecturer in Modern History, Fernuniversität Hagen. Author of *Internationalismus und nationale Interessenvertretung. Zur Geschichte der internationalen Gewerkschaftsbewegung,* Cologne (Bund-Verlag) 1991 (with Sabine Hanna Leich); *Krieg und nationale Integration. Eine Neuinterpretation des sozialdemokratischen Burgfriedensschlusses 1914/15,* Essen (Klartext) 1993; (editor and main author) *Eine Welt von Feinden. Der Große Krieg 1914–1918,* Frankfurt am Main (Fischer) 1997.

HANS MOMMSEN, Professor Emeritus of Modern History, Ruhr-Universität Bochum. Among his more recent publications are *Der Nationalsozialismus und* *die deutsche Geschichte*, Reinbek (Rowohlt) 1991; *From Weimar to Auschwitz. Essays in German History*, Cambridge (Polity Press) 1991; *The Rise and Fall of Weimar Democracy*, Chapel Hill (University of North Carolina Press) 1995; *Das Volkswagenwerk und seine Arbeiter im Dritten Reich*, Düsseldorf (Econ) 1996 (with Manfred Grieger); *Von Weimar nach Auschwitz. Zur Geschichte Deutschlands in der Weltkriegsepoche*, Stuttgart (Deutsche Verlags-Anstalt) 1999.

REINHARD RÜRUP, Professor Emeritus of Modern History, Technische Universität Berlin. His publications include *Emanzipation und Antisemitismus. Studien zur 'Judenfrage' der bürgerlichen Gesellschaft*, Frankfurt am Main (Fischer) 1987; *Volksbewegung und demokratische Neuordnung in Baden 1918/19*, Sigmaringen (Jan Thorbecke) 1991 (with Peter Brandt); (editor) *Jüdische Geschichte in Berlin. Essays und Studien*, Berlin (Edition Hentrich) 1995; (editor) *Jüdisches Leben auf dem Lande. Studien zur deutsch-jüdischen Geschichte*, Tübingen (Mohr und Siebeck) 1997 (with Monika Richarz).

HANS-ULRICH WEHLER, Professor Emeritus of Modern History, University of Bielefeld. His many books include *The German Empire, 1871–1918*, Oxford (Berg) 1985; *Deutsche Gesellschaftsgeschichte*, vols 1–3, Munich (C. H. Beck) 1987–1995; *Entsorgung der deutschen Vergangenheit? Ein polemischer Essay zum 'Historikerstreit'*, Munich (C. H. Beck) 1988; *Aus der Geschichte lernen? Essays*, Munich (C. H. Beck) 1988; *Die Gegenwart als Geschichte*, Munich (C. H. Beck) 1995; *Die Herausforderung der Kulturgeschichte*, Munich (C. H. Beck) 1998; *Politik in der Geschichte*, Munich (C. H. Beck) 1998.

HEINRICH AUGUST WINKLER, Professor of Modern History, Humboldt-Universität Berlin. Among his many publications are *Die Sozialdemokratie und die Revolution von 1918/19*, 2nd edn, Berlin (Dietz) 1980; *Arbeiter und Arbeiterbewegung in der Weimarer Republik*, 3 vols, Berlin (Dietz) 1984–1987; *Weimar, 1918–1933. Die Geschichte der ersten deutschen Demokratie*, 2nd edn., Munich (C.H. Beck) 1994; *Streitfragen der deutschen Geschichte. Essays zum 19. und 20. Jahrhundert*, Munich (C. H. Beck) 1997; *Der lange Weg nach Westen. Deutsche Geschichte vom Ende des Alten Reiches bis zur Wiedervereinigung*, 2 vols, Munich (C. H. Beck) 2000.

Printed in the United Kingdom
by Lightning Source UK Ltd.
115916UKS00001B/71